FIGHTING IN FAITH

FIGHTING IN FAITH:

A Practical Guide for Successful Spiritual Warfare

By Pastor A. W. Barlow, Attorney at Law

© 2015 by Pastor A. W. Barlow, Attorney at Law

All rights reserved.

This book or any portion thereof may not be reproduced or used in any manner whatsoever without the express written permission of the publisher except for the use of brief quotations in a book review.

ISBN-13:978-0692455487
ISBN-10:0692455485

DEDICATION

I dedicate this book to my late parents, Arthur Welton Barlow Sr. (February 13, 1927–February 7, 2005) and Annie Mae Davis Barlow (May 12, 1926–June 1, 2015). Dad was a meek and humble man who loved to serve, while Mom had a heart full of grace and compassion. Both were sources of comfort and strength throughout my entire life. Without any doubt whatsoever, almighty God used them both to shape, mold, and prepare me to be the person I am today.

TABLE OF CONTENTS

Introduction ix
1. Conquering Doubt, Fear, Pride, and Unbelief 1
2. The Natural and Supernatural Realms 9
3. My Burning-Bush Moment 17
4. My Separation for Ministry 25
5. Prophetic Ministry 41
6. Tongues and Interpretation of Tongues 51
7. Power Ministry Part I: A Biblical Foundation 71
8. Power Ministry Part II: Manifestations: 91
   Signs, Wonders, Healing, and Deliverance Ministry
9. Power Ministry Part III: The Great Commission 113
10. Ministering to Men, Husbands, and Fathers 127
11. Ministering to Women, Wives, and Mothers 135
12. Ministering to Children 153
13. Ministering to Homosexuals 173
14. Maintaining Deliverance 191
15. Testimonies: Domestic Mission Works 215
16. Testimonies: Foreign Mission Works 245
Acknowledgments 281
Author Biography 283
References 285
Scripture Index 287

INTRODUCTION

[O]n this rock I will build My church, and the gates of Hades shall not prevail against it. And I will give you the keys of the kingdom of heaven, and whatever you bind on earth will be bound in heaven, and whatever you loose on earth will be loosed in heaven. (Matt. 16:18–19)

Deliverance ministry is spiritual cleansing from the negative and soul-damning presence, power, and influences of the world, the flesh, and demonic spirits. If you are reading this book, there is absolutely no doubt that God has in some way stirred your spirit to be interested in this very powerful ministry. Demons are disembodied, malevolent spirits specifically sent by Satan "to steal, and to kill, and to destroy" every good thing God has ordained for mankind. (John 10:10) This is especially true with respect to eternal salvation of the soul. Such destruction specifically targets the human body through sickness and disease, while the soul and spirit are tormented through anxiety and many other types of mental anguish. Satan's ultimate goal is to permanently separate our souls from God in the lake of fire. This is the bad news.

However, the very good news is that the Son of God manifested Himself on Earth in the person of Jesus Christ "that He might destroy the works of the Devil" so that we might "have life, and that [we] may have it more abundantly." (1 John 3:8, John 10:10) Notice that Jesus's objective is for us to "have" life as opposed to life having us.

Mankind is locked in an eternal battle with a trifecta of an enemy the Holy Bible identifies as the "World," the "Flesh," and the "Devil." On the other hand, mankind has awesome and unlimited help in the triune of God the Father, Jesus the Son, and the Holy Spirit. God has ordained deliverance ministry to set free those who have been made captive by the very subtle wiles, schemes, plots, and evil plans of Satan and his legions of fallen angels more commonly identified as demons. However, "… greater is He that is in you than he that is in the world." (1 John 4:4)

Deliverance ministry is not something separate and distinct from the ministry of preaching and teaching God's Holy Word. To the contrary, deliverance ministry is simply having an ever-present, Bible-based understanding that as we go about our normal lives at work in vocational ministry or secular service, there will be opportunities to put the word of God into active practice to bring God's kingdom to Earth. This is often accomplished by laying hands on the sick for healing and casting out demons for deliverance from satanic or demonic powers or influences. Accordingly, it goes without saying that the same should be performed as a natural part of our daily lives and especially when apostles, prophets, evangelists, teachers, and pastors preach and teach the Word.

A classic example just happened last week when I went to a print shop to review a proof of the artwork for this book. The owner had had gastric bypass surgery well over two months prior and was having multiple problems that greatly interrupted his normal life. Upon him articulating this, my left hand was on his right shoulder before I realized it and my right hand was on his forehead while I spoke, "Be healed in the Name of Jesus." He looked at me with a huge smile on his face and said, "Thank you very much, Mr. Barlow, I really needed that today." This happened at the front counter of the business. After leaving I emailed several prayer intercessors asking them to join me in praying for him immediately upon their receipt of the request. Upon returning to the shop the next day, the owner approached me with a huge smile on his face, saying, "The prayers worked; the last twenty-four hours have been the best I've had since the surgery!"

This book is written with two primary objectives. First, to demonstrate how to utilize the Holy Bible to teach God's eternal truths about how Satan and his demons operate in our daily lives—whether we believe it or not. Second, to provide very practical means by which to both activate and operate our faith in God to engage and completely conquer demonic forces through Bible-based spiritual warfare. There are many great books on spiritual warfare, healing, and deliverance ministry and how to recognize demonic activity in our daily lives. There is also a plethora of books, writings, and written and preached sermons describing each article of the "Whole Armor of God." I can attest to this fact as I have read and greatly appreciate many of them. However, there appear to be few that concentrate on intensely practical and Bible-based strategic means to learn and immediately apply the same in the art of healing and deliverance ministry. This being the case, there are very few that not only teach practical application strategies but also include actual testimonies from those who have been miraculously healed, delivered, and otherwise touched by God through such "power ministry." Fortunately, this work contains the full gamut.

Who Should Read This Book

Fighting in Faith is written with the healing and deliverance practitioner in mind, along with those who are not too afraid of Satan to obey God in this area of ministry. If you discern that God has gifted you to operate in the prophetic, healing and deliverance, or "power" ministry, including the performance of miracles and the casting out of demons, this book is specifically written with you in mind. If you have never operated in power ministry before but strongly believe God is moving you in this area of godly service, this book is for you too.

However, if you are the type of person who simply likes to constantly learn biblical principles or new things about God but is never motivated to put them into active practice, then I can assure you that this book is not for you! This book is specifically written under the guidance of the Holy Spirit for those who earnestly desire to put feet to their faith by actively doing the Word of God as opposed to being "forgetful hearers" who only deceive themselves. God faithfully promises to bless each and every one who "… looks into the perfect law of liberty and continues in it, and is not a forgetful hearer but a doer of the work." (James 1:25) Ask yourself right now: am I a doer of God's will, or am I a forgetful hearer?

As moved by the Holy Spirit of Christ Jesus, it is my goal to provide sound biblical instruction and hands-on practical strategies that have already proven to be successful in conducting spiritual warfare, even under the most dreadful and seemingly insurmountable circumstances. One caveat: everything you are about to learn presupposes that you have FAITH (belief plus trust) in Jesus and a desire to OBEY God regardless of what others think, have been filled with the Holy Spirit, and have already been delivered from doubt, fear, pride, and unbelief. If you do not meet all of these qualifications, please do not try to perform anything written in this book until you have done so. Otherwise you will be effectively playing with hellfire at the risk of your soul being eternally separated from God in the lake of fire.

A Solemn Promise

I solemnly promise that if you have and maintain mustard-seed faith as you read through this book, by the time you are done reading and completing the practical exercises, the Holy Spirit will have fully equipped you to "move mountains" as Jesus promised every believer in Mark 11:22–26. One of the most fascinating aspects of this book is that it freely shares the spiritual wealth God has bestowed upon me over the past fifteen years. God has inspired me to use this book to pour into as many people as He wills the same type of

Fighting in Faith

supernatural abilities with which He has empowered me. You are about to be exposed to some of the most miraculous things you have ever seen, heard, or read. Stay with me on this journey to God's awesome power and ability to change lives, heal sick minds and bodies, perform unheard-of miracles, and most importantly save lost souls from Hell and the lake of fire.

Note: All Scripture citations in this book are from the New King James Version (NKJV) unless specified otherwise.

Chapter 1

CONQUERING DOUBT, FEAR, PRIDE, AND UNBELIEF

"There is no fear in love; but perfect love casts out fear, because fear involves torment. But he who fears has not been made perfect in love." (1 John 4:18)

If you believe in God, Jesus, and the Holy Spirit but do not believe Satan or demons exist and play active roles in our daily lives, then you do not believe 100 percent of the Holy Bible. I will further unequivocally state that if you have difficulty believing in the existence, influence, and activity of Satan and his fallen angels, more than likely you are already under the deception of doubt, which can be generated by a demon.

I often ask people if they believe God exists, and the usual answer is yes. However, when the same question is posed with respect to whether they believe Satan or demons are real, I notice a very skeptical look on their faces immediately followed either by an outright no or an equivocal response that's bathed in doubt or very strong disbelief, which is really faith against faith. They doubt that which God would have them believe and know, while they simultaneously believe that which Satan would have them accept. When this occurs the demon spirit of doubt literally cancels out the faith that God would have them retain in their hearts.

Without any doubt whatsoever, each of the responses confirms that the person's mind has been blinded to the truth of what the Bible says about Satan and demons, which like to operate in complete darkness that manifests in doubt and ultimately unbelief. This is what the Holy Bible refers to as a "blinded mind." Satan instills doubt, uncertainty, and skepticism in the minds of those who have difficulty believing 100 percent of the Bible "lest the light of the glorious gospel of Christ, who is the image of God, should shine unto them." (2 Cor. 4:3–4)

No doubt when our spiritual eyes (minds) are blinded, our hearts become hardened and very resistant to God's eternal truths and His gospel of eternal salvation through faith in Christ Jesus. The word "faith" is used throughout this book. In this regard, please understand that I am referring to belief plus trust whenever this word is used. When spiritual eyes are opened and hearts can accurately discern right from wrong and truth from error, faith can progress exponentially. When this occurs, we can see with our spiritual eyes, understand with our hearts, be healed of our sin or problem, and be converted to salvation in Christ Jesus. (John 12:40) Salvation in Greek is "sozo" which basically means blessed, protected, and delivered—not only from the ravages of Hell but also healed and cured of all afflictions, sicknesses, diseases, mental illnesses, and all other means whether caused by the wayward world or by the condemned flesh or by Satan and his demons. (www.blueletterBible.com)

The Spirit of Doubt

Several of Satan's most effective weapons are doubt, fear, pride, and unbelief, all of which are demonic spirits that are addressed in this book. Doubt is a spirit that causes its victim to have at least two opinions on a particular subject that requires only one. Having differing opinions on a single subject invites confusion, which can also be generated by a demon. Having a spirit of confusion substantially reduces the possibility of the victim possessing a solid opinion or belief, resulting in "double mindedness," which is a real blessing blocker. The Bible says one who doubts is "double minded" and should not expect to "receive anything from the Lord" because "he is a double-minded man, unstable in all his ways." (James 1:7–8)

Doubt cancels faith, and faith cancels doubt. The more doubt, the less faith—and the more faith, the less doubt. Accordingly Satan knows he can hinder our prayers and therefore potentially block blessings by instilling just a little doubt in our comprehension of God's promises in the Holy Bible.

The Spirit of Fear
With respect to fear, 2 Timothy 1:7 boldly proclaims, "…God has not given us the spirit of fear, but of love and of power and of a sound mind." The first eternal truth revealed is that fear is a spirit. Second, this spirit does not come from God, which means that it comes from Satan. Third, love, power, and a sound mind come from God. Please note that the scripture reads: "of love," "of power," and "of a sound mind," which effectively translates to "God has given us the spirit of love and the spirit of power and the spirit of a sound mind." Each of these spirits from God is an antidote to the spirit of fear that Satan wants to instill in everyone to preclude them from obeying and operating in the awesome and unlimited power of almighty God.

The Spirit of Pride
Concerning pride, the Bible declares that "pride goes before destruction and a haughty spirit before a fall." (Prov. 16:18) Pride was the original sin that welled up in Lucifer and moved him to lust after (which means covet) God's glory and be cast out of his heavenly estate. Could this be why God says "you shalt not covet" as the tenth commandment? (Exod. 20:17) Accordingly, to this very day, spirits of pride and arrogance are generated by Satan and his demons in their strategic plans to subtly entice mankind to exalt self above

God, knowing full well that God will crush such rebellion by abasing the rebels. Conversely God promises to exalt us before our enemies if and when we humble ourselves in submissive obedience to Him. (James 4:10)

The Spirit of Unbelief
With regard to the spirit of unbelief, the Bible clearly informs us that it is absolutely impossible to please God without faith. The opposite of faith is unbelief. Satan is fully aware that if he can get human beings into the position of strongly disbelieving the Bible, he has secured a soul for the damning eternal separation from God in Hell and ultimately the lake of fire. It is for this reason that the Bible says "…without faith it is impossible to please Him, for he who comes to God must believe that He is, and that He rewards those who diligently seek Him." (Heb. 11:6)

No doubt the ultimate goal of Satan is to methodically move human beings into doubt, fear, or pride so that they form a solid unbelief in the existence and love of God and end up in a hardened state of soul-damning unbelief. God's ordained remedy to address this matter and rescue His children from such deception and destruction in general is the concept of spiritual warfare. Healing and deliverance ministry, also called power ministry, is a very important aspect of spiritual warfare. Power ministry involves mano-a-mano battles with demonic spirits that have very subtly taken up residence in the human psyche without the victim's knowledge. These forces attack and influence the mind, will, emotions, longings, lusts, tendencies, proclivities, and desires. This kind of spiritual warfare entails protecting ourselves from the wiles of the devil and proactively eradicating all vestiges of his evil influences in our daily lives. Most have faith in God, and some have the will and desire to obey God at all costs, but few have conquered Doubt, Fear, Pride, and Unbelief. Have you?

Self-Deliverance Practicum
If you are unsure whether you have overcome doubt, fear, pride, and unbe-

lief, self-deliverance is the remedy. Are you ready to see, determine, and/or understand whether you are being hindered by satanic or demonic influences? In other words, are you ready to experience deliverance ministry for yourself? If so, let's do it right now by saying these words out loud:

Father God, I confess having some doubt, fear, pride, and unbelief in my spirit about the activity of Satan and demons in my daily life. I therefore renounce all doubt, fear, pride, and unbelief as it relates to what your Holy Word says about satanic and/or demonic activity in our daily lives. I break all agreements I may have allowed to come into my spirit related to doubt, fear, pride, and unbelief. Doubt, come out of me in the name of Jesus. Fear, come out of me in the name of Jesus. Pride, come out of me in the name of Jesus. Unbelief, come out of me in the name of Jesus.

Now please take at least six very deep breaths as follows:

Close your mouth.

Inhale through your nostrils until your lungs are completely filled with air.

Open your mouth and exhale until all of the air has been expelled.

Now please take a few moments (as long as you like) to thank Jesus for delivering you from doubt, fear, pride and unbelief. This is a step of deliverance that many people fail to take sufficient time to practice. Many times people receive their greatest deliverance and ultimately their complete freedom from sickness, disease, and demonic oppression when they simply take sufficient time to thank God for that which He has already done. This should always be done well before we start expecting God to do something else.

While undergoing this exercise, it is not uncommon to repetitively yawn, cough, or vomit, depending upon the level of entrenchment of doubt, fear, pride, or unbelief. However, the probability of the same is substantially reduced due to confession, renunciation, and the Breaking of agreement with each. If you underwent this deliverance exercise in spirit and in truth, you should feel much better now than you felt before you started. The greatest sign that you have been delivered (the malevolent spirits have been expelled) is that you feel spiritually and emotionally free or much lighter than you felt before you started this process.

The usual question is why? The reason most people feel lighter after having gone through deliverance is because all of the spiritual and emotional weight of years of unconfessed and unrepented sin has been lifted off the spirit or the mind, will, and emotions. Over the years God has graciously provided me with a somewhat easy way of explaining how this process works. Basically, each and every time a human being sins against God, it's like placing a single sheet of paper on the back side of your outstretched hand. While the weight of a single sheet of paper is barely noticeable, after years of sin, stubborn disobedience, and outright rebellion, the result will be the equivalent of a four-inch-thick telephone book on your hand. As you can imagine, that hand will have been slowly and very incrementally weighed down. However, when the person undergoes deliverance ministry, all of the paper comes off at once, which raises the hand back up to the level it was when the very first sheet of paper was placed there after the initial sin was committed. Accordingly the person feels light, free, and greatly refreshed spiritually, physically, emotionally, and psychologically. It is at this point that the victim can discern just how far they had been weighed down by years of stubbornness, rebellion, and sin against God. It also goes without saying that the person is very, very thankful for the goodness, grace, and mercy God demonstrated by delivering them from demonic powers they never really understood were weighing them down until they were cast out.

Being Filled with (and Controlled By) the Holy Spirit

If you have yet to be filled with the Holy Spirit, why not do so now? Receiving the Holy Spirit will substantially help you to spiritually comprehend this material and be motivated and equipped to successfully apply the same consistently. Please follow these instructions to receive an infilling of the Holy Spirit:

Go to a very private place where you can be alone with God for at least two hours with no telephone, television, radio, email, social media, or any other distractions. Prostrate yourself (lie face down on the floor) before God in complete silence for ten to fifteen minutes, just listening for God's very still, small voice. Think about the span of your entire life from your conception to the present. Say, "Thank you, Lord Jesus, for filling me with your Holy Spirit" (this is an act of faith), then start thanking God for every year of your life and every blessing the Holy Spirit brings to your memory. For example: "God, I thank you for my conception in 19__ or 20__. Thank you, God, for the first full year of my life in 19__ or 20__."

After coming up to the present time in your life, start rapidly repeating the words "thank you, Jesus, thank you, Jesus, thank you, Jesus" until the Holy Spirit activates your prayer language. This may take some time, depending upon how strong your desire is to speak in tongues, but don't give up; keep repeating these words until your tongues start to flow! This is something you really have to want very deeply within your soul and will definitely receive in due time, so please be patient. God promises "… whatever you ask for in prayer, having faith and [really] believing, you will receive." Matt. 21:22, Amplified Version)

Speaking in tongues and the issue of whether a Christian can be taught how to speak in tongues are addressed more thoroughly in chapter six.

This book is specifically designed to reveal God's truth about the awesome power genuine believers have in Christ Jesus to bring God's kingdom to Earth to conduct spiritual warfare and win the war, although we may lose a few battles between each victory. If you want to fulfill your God-given calling in life and be all you can be in Christ Jesus, please put on your spiritual seat belt. Upon learning the art of spiritual warfare, you can start fighting in faith and successfully execute Bible-based healing and deliverance ministry that God has ordained for every believer in Christ Jesus.

CHAPTER 2

THE NATURAL AND SUPERNATURAL REALMS

"Assuredly, I say to you, whatever you bind on earth will be bound in heaven, and whatever you loose on earth will be loosed in heaven." (Matt. 18:18)

Why is healing and deliverance ministry so very controversial and misunderstood? The short answer is that it is specifically designed to quickly, powerfully, and very effectively bring God's kingdom (His awesome power, protection, and peace) to conquer any issue, problem, or negative circumstance any human being may have.

When God's kingdom is brought to Earth, it immediately proceeds to eliminate every issue, problem, sickness, and disease generated by the fallen world, man's condemned flesh, or Satan and his legions of demons. Healing and deliverance is "power ministry" because it overpowers and conquers evil, sickness, disease (or as I call it "dis-ease"), and demonic activity in our daily lives. This is precisely the reason Satan and demons constantly fight to dissuade human beings from ever gaining a godly knowledge of the truth with respect to the power God so freely gives us to conquer dark forces through healing and deliverance ministry. Jesus said, "...you shall know the truth, and the truth shall make you free." (John 8:32) He specifically articulated this to people who were by all outward appearance not in any kind of bondage. This was declared to the Pharisees back then and to us now because many are slaves in thought, word, and deed, yet are oblivious to their true spiritual condition.

There is an art to conducting healing and deliverance ministry. Unfortunately the vast majority of "believers" are absolutely oblivious to the presence of evil spirits due to demonically driven feelings of doubt, fear, pride, and outright unbelief. Satan and his legions of demons have bewitched and blinded the minds of many to the fact that these evil spirits are real and play active roles in our daily lives. Jesus plainly warns, "The thief does not come except to steal, and to kill, and to destroy." (John 10:10a)

This warning is not to be taken lightly, because it is a literal statement that demonic spirits like doubt, confusion, and/or unbelief can and will deceive the ignorant, unsuspecting, or lackadaisical reader into blowing past any mention of these things without much cognition or spiritual meditation. The very good news is that the spiritual antidote for this eternal ailment is found in the next sentence: "I am come that they might have life, and that they might have it more abundantly."(John 10:10b) Jesus uses this single verse of Scripture to concisely and very powerfully describe the cosmic battle that plays out in the invisible spirit realm twenty-four. seven, whether human beings realize it or not.

Two Critical Facts

Unfortunately, most people on Earth are absolutely clueless of two critical facts that can make a world of difference in our lives on a daily basis. One, there is a supernatural or spirit realm. The terms "spirit realm" and "supernatural realm" are synonyms and will be used interchangeably throughout this book. Two, the spirit realm influences, motivates, controls, and often exercises dominion over the natural realm. Jesus Himself confidently confirms this with these words: "…assuredly, I say to you, whatever you bind on earth will be bound in heaven, and whatever you loose on earth will be loosed in heaven." (Matt. 18:18)

Jesus solemnly informs us of the reality of the spirit realm and reveals the interconnectivity between it and the natural realm. He further explains the awesome power we have when we agree with each other: "Again I say to you that if two of you agree on earth concerning anything they ask, it will be done for them by My Father in heaven." (Matt. 18:19)

In Matthew 18, verses eighteen and nineteen reveal two very important doctrinal truths that we will either believe, embrace, and use to our benefit or reject—and be severely harmed to our personal detriment. These spiritual truths are very real, whether we acknowledge and accept them or not. In verse eighteen, Jesus reveals there is direct connectivity between the natural and the supernatural realms, and that human beings can bind or loose powers in Heaven that will manifest results on Earth. In other words, that which mankind does in the natural realm has direct impact and influence in the supernatural realm.

For example, if demonic spirits are negatively influencing a person to be addicted to drugs, alcohol, or any form of sexual immorality and that person renounces his or her sinful misconduct, the renunciation binds those spiritual forces and forbids them to continue their assault on that person's mind, will, and emotions. This has the ultimate impact of setting that human soul free from the bondage of sinful misconduct. Man's equivalent of this is called the power of positive thinking. However, this is much more than positive thinking. This is an act of man's God-given will and ability to decree things into existence, thereby greatly impacting what will transpire in the heavenly realm.

The other side of the coin is "loosing," which can be positive or negative, beneficial or detrimental to the human body, mind, soul, or will. For example, if God has called on and equipped a person to serve Him as a medical doctor, the person has received divine authority to minister to the world in that capacity. However, if the person allows devilish thoughts of fear (of failure), doubt (that she or he cannot make it through college), or unbelief (that she or he can successfully pass the state medical licensing exam), this person will fail to fulfill her or his purpose. This will be true chiefly because the person failed to bind those malevolent spirits of doubt, fear, and unbelief. These are all supernatural forces specifically designed to negatively impact, influence, control, and/or dominate matters taking place in the natural realm.

As you can discern, this spiritual warfare plays out on a daily basis, which means those who lack sufficient knowledge pertaining to binding and loosing are being attacked and often devastated spiritually, emotionally, and psychologically. Without question, being clothed in just a little knowledge of the power believers are authorized to wield in the name of Jesus can make a world of difference in our daily lives.

Spiritual Slavery
Jesus confirms that a cosmic battle is taking place between the natural realm and the spirit realm with these solemn words: "Most assuredly, I say to you, whoever commits sin is a slave of sin." (John 8:34)

Many fail to grasp that this statement is not metaphorical but spiritually factual. Here Jesus reveals the true nature of spiritual slavery, which is much more dangerous and deadly than slavery in the natural realm. To be a slave is to be under the influence, control, or domineering power of another. Because no physical confinement is required for spiritual slavery, many (if not most) people are deceived into believing they are free to do as they please when they are in fact bound in the worst of ways.

For example, have you ever heard a person addicted to nicotine say words to this effect: "I'm not addicted to smoking—I can quit anytime I want to" or "I've quit before, so I know I can quit?" This is a classic example of a person whose mind has been so deceived that they absolutely deny they are addicted when they are in the worst way. To stop means to bring something to a complete end. Here the person has been deceived into believing that taking breaks from smoking is the same as quitting cold turkey. The reality is they have never actually stopped, so they are comfortable with the idea of continuing to smoke because they falsely believe they can stop at will. This kind of demonic deception is specifically designed to lull the person into such a deep spiritual sleep over their perilous condition that they continue to smoke until it slowly and methodically kills them, thereby fulfilling John 10:10: "The thief does not come except to steal, and to kill, and to destroy."

This is spiritual slavery, which is much worse than physical slavery because the victims fail to understand that they are living in bondage. The victims are unduly influenced, addicted to, and thereby controlled by cravings, lusts, and perceived needs that dominate the mind, will, and emotions. They are therefore slaves to the satanic and demonic forces that motivate them to think and therefore act on their wayward thoughts. With respect to smoking, this is especially true if and when they come under any kind of stress or anxiety. The first thing they will reach for to get relief is their little-*g* god called nicotine.

You can replace nicotine addiction (smoking or chewing tobacco) with just about any other habitual sin, and the fact will remain the same. For example, people are spiritual slaves to the cravings of adultery, alcohol consumption, assault, battery, bestiality, fornication, homosexuality, fetishes, infidelity, masturbation, pyromania, suicidal thinking, whoredom, and many, many others. Jesus warns us that Satan and his demons come "to steal and to kill and to destroy." (John 10:10) This being the case, how is it that addictions are so powerful despite the fact that Jesus solemnly warns us of them?

The short answer is that Satan and his demons have bewitched what appears to be the vast majority of people on Earth into having doubt, fear, pride, and unbelief. These demonic spirits are specifically released into the lives of stubborn, ignorant, unbelieving, and/or rebellious people who reject

God's truth. God's absolute truth is either negligently avoided through biblical ignorance or outright rejected in stubborn or rebellious disobedience. Please forgive such stern language, but it is quite necessary to employ it to wake you up to receive that which God has ordained to empower you to "fight the good fight of faith." (1 Tim. 6:12)

Unfortunately, if and when people continue rejecting God's love and truth through doubt, fear, pride, unbelief, or otherwise, after a certain point, God will "send…strong delusion, that they should believe the lie" so that "they all may be condemned who did not believe the truth but had pleasure in unrighteousness." (2 Thess. 2:12)

This verse plainly warns that when mankind continues to reject God's love and truth, God himself will make sure they receive the lies of the enemy, which fosters their ultimate damnation in the lake of fire because they refuse to accept God's holy truth. The million-dollar question is, Why and how did they reject God? The answer is that they allowed demonic spirits of doubt, fear, pride, and unbelief to influence, control, and ultimately destroy their entire lives.

Human Beings Are Instruments of War
God created mankind to fight evil forces face to face in hand-to-hand combat with the aid, guidance, comfort, counsel, and empowerment of the Holy Spirit. Jesus immediately established this mode of ministry after having been baptized in the Jordan River then "led up by the Spirit into the wilderness to be tempted by the devil." (Matt. 4:1) Yes, you read that right. The Holy Spirit led Jesus into the wilderness to be tempted by Satan himself, and it all took place immediately after Jesus was baptized and heard God say, "This is my beloved Son, in whom I am well pleased." (Matt. 3:17)

This begs the question that if God is well pleased with His only begotten son, then why is He setting him up to be tempted by Satan? The answer is for the exact same reason God placed Adam and Eve in the Garden of Eden to face Satan mano a mano and conquer each and every wile, plot, and devilish scheme he would launch against them. Unfortunately, the first Adam fell for those temptations which Satan is still using to hunt down, deceive, and enslave lost souls to do his evil bidding and then ultimately destroy them in Hell: namely, the "lust of the flesh, the lust of the eyes, and the pride of life." (I John 2:16) Eve was tempted and overtaken by all three of these evil temptations when she "…saw that the tree was good for food, that it was pleasant to the eyes, and a tree desirable to make one wise, [and] she took of its fruit and ate. She also gave to her husband with her, and he ate." (Gen. 3:6)

When Adam and Eve ate of the single tree from which God specifically forbade them to eat, they failed a very important test that God Himself had authorized. As will be discussed momentarily, God had already dethroned Lucifer, one of his three archangels, from his heavenly estate. The eternal punishment was that Lucifer was to be cast down to Earth to be ruled over by man under the aid, guidance, counsel, and inspiration of the Holy Spirit. However, Lucifer, who became Satan, flipped the script by deceiving Eve while Adam, the head of the household, sat idly by and allowed his wife and himself to fall into temptation. Unfortunately this scenario is still playing out in households around the entire world today, which is replicative rebellion and disobedience.

Men Are to Serve as Priest, Prophet, and King

God created and ordained men to serve three very important roles in the family: priest, prophet, and king. As priest of the household, men—and especially married men—are to be servant leaders in the things of God such as leading family prayer, taking charge in biblical instruction, and most importantly setting an example by living out a Christian life. As prophet a man is supposed to have a personal relationship with God in the person of Jesus and therefore hear from and obey the promptings of the Holy Spirit. Finally, as king a man is to be the chief protector and provider for the family in both the natural and supernatural realms.

When men are consistently and comfortably serving in all three capacities, it is virtually impossible for either Satan or any demon to even get a toehold, let alone a foothold or any stronghold in the family. However, when there are chinks in any one of these areas of a man's service as priest, prophet, or king, Satan will come in and wreak as much havoc as possible. Chinks in the armor are any kind of sin or unrighteousness whatsoever. This relates to both sins of commission and sins of omission. Sins of commission are perpetrated when we actively do that which should not be done according to God's Holy Word. Sins of omission involve our negligent failure or willful refusal to do that which is right when we know it should be done. Either one is more than enough to authorize evil forces to enter into the mind, will, and emotions and cause chaos.

Unfortunately, this is what happened to Adam, and the horrendous results have been reverberating ever since. For example, a lack of contentment in Eve allowed her to fall into satanic temptation. She was enticed and then seduced her husband to follow suit. This generated a spirit of fear in both of them that caused them to sew fig leaves together to make aprons to try to hide themselves from God in their sinful state. It was the spirit of rebellion that led them to disobey God in the first place, along with the spirit of idolatry that enticed them to desire to "be like God, knowing good and evil." (Gen. 3:5) Could this have been the exact same spirit that caused Lucifer to be cast out of his heavenly estate?

Finally, this sinful misconduct ultimately produced the very first recorded murder when demonic spirits of jealousy and envy seduced Cain to rise up in unjustified anger and kill his righteous brother, Abel. (Gen. 4:8) As we can now discern, the fact that Adam failed in his duties as priest, prophet, and king led to curses of sibling rivalry and disunity that have been going on for thousands of years. Fortunately, the second Adam came in the flesh to finish the eternal work that Satan successfully kept the first Adam from completing.

Chapter 3

MY BURNING-BUSH MOMENT

> Now Moses was tending the flock of Jethro his father-in-law, the priest of Midian. And he led the flock to the back of the desert, and came to Horeb, the mountain of God. And the Angel of the Lord appeared to him in a flame of fire from the midst of a bush. So he looked, and behold, the bush was burning with fire, but the bush was not consumed. (Exod. 3:1–2)

God loves to employ a measure of His miraculous divine power to interrupt the normal course of life to focus or refocus our attention on Him and matters of the spirit realm. This is what is commonly called a burning-bush moment. God uses burning-bush moments to "stir up our spirit man to focus on things on a much higher spiritual plane." For instance, when Moses observed a bush that was on fire, yet the flames had absolutely no power over the bush, God successfully gained 100 percent of his undivided attention. This was plainly evident because Moses stopped everything he was doing and said, "I will now turn aside and see this great sight, why the bush does not burn." (Exod. 3:3)

After Moses properly responded to the sign, wonder, and miracle, God spoke to Moses. Moses spoke back to God, which then providentially allowed God to speak to many others through Moses's obedience. This wonderful exchange between Moses (man) and God (man's creator) is recorded: "So when the Lord saw that he turned aside to look, God called to him from the midst of the bush and said, 'Moses, Moses!' And he said, 'Here I am.'" (Exod. 3:4)

My Burning-Bush Moment
God spoke to me powerfully the day our twenty-three-month-old daughter started walking on her own for the first time in March of 2001. My wife, Cassandra, had given birth to her in April of 2000. Our daughter started walking approximately a year and a half before I would have my next miraculous moment with God. The second took place during an intercessory prayer and prophetic ministerial session at a Marketplace Ministries conference in St. Augustine, Florida, conducted by Os Hillman, president of Marketplace Leaders. More about this will be covered in the next chapter.

This is our only child but my third, the first two of which were born over eighteen years before while I was in college. My first child was conceived when I was an eighteen-year-old high school student but born while I was away in my first year of college. My second was born three years later when I was a junior in undergraduate school. I was neither saved, sanctified, nor filled with the Holy Spirit back then. In fact it would be quite accurate to say I was a heathen, although I had initially confessed faith in Jesus during an encounter with a door-to-door evangelist walking the streets of our neighborhood while I was home on brief break from college in 1981. However, I went back to college and continued living the same wayward, rebellious, slick, whorish lifestyle I had been living before I met that bold evangelist on that fateful day. What I failed to realize was that a spiritual hook had been placed in me that God would later use to literally reel me in, pick me up, turn my life upside down (in reality right side up) and place my spiritual feet upon solid ground. All this would be done so

He could send me back out into the world to help others know Jesus of Nazareth the Christ and thereby be "partakers of the divine nature, having escaped the corruption that is in the world through lust." (2 Pet. 1:4)

I missed many firsts in the lives of my first two children because I was away from home attending college and doing the things that eighteen- to twenty-year-olds do—drink, party, and lie to and play around with females. I missed witnessing my first two children's births and first steps, helping them tie their shoes, taking them to their first day of school, and on down the line. Upon hanging up the phone back in 1982 with my second child's maternal grandmother, who called to tell me the gender and health of my second child, I vividly recall thinking, "I'm really messing up my life. Part of me is doing very well in college, but another part of me is really not doing good at all."

I was assessing my life, and I did not like what I was becoming. Although I was in no way living right, neither going to any church nor reading the Bible, I felt guilty and very remorseful for having missed witnessing the births of my first two children. What I did not know at the time was that the Holy Spirit was convicting me "of sin, and of righteousness, and of judgment." (John 16:8) In response to such conviction, I recall having said a prayer along these lines:

> "God, I'm really messing up my life. If you ever bless me to have a wife and another child, I want to make every first. I want to see that child being born, start walking, tie shoes, go to school, and down the line."

Afterward, I graduated from college in 1983 and law school in 1985. I started practicing law in 1986 and married my wife, Cassandra, in 1988. My wife conceived in 1999 while I was in the middle of a campaign for the Florida House of Representatives. She gave birth the following year. The campaign was from 1999 through the date of the election in September of

2000. This was a state-level office, which meant I would need to temporarily live away from home while the legislative session took place in another city located about 170 miles away. The legislative sessions run March through April, and members are required to be present in the city during the sessions. Needless to say, I had forgotten about the prayer that I prayed in my college dorm room back in 1982.

I ran for this position with everything in me. I was fully dedicated to the cause, as I intended to go and represent the people. I was determined to win; I thought I would win; I knew I was going to win. I lost! The loss was a very hard loss. In fact it had me wondering about my entire life. I was thinking, "How could I have lost this election? Everything was set in place for me to win and I should have won." I had prayed about running and prayed about winning and felt very good about everything that had taken place except the actual election returns. Just before going to bed that fateful night, I prayed, "God, why did I lose this race, why? I don't understand why I lost." I received absolutely no response from God that night, the next day, the next week';, or the next month, which was October 2000. I can't say this really surprised me because I did not have a close relationship with God at that time but had sense enough to pray. After having received no answer whatsoever, I went on with my life, continuing to practice law and going to church sporadically but never attending Sunday school or midweek Bible study or going out with any of the church's door-to-door witnessing teams on Saturday mornings.

The Hand of God
In March of 2001, our baby picked herself up and started walking while the three of us were in the den. In complete excitement, my wife and I started clapping our hands, praising God and encouraging her to keep walking. As I was in the highest happiness watching her take those first several baby steps, I saw a very large hand that was about two feet in both height and width pointing at our daughter while she was walking. The hand was transparent,

which meant I could see both it and my daughter while looking through it, for it was between us as she was walking. My great excitement about her taking her very first steps suddenly changed to great fear—even terror—because I knew neither what this giant hand was nor what this meant.

I had mixed emotions. On the one hand, I was excited about the fact that our daughter was taking her first steps right in front of both me and my wife. On the other hand, I was terrified about the meaning of this giant hand with its index finger pointing at my baby girl. All of a sudden, I heard this voice in my mind saying these very fateful and true words: "That's why you lost!"

As these words were being spoken to my mind, the hand vanished, and I was left with a clear and unobstructed view of our baby walking across the room. Things were happening so quickly that I did not immediately relate these four words to the election that I had lost seven months prior. As I was meditating on the meaning of these four words, the voice spoke to my mind again, asking me, "Where would you be right now had you won the election?" All of a sudden, God then reminded me of the prayer that I had prayed to Him way back in 1982 when I had said that I would be there for every "first" if He would ever bless me to have a wife and another child. Simultaneously God also reminded me of the prayer that I had prayed to Him back in September of the previous year asking why I had lost that election. God then focused my attention on where I would have been at this very moment had I won that election.

All of a sudden, great awe and reverence for God filled my entire being. God showed me a vision of what would have happened to me had I won that election. Our daughter would have started walking that same day, and I would have been out of town for the third time one of my children took their first steps without me being present. My wife would have called to tell me, and I would have felt like the complete failure that I would have been—successful on the political side but a failure on the marriage and family side of life, which is vastly more important.

I was now beginning to appreciate the absolute reality of God and how He loved me more than I loved myself. This was proven in that He remembered a prayer that I had prayed nineteen years before that I had completely forgotten. This was my very personal and customized burning bush moment. This awesome experience arrested my attention to the point that I could no longer question, wonder about, or deny the supernatural presence, impact, influence, and absolute love God was demonstrating in my life. Even as I recalled this very pivotal moment in my life for this book, I had to stop typing, fall to the floor in tears, and thank God again for having reached down from Heaven to touch my heart and forever change my life that fateful day in March of 2001.

Awestruck

"He is your praise, and He is your God, who has done for you these great and awesome things which your eyes have seen." (Deut. 10:21)

I was completely awestruck for several reasons. First, I was in awe because God remembered that first prayer that I had prayed way back in 1982 at the birth of my second child, saying that I wanted to witness every first if He ever blessed me with a wife and another child born in that marriage. He remembered it, despite the fact that I had completely forgotten. Second, I was awed because God simultaneously and very providentially answered the second prayer that was delivered to Him seven months prior, asking Him for the reason I lost the 2000 election. Finally, I was greatly humbled, appreciative, and absolutely thrilled that God loved me so much that He mercifully allowed me to lose the election (one of many battles) so I could win the war—quality time with my family while simultaneously witnessing our daughter's firsts. Speaking of which, she's currently fifteen, and just two weeks ago, I witnessed her putting contact lenses in for the first time, which was a huge accomplishment for her. These firsts never ever get old.

Fruit Production

"…the fruit of the Spirit is love, joy, peace, longsuffering, kindness, goodness, faithfulness, gentleness, self-control…" (Gal. 5:22, 23)

This burning-bush moment stirred up my spirit and caused me to focus on things on a much higher spiritual plane. It strongly impacted my entire being. I began to thank God for so many things that I had taken for granted—excellent health and physical fitness, my marriage, my family, my degrees, my career, and many other things. Most importantly this burning-bush moment caused me to pursue God with everything in me—my heart, mind, soul, spirit, and strength. I made a commitment to regularly attend Sunday school and Bible study on Wednesdays. I made a commitment to regularly read the Bible, which turned out to be every night. I moved on to take discipleship classes at church, the most powerful and life changing of which is called Master Life. I started fasting, witnessing to anyone who didn't refuse to listen, and leading complete strangers to Christ. I actively participated in church sponsored door-to-door witnessing projects and started praying over and leading clients to Christ at my law office, at the courthouse, at the jail, and anywhere else God would provide me with such opportunity.

My demeanor and overall disposition changed. I was starting to experience peace in my life. God's providential sanctification process was starting to set in. My values, attitudes, and overall temperament changed. My pastor noticed these virtues and decided to invite my wife and me to a Marketplace Ministries conference in St. Augustine, Florida, about which I testify in the next chapter. I was at this conference when I had what I consider to be a second burning-bush moment in which God again used a word of knowledge about my infant daughter to arrest my attention. (1 Cor. 12:8) It was after that conference that I had a third burning-bush moment with God, and He ordained me to preach and teach the gospel.

Chapter 4
MY SEPARATION FOR MINISTRY

The anointing which you have received from Him abides in you, and you do not need that anyone teach you; but as the same anointing teaches you concerning all things, and is true, and is not a lie, and just as it has taught you, you will abide in Him. (1 John 2:27)

My Introduction to Spiritual Gifts in Active Operation
In September 2002, my wife Cassandra and I attended a Marketplace Ministry conference in St. Augustine, Florida, which is within an hour's drive from where we live in Jacksonville. The theme of the conference was that ministry and godly service are not limited to the four walls of church buildings. Likewise the mantra of Marketplace Ministries is that God ordains, gifts, equips, empowers, and strategically places people in positions of power, authority, and influence in the secular marketplace. This anointing is for the specific purposes of witnessing and sharing the gospel message with people we meet and with whom we converse Sunday through Saturday in our regular endeavors at work and social events.

A very interesting part of the conference was a fifteen-minute session with several ladies who were gifted in prophecy. Conference attendees could sign up for a brief intercessory prayer session and be prayed over and prophesied to by these very gifted women. My wife and I were interested but simultaneously very skeptical. In this regard, we both agreed not to reveal to these ladies any information about anything related to us. We agreed that if they were as good as they were reputed to be, they would be able to tell us everything without us having to tell them anything. We went in and sat down before four women. Almost immediately they focused on me, with the first lady asking, "Are you a minister?" to which I said no," as God had yet to set me apart for ministerial service at that time. To be frank, I answered the question with much disdain because I never, absolutely never in my wildest dreams, had wanted to be a minister. In fact I grew up hating all ministers, preachers, and especially pastors because of the sexual sins, repetitive criminality, and ultimate suicide of the person who pastored a church my family briefly attended when I was a child.

Another lady asked, "Are you an evangelist?" I again said no. Despite my truthful answers, one by one these ladies began saying words to this effect: "I see you standing up, preaching God's word very powerfully, and people are responding and giving their lives to Christ." They continued on, saying, "While you're preaching and doing God's work, you must remember that you will be speaking for God and not yourself." They further cautioned that often when God uses people in such very powerful ways, they forget that the power is God's power and that it's God doing miraculous things through them and not themselves who are doing such wonderful things.

Quite frankly, I laughed in my spirit while thinking these ladies were complete quacks. Just about the time I entertained this doubt, the Holy Spirit spoke a word of knowledge through the youngest of the ladies, which was like a bolt of lightning to my spirit. It really jolted me into the spiritual authenticity of these ladies' awesome gifting from God. She said, "You have a minor daughter at home, right?" By this time our daughter was approximately two and a half years old. At that time she was back home with her

Fighting in Faith

grandparents. We had just met these people in St. Augustine, so we fully realized they knew nothing about us, nor did we know anything about them. We were all complete strangers to one another. However, this was very accurate as to both the gender and approximate age of our daughter.

Although this was laser-like accuracy, I recall thinking to myself, "That was a lucky guess." I would later come to realize that such skepticism was really an outright demonic attack from the evil spirit of doubt that was warring in my mind in a very strong and concerted attempt to convince me to ignore or completely discount that wonderful and amazing information the Holy Spirit was pouring into my spirit through these women. No doubt, each of these ladies was operating her spiritual gifting at optimal levels.

As previously stated, doubt is a demonic spirit whose specific job is to generate a stronghold of skepticism in one's mind, will, and emotions about the inerrancy of God's Holy Word, His promises, and His awesome power. This is especially true for those whom God ordains to be saved and those who are called and sent to be used by God to help save others. Satan knows the absolute veracity of Hebrews 11:6, which says, "Without faith it is impossible to please Him, for he who comes to God must believe that He is, and that He is a rewarder of those who diligently seek Him." A great battle of the mind was going on in that intercessory prayer session. On the one hand, the Holy Spirit was using those faithful and very spiritually gifted women to speak godly prophecy into our lives. Conversely, satanically driven demons were simultaneously battling the truth with evil thoughts of doubt, fear, pride, and unbelief.

We confirmed that we had a child in the home, but we were both still very skeptical of what we were hearing until the same young lady spoke her next words, which shocked me and almost made me fall out of my chair. She then said, "And she likes American flags, doesn't she?"

Our daughter, who is fifteen at the writing of this book, absolutely loved American flags when she was a toddler. We never knew why, but she loved to hold them and run around the house, jumping up and down waving them. She did it all the time. She loved them so much that no matter what store we were in, if she saw an American flag, she would want us to buy it for her. Accordingly this spoken word had such pinpoint specificity that I could not deny it with a clean conscience. I recall thinking, "What on Earth could have given this lady such accurate information?" I was kind of fearful and simultaneously joyful, which bespeaks just how awesome an experience this was. This is precisely what reverence means, as it was pure awe that I was experiencing.

No doubt these ladies were actively operating in their spiritual gifting at the absolute highest levels. My wife and I were quite spellbound because of the exceptional accuracy of the information they were speaking under the apparent inspiration of the Holy Spirit of Christ Jesus. By God's awesome providence, I would later come to realize that God used this bit of information to arrest my attention so that I could start giving heed to that which was being spoken to us by the Holy Spirit through these gifted ladies.

Word of Wisdom, Word of Knowledge, and Prophecy
The information relayed about our daughter was a word of knowledge, while the message about me preaching was a prophecy of things that were surely to come in the future. These were the fulfillment of Scripture in our hearing and comprehension. 1 Corinthians 12, verses 8–11 read as follows:

> For to one is given the word of wisdom through the Spirit, to another the word of knowledge through the same Spirit, to another faith by the same Spirit, to another gifts of healings by the same Spirit, to another the working of miracles, to another prophecy, to another discerning of spirits, to another different kinds of tongues, to another the interpretation of tongues. But one and the same Spirit works all these things, distributing to each one individually as He wills.

My wife and I had just witnessed and personally experienced the active, accurate, and very awesome operation of spiritual gifting in these women of God. The inquiries about whether I was a minister or an evangelist were in fact prophetic words telling what would surely come to pass—and much sooner than I would ever imagine. The statements about our daughter were words of knowledge which, by definition, is information revealed by the Holy Spirit that is already in existence presently or has existed in the past. Finally, the statements cautioning and warning me about being ever mindful of the fact that the very powerful evangelistic work and the successes of the same will be God's work, power, authority, and influence flowing through me and not my own were words of wisdom. By definition a word of wisdom is when the Holy Spirit gives godly advice as to how to go about handling situations and circumstances to bring about righteous results. When such godly spiritual advice is followed, mankind will be comforted, edified, encouraged, and strengthened, but most importantly God will be glorified, which is why human beings exist in the first place. This encounter with the Holy Spirit speaking into our lives through those women would have a very deep impact on my life and ministry for years to come. Within just two months from that meeting with those gifted women, God would shock me again by commissioning me to do the very things that were spoken.

Fulfillment of Prophecy: My Separation for Service to Preach, Teach, and Minister God's Holy Word

On Friday, November 1, 2002, at approximately 8:15 a.m., I was preparing breakfast and repetitively singing (make that trying to sing) the hymn "Lift Him Up," the chorus of which goes "And I, if I be lifted up from the earth, will draw all men unto me." While in the process of repetitively "singing" this hymn, I suddenly heard these words from the Lord: "I am separating you for service in the kingdom to teach the word with the aid, guidance, and counsel of the Holy Spirit as opposed to man's finite wisdom."

While these words were registering in my spirit, it seemed as though I lost all strength in my body, and I became very weak. It was beginning to dawn on me that I was being spoken to by the author and finisher of the universe. I was forced to recognize it, as every part of my entire being immediately fell into a complete state of reverence. I suddenly fell prostrate as I was hearing those very solemn words in my mind. I soon found myself praying, telling God, "Yes, I will do what you want me to do." I further prayed, asking God to keep me humble and real in my calling.

I immediately called my wife, then my parents to tell them the wonderful and shocking news of my separation for service, and they were all very excited. I then called my home church to speak with my pastor, but he was traveling. However, I was able to speak with his second-in-command, who was not at all surprised at the news I shared. To my surprise, he said that he and my pastor had already discussed how they perceived that the Lord was moving in me and preparing me for the ministry. I asked why they never told me, to which he replied, "We can't tell you; God has to tell you." God had in fact just told me in a very loving and powerful way that I will never ever forget!

Looking back to the prophecies I received at the Marketplace Ministries conference in St. Augustine, which was in September of 2002, I see that this divine encounter with God was the beginning of the fulfillment of those prophecies which were delivered to me just sixty days before God spoke to my heart, commissioning me to preach, teach, and minister. I was very much interested in finding these ladies and sitting down with them again for three primary reasons. First, I wanted to wrap my mind around how in Heaven they could have known that God was going to commission me to be a minister. Second, I wanted to hear more details about what they saw God doing with me in the future. Third, I wanted to know if it was possible for me to learn how to minister to people and prophesy over them with the same pinpoint accuracy these ladies had delivered to me. I was able to make contact with the leader of the group. She later trained me in the ways of Bible-based spiritual gifts activation, accurate prophecy, and healing and deliverance ministry. This will be addressed more fully in the next chapter.

A Divine Appointment on the Day I Was Sent to Preach
Sometime between ten o'clock and eleven o'clock in the morning on the day I was ordained as a minister, God spoke again, telling me to immediately go to an election polling site. I already had an appointment to meet my team at one at 1:00 p.m. to go over procedures for the general election that would take place the next Tuesday. I was the designated precinct captain at a polling site located in a local senior citizen center. However, God was telling me to go there two to three hours early, when not one of the people I was supposed to meet at one o'clock would be there.

I obeyed God and went to the site. I recall going into the room where I would later meet the people, and the room appeared to be in order, but no one was there—nor should they have been, as I was a few hours early. I was very perplexed, so I went out in the main lobby and sat down on a bench, pondering why I was there. Shortly after I sat down, a man who was seated to my right said, "I hope everything goes well."

Without even looking in his direction, I replied, "Yeah, I hope the election goes well next week too."

To this he replied, "I'm not talking about the election. I'm having surgery next week."

Hearing those words caused me to stop, turn, and look him straight in the eye. Something within me said, "This is why you're here." I immediately thought to myself, "He might need salvation," so I asked him if he knew Jesus. He replied yes and that he had been saved for well over forty years. I was obviously not sent to lead him to confess faith in Jesus. Still perplexed, I then asked if I could pray for him concerning his surgery, and he said, "Yes, we all need prayer." I then placed my right hand on his left shoulder, bowed my head, closed my eyes, and began to pray for his surgery to be successful.

Just as I started to pray, another man sat down very close (too close) to me on the opposite side, squeezing me between himself and the other man. This man said, "I need some of that too." By his voice I discerned that he was African American, but I had yet to actually see him as my eyes were still closed as I prayed for the first gentleman, who happened to be white. So there I was, sandwiched between two men and praying with my eyes closed while people were passing back and forth. This was way, way outside of my comfort zone, but I was just going with the flow of what I would later understand was a divine setup to point me in the right direction in the ministerial services God had commissioned me to perform just two hours or so before that time.

As I finished the prayer, the man to my right immediately and joyfully said, "I know my surgery is going to go well next week."

In complete surprise I asked, "How do you know that?"

He then said words to this effect: "As soon as you touched me, I felt heat in your hand, and I know heat when I feel it because I used to do massage therapy for years in New York." I was completely speechless, as no one had ever said such a thing to me before.

Having been encouraged, strengthened, and further motivated by these very gracious words, I then eagerly turned to face the man to my left and asked him why he needed prayer. He said, "I have a bad heart" or "a weak heart." I then took my right hand—the same hand from which the other gentlemen had said he felt heat—placed it on his chest over his heart, and prayed for God to heal, strengthen, and bless his heart. He smiled and said that he felt much better. So there I was sitting on a bunch between two complete strangers, one white and the other African American, conducting what I would later come to know as healing and deliverance ministry in a public place which happened to be a senior citizen activity center.

After this encounter I went back to my law office to finish the work that I had been doing when God had interrupted everything earlier and sent me to the senior citizen center for what I would soon realize was a divine appointment with two messengers from Heaven. Scripture warns believers, "Do not forget to entertain strangers, for by so doing some have unwittingly entertained angels." (Heb. 13:2) I would soon discover the literal accuracy of this passage of scripture from the Holy Bible.

As I worked on legal matters for clients in my law office, my mind would not leave that encounter I had had with those two complete strangers. Something inside of me kept saying, "More happened there than you understand," which made me want to see those men again and ask them some questions about what had happened to them when I was praying over them. I could hardly wait to return to that place to talk to them again. Something kept telling me that what transpired between the three of us was very, very important, though I could not discern it as it was taking place. I returned to the senior citizen center approximately thirty minutes before the time I had set to meet my team to go over election procedures. I went early so I would have some time to speak with those two gentlemen again. However, I could not find them anywhere in the entire facility. I then went to the receptionist's desk to describe the men and ask if she knew either of them. Her desk was directly across the walkway from where we had been seated hours earlier, and she had been there then, so I figured she might have seen me sitting there talking and praying with them.

When I asked her about the two men who were seated with me on the bench earlier that morning, she said that no one there fitted those descriptions. I then said, "But I was sitting down on that bench right there talking with them earlier this morning."

Here's the kicker: she then said, "Yeah, I saw you sitting over there earlier, but no one was with you. You were by yourself."

As you can imagine, her reply caused me to lose strength in all of my being for the second time that day. It was at this very moment that my suspicions were confirmed: there was much more to this meeting than had originally registered with me. I had in fact entertained two angels from

Heaven, both of whom had allowed me to pray for them for healing.

The encounter with these two messengers from Heaven would ultimately prove to be exceptionally important in the type of miracle-working and miracle-receiving ministry God would progressively usher me into and ultimately have me share all over the world through ministering, preaching, and teaching (spiritual gifts activation locally and abroad) and now via my first book.

Just think about the dynamic of what happened and how quickly it transpired in just a few short hours in a single day! That morning God spoke to my mind and commissioned me to preach His word through the infinite wisdom of the Holy Spirit, as opposed to man's very limited wisdom. Within just a few hours, He sent two angels to an orchestrated divine appointment to test me. I have absolutely no doubt in my mind that God was testing the veracity of what I had told him earlier that morning when I replied, "I'll do what you tell me to do!" Looking back on what happened that day, I am very blessed to have simply obeyed the promptings of the Holy Spirit to go there, listen to those two messengers from Heaven, and pray.

The Insignificance of Race

With God no matter is insignificant when it involves the concept of preparing one for ministry or godly service. Even the race of the angelic beings I encountered would later hold great significance, as God began to send me out into the vineyard (the world) to minister to the lost, diseased, tormented, rich, middle class, poor, destitute, and deceived. From day one my ministry has been completely color blind. In other words, one of the very first significant spiritual truths God divinely delivered to me is there are no different races on planet Earth. One of the greatest spiritual truths of the Bible that Satan and his demons spend much energy trying to defeat is the fact that there are no such thing as different races with God. God created a single race of people called the human race. The confirming scriptural foundation for this spiritual fact is Colossians 3:9–11:

> Do not lie to one another, since ye have put off the old man with his deeds and have put on the new man who is renewed in knowledge according to the image of Him who created him, where there is neither Greek, nor Jew, circumcised nor uncircumcised, barbarian, Scythian, slave nor free, but Christ is all and in all.

If one genuinely believes God and 100 percent of His Holy Word, there are absolutely no differences between people. In the name of Jesus, we are all children of God whether we realize it or not! With this undisputed spiritual fact in mind, God has had me meet, befriend, receive from, impart into, teach, minister to, and bless and be blessed by and through people of all races, colors, creeds, nationalities, and socioeconomic backgrounds around the entire world, in person, on the World Wide Web, and now via this very book. Everything you have read and are about to read in these pages has foundations in the divine appointments that I had with God on the morning of November 1, 2002. If this is too much for you to believe, then you're going to have great difficulty believing the rest of this book.

Laying On of Healing Hands
Within just a couple of weeks of my commission from God to serve Him as a minister, followed by that divine encounter with His two messengers, the Holy Spirit gently ushered me into what many call faith healing. I recall one evening when I was home awaiting the arrival of my wife's return flight and wanted to get some Bible study in before I had to go to the airport. I had a massive migraine, which was very unusual because I seldom get headaches. Even when I do, they are usually mild and do not last very long, but this was not a normal headache. Looking back on it in the context of this subject matter, I now know it was demonic in origin. I vividly recall sitting down at the dining room table and trying to read the Bible, but each time I started

reading, both sides of my head would throb in pain. The more I tried to read, the greater the throbbing and the pain.

I recall having the Bible open and leaning over it with my head resting between my hands and my eyes closed, thinking to myself, "I'm not going to be able to read like this." Just as I was about to give up trying, I heard a very faint voice in the back of my mind repeating, "Physician, heal thyself" several times in rapid succession. I immediately recognized that this was Scripture that Jesus Himself spoke in one of the Gospels (Luke 4:23, King James Version), but I did not immediately relate it to anything that had to do with me. After pondering it for a few minutes or so, I recall thinking to myself, "Physician, heal thyself—what does this mean?" Before I could even complete the thought, it was as if I heard that same faint voice in the back of my mind saying, "Fool, pray!"

God Speaks Uniquely and Intimately

Please understand that God created us and knows us very well. He therefore communicates with us on a very intimate and personal basis. With respect to myself, I happen to have a very aggressive type A personality which allows the Holy Spirit to speak to me in the type of language I am accustomed to using myself. Accordingly, when I heard "Fool, pray!" it was not shocking to me at all. In response to that directive, I recall placing both hands on my temples, rubbing my head, and saying, "Headache, go away in the name of Jesus" or "Headache, I cast you out of me in the name of Jesus."

I admit that I was just going through the motions in obedience to the voice I heard in the back of my mind; I honestly did not expect or even believe it would make any difference whatsoever. This was simply an act of mustard-seed faith (Matt. 17:20) that involved a simple act of obedience—trusting that still, small voice I heard in the back of my mind. After I articulated those few words, the headache left me immediately. I recall shaking my head back and forth and up and down trying to detect the pain, but it was gone. I was completely healed, in the name of Jesus, so I thanked and praised God. This is how the Holy Spirit providentially walked me into the healing and curing side of spiritual warfare, which is more accurately called healing and deliverance ministry or power ministry.

Deliverance from Demons

My first known encounter with the deliverance (from demons) side of spiritual warfare came without any warning whatsoever. Looking back now—more than ten years later—however, it is quite clear that it was a divine setup for me to be ushered into healing and deliverance ministry, one of many spiritual tools with which God equips believers to demonstrate the awesome power of the gospel message to save lost souls.

I was an associate minister standing before the congregation of my church family while my pastor was conducting an altar call at the end of his sermon. This altar call initially appeared to be no different from the scores of others I had previously witnessed. However, it would very quickly turn out be anything but routine. A lady came forward, crying and in great travail, saying words to this effect: "You can't have my child, no, Devil, you can't have my baby, no, no!" In response to her cries, one of the other associate ministers went over to minister to her. While he was trying to console her, she either struck him or came very close to doing so, which caused me to go over to help him as he was trying to minister to her.

She immediately grabbed me in a bear hug from which I could not break free. It seemed that she had superhuman strength. Although she was a very small-framed woman, I felt as if I was being squeezed by several large and very powerful men. Mind you, all of this was taking place in the front of the church during the altar call. I wrestled, trying to break free, and we hit the floor and rolled under the first pew. As I struggled to free myself, I heard a very faint voice in my mind telling me, "Say, 'Come out in the name of Jesus.' Just say 'Come out in the name of Jesus,'" which I hurriedly obeyed. Almost as quickly as the last *s* in Jesus proceeded from my vocal chords, the woman released me, passed out completely for fifteen to thirty seconds, and then awakened, praising and thanking God in a very loud voice. I immediately noticed a very foul odor emanating from her but could not discern from where it came. All I could do was think, "What just happened? What in the world was that all about?"

I went home after that service and was immediately led by the Holy Spirit to crack open the Bible and find out what had just happened. If I recall correctly, the Holy Spirit gently directed me to Mark 3:13–15, which says:

> And He went up on the mountain and called to Him those He Himself wanted. And they came to Him. Then He appointed twelve, that they might be with Him and that He might send them out to preach, and to have power to heal sicknesses and to cast out demons.

The Holy Spirit heavily focused my attention on verse 15, which involves Jesus giving His apostles "power to heal sicknesses and to cast out demons." A little doubt rose up in my mind, saying, "Yes, but this Scripture does not relate to regular believers but only to the original twelve apostles." Reflecting back on this scenario after having well over a decade of experience in the art of spiritual warfare, I am fully cognizant that demonic forces of doubt, fear, pride, and unbelief were at work in me as I read up on this matter. In my reading that day after church, the Holy Spirit eventually focused my attention on Luke 10, where Jesus gave the exact same authority (*exousia*) and power (*dunamis*) to seventy others who obeyed His commands by healing sick people and casting out demons. Luke 10:17–20 says:

> The seventy returned with joy, saying, "Lord, even the demons are subject to us in Your name." Jesus replied, "I saw Satan fall like lightning from heaven. Behold, I give you the authority to trample

on serpents and scorpions, and over all the power of the enemy, and nothing shall by any means hurt you. Nevertheless, do not rejoice in this, that the spirits are subject to you, but rather rejoice because your names are written in heaven."

As if this was not enough, the Holy Spirit finally took me over to the Great Commission in Mark 16:15–20:

And He said to them "Go into all the world and preach the gospel to every creature. He who believes and is baptized will be saved; but he who does not believe will be condemned. And these signs will follow those who believe: In My name they will cast out demons; they will speak with new tongues; they will take up serpents; and if they drink anything deadly, it will by no means hurt them; they will lay hands on the sick, and they will recover." So then, after the Lord had spoken to them, He was received up into heaven, and sat down at the right hand of God. And they went out and preached everywhere, the Lord working with them and confirming the word through the accompanying signs. Amen.

Verse 17 promises that "signs will follow those who believe" and that believers will "cast out demons" in the name of Jesus, while verse 18 says, "they will lay hands on the sick and they will recover." The climax of these promises is verse 20, which testifies that upon their obedience in going out to preach the gospel, Jesus Himself would be "working with them and confirming the word through the accompanying signs."

Looking back on my experience during the altar call at church, it became crystal clear that the Holy Spirit had taught me how to perform deliverance ministry that very day in the presence of hundreds of people who were probably clueless as to what was going on. In a very short period of time thereafter, it also became clear that this was not just a fluke but would ultimately become a very significant part of my personal ministry. The same has come to pass, the fruit of which is contained in this book. There is no doubt that God ordained me to operate in healing and deliverance ministry. This calling in ministry includes the duty to motivate, equip, and train others who are willing and obedient to God's calling and to commission them to go out into the entire world to do the same. There is no way on Earth I would have chosen to operate in this very dangerous and highly controversial area of ministry but for God having purposed it in my mind, will, and emotions!

If you are torn between a burning desire to powerfully serve God in miraculous and meaningful ways and doubt as to whether this type of ministry is for you, then you are in the right place. Doubt, fear, pride, and unbelief are demon spirits that usually try to attack those whom God has designated, gifted, or otherwise anointed to serve Him in mighty ways. Please keep reading, and you will be convinced by the time you finish that "…greater is he that is in you, than he that is in the world." (1 John 4:4, KJV)

Chapter 5

PROPHETIC MINISTRY

"Having then gifts differing according to the grace that is given to us, let us use them: if prophecy, let us prophesy in proportion to our faith." (Rom. 12:6)

Hindsight always seems to be twenty twenty. After I was ordained by God as a minister of the gospel on November 1, 2002, I had a deep and burning desire to know more about how those wonderful ladies at that Marketplace Ministries conference the preceding September could have possibly known that I was going to be used by God to preach and evangelize. I contacted the person who invited our church to the conference and inquired about the ladies who had conducted the prophetic prayer intercessory session. I was given the name of the leader, who was a trained prophetess. In January of 2003, Cassandra and I met up with her and another of the ladies whom we had met at the conference. We let them know that God had divinely commissioned me to minister since the time they prophesied to me just two months prior. They were excited to have at least some of their prophecies confirmed in such a very short time frame.

I primarily wanted to know just how in Heaven they could have done what they did with such grace, assurance, and accuracy. The prophetess explained that it was a matter of spiritual gifts activation. She proceeded to tell us that she conducts spiritual gifts activation classes and would let us know when the next class would be conducted locally so we could attend. I recall thinking to myself, "God, if you want me to take this class, I'll do it and whatever else you want me to do too." The precise accuracy of the prophetic words that were delivered to us back in September of 2002 further melted my heart toward the Lord and ushered me into a place of complete belief and trust in Almighty God.

These two wonderful women prophesied over us again. This time I brought my digital recorder so I could capture every word they spoke. Unlike my first encounter with them, this time I was very serious about our session and made sure I listened very attentively to every word they said, for I was convinced that God would speak through them again as He did the first time.

Second Prophetic Session: Part One
Here's a brief transcript of what Cassandra and I were told that day in January of 2003. The women started with a prophetic disclaimer:

> The Bible says we know in part, and we prophesy in part, and we see through a glass darkly. We will do our best to hear the heart of God for you. Whatever we speak will not be the whole wisdom and full counsel of the Lord on any subject. We might make a mistake and miss it completely, and for this reason you need to judge this word and take it to those who know you the best and ask them to help you judge it. If it is of God, then you should pray it through until you see it come to pass, and if it's not, throw it away.

The prophetess next quoted Psalm 1, saying these exact words:

The scripture that the Lord is giving is Psalm 1. Blessed is the man that walks not in the counsel of the ungodly, nor stands in the way of sinners nor sits in the seat of the scornful, but his delight is in the law of the Lord and in His law, he meditates day and night. He shall be like a tree planted by the rivers of water that brings forth fruit in his season. His leaf also shall not wither and whatsoever he does shall prosper.

She continued speaking with much grace and ease, saying,

The word that I had for you is that the two of you are like a tree planted by the water, and your roots are very deep and they're very strong, and that you will bring forth your fruit in your season. Your leaves shall not wither and whatever you do will prosper. So I think the Lord is going to give you insight, and he will give you revelation to bring others into the kingdom of God. He's going to allow you to see things and to hear things about people, and through the spirit of God you are going to be speaking those things forth to these individuals that will be a sign and a wonder to them. God is going to broaden your evangelism through prophetic words and words of knowledge. I guess basically that's what it would be.

Word of Knowledge
I will digress from this briefly, as this is a teachable moment with respect to spiritual gifting, biblically identified as a word of knowledge. Verses 7 through 10 of 1 Corinthians 12 proclaim:

But the manifestation of the Spirit is given to each one for the profit of all: for to one is given the word of wisdom through the

Spirit, to another the word of knowledge through the same Spirit, to another faith by the same Spirit, to another gifts of healings by the same Spirit, to another the working of miracles, to another prophecy, to another discerning of spirits, to another different kinds of tongues, to another the interpretation of tongues.

This book covers instruction, practical application, and actual testimonies pertaining to each operation of activated spiritual gifts in Bible-believing Christians. Right now, however, I will briefly focus on the specific gifting that was mentioned in the prophecy Cassandra and I received in January 2003. This was delivered just two months after God ordained me to preach and less than a month after I had preached my very first sermon in December of 2002.

The prophetess said that the Holy Spirit would speak words of knowledge to others through me, and the same would be a sign and wonder to the hearers as a means of being drawn into God's kingdom. A word of knowledge is specific information that is either from the past or the present, as opposed to a future occurrence. A word of knowledge is something that has already taken place or something that is taking place now or presently exists. Holy Spirit–given words of knowledge can be very powerful indicators that something supernatural is at work in a person's life. The accuracy of the articulated information cannot be denied, which then leaves the recipient wondering, How in the world did this complete stranger know this about me? The immediate effect is to arrest the person's attention, much akin to how God got Moses to stop everything he was doing and focus 100 percent of his attention on a bush that was engulfed in flames yet remained intact (Exod. 3:1–3). Witnessing this miraculous event was a wonder to Moses and a sign that something was completely out of the ordinary about this bush that was on fire yet not being destroyed by the flames. It was so shocking to Moses's conscious that he said, "I will now turn aside and see this great sight, why the bush does not burn."

Fighting in Faith

Going back to the first time I met these prophetesses in September of 2002, this lady who prophesied over me at our second meeting was the same lady who delivered the word of knowledge about our daughter who loved American flags. Hearing a very precise and accurate word of knowledge about our infant daughter being spoken by a complete stranger, at a conference full of complete strangers taking place in another city, gained my focused attention.

The Holy Spirit's goal of getting 100 percent of my attention and focus worked so well that I made it a point to seek out these ladies for another prophetic intercessory. Not only that—I came with a recorder to make sure I did not miss a single word of knowledge, prophecy, or anything else they spoke.

Word of Wisdom

Now let's go back to my second session with these women of God. The younger lady continued prophesying to me, but this time the Holy Spirit had her shift gears and start giving a word of wisdom as found in 1 Corinthians 12:8. By strict definition, a word of wisdom is Holy Spirit–given advice for something to be done either now or in the future to bring about godly results. Such godly results often concern convicting man's conscience of sin—the ultimate judgment to come due to sin, salvation, edification, exhortation, comfort, counsel, confirmation of righteousness when the world speaks and believes otherwise, and many other godly virtues. (See John 16:8.) Please highlight this definition now and place it in your memory, as it is vitally important. No doubt you will need it in the future if you plan to have your spiritual gifting activated and mightily used by God to witness; minister; preach; teach; and perform signs, wonders, miracles, healings, and deliverances.

Second Prophetic Session: Part Two

The prophetess went on prophesying to me about things that would start to happen in the future and about the particular ways God would use me to minister to others. She got specific about how God would have me minister to people by saying,

> You're sitting and you're talking to someone, and the Lord would say thus and so about this person and you will say, "Have you ever or did you…?" and then say, "I believe that the Lord is showing me _____." And as you share this with them, it will be a sign and a wonder. I think that's where the fruit in due season is coming, and by being obedient and speaking out on these words (of knowledge and wisdom), you're going to see fruit that you've never seen before. The Lord is going to use words of knowledge to minister to others.

Here the prophetess was simultaneously exercising at least three spiritual gifts. A more accurate way to state this is that the Holy Spirit was manifesting Himself through her in three different operations. First, she was delivering what would ultimately come into fruition in the form of very accurate prophecies specifying in detail how God would use me to minister in the future. As I write this sentence on July 3, 2015, over thirteen years have gone by since this second prophetic session. I can attest that each and every word these two ladies delivered to us that day has come to pass time and time again.

Second, she was delivering words of knowledge, as what she described was already happening in my life before I first met the prophetesses in September of 2002. Prior to my separation of service to preach, I would often receive personal and intimate information from the Holy Spirit about people as I would speak with them. This information would come whether we spoke in person or by telephone. I would often silently ask God, "Why did you reveal this to me?" I would never get an answer to my question. I would simply be instructed, "Just say it" or "Just ask the question."

As you can imagine, this was a sign and a wonder to me because that had been happening to me on a regular basis. I would speak that which I heard from the Holy Spirit, and then the person would confirm its accuracy, emotionally break down, and give their lives to the Lord Jesus. It would happen so easily and so very quickly that sometimes I could hardly mentally process it myself. It was as if I could read deeply into people's minds to discern their mindsets, backgrounds, family, social relationships, occupational history, successes, failures, and on down the line. When I would obediently say whatever the Holy Spirit had led me to speak, it was as if the person's heart had been pricked, which caused them to be very receptive to the gospel message of salvation through faith in Christ Jesus.

Third and finally, the prophetess was speaking forth words of wisdom, articulating exactly how the Holy Spirit wanted me to continue to hear from Him and boldly repeat that which I would hear so as to bless the recipients with this information from Him. As you progress through this book, you will read actual testimonies of these seamless operations manifesting in prophecies, words of knowledge, words of wisdom, miracles, healings, deliverance from demons, and many other operations of the spiritual gifts. This will be readily noticeable in chapters fifteen and sixteen, which particularize healing and deliverance ministry that took place in both individual and congregational settings.

As you can discern, the operational methodology of the Holy Spirit with respect to spiritual gifting is often seamless. In a single breath, one can deliver a prophecy that is all inclusive of a word of knowledge (that which is past or present), a pure prophecy (that which will surely come to pass in the future), and a word of wisdom (godly spiritual advice about how to go about handling a situation that will take place in the future).

Prophecy

The words *prophecy*, *prophetic*, *prophesy*, and *prophecies* are some of the most confused, maligned, and misused terms in the entire Holy Bible. According to Strong's Concordance, the King James Version of the Holy Bible uses *prophecies* 2 times, *prophecy* 21 times, prophesied 50 times, *prophesieth* 7 times, *prophesy* 90 times, *prophesying* 6 times, *prophesyings* 1 time, *prophet* 242 times, *prophetess* 8 times, *prophet's* 2 times, and *prophets* 239 times for a grand total of 668 times. Prophecy is very significant in the things of God. No doubt, of all the spiritual gifts God avails to believers, the ability to accurately prophesy is the most important. The Apostle Paul confirms the same with these very words:

> Pursue love, and desire spiritual gifts, but especially that you may prophesy. For he who speaks in a tongue does not speak to men but to God, for no one understands him; however, in the spirit he speaks mysteries. But he who prophesies speaks edification and exhortation and comfort to men. He who speaks in a tongue edifies himself, but he who prophesies edifies the church. (1 Cor. 14:1–4)

The ability to accurately prophesy is a very important spiritual gift because prophecy is the Holy Spirit's ability to divinely inspire human beings with the power to declare and decree God's divine plans and purposes in our daily lives. Such a divinely inspired ability can be directed toward reproving and admonishing stubborn and rebellious sinners, comforting the afflicted, revealing matters that are spiritually obscured, and/or foretelling future events. With respect to foretelling future events, I will take the liberty of tweaking Mr. Strong's definition. There are major differences between fortune-telling, which is a forbidden occult practice from Satan, and prophetic ministry, which God ordains. Fortune-telling is the unrighteous business of trying to capture and deliver hidden information from the spirit realm through evil sources that are demonic in origin. Fortune-telling is the practice of "predicting" events that are supposed to happen in the future.

The word *predict* in and of itself has a connotation of uncertainty. *Prophecy*, however, describes the Holy Spirit's enablement of a person to tell forth that which God has already ordained in the supernatural (heavenly) realm to transpire or manifest in the natural (earthly) realm. Put another way, a very practical definition of *prophecy* is the ability to speak on God's behalf concerning that which He has ordained. However, this is not always relegated to the future but could be related to that which has already occurred or is now occurring, both of which are by definition words of knowledge revealed by divine inspiration.

The major reason prophecy is considered the most important Spiritual gifting is that it has the intended purpose and awesome power to deliver souls from Satan to Almighty God. Whereas many of the other gifts—such as healing, working miracles, and the like—produce signs and powerful wonders that God is at work, the ability to accurately prophesy what "thus says the Lord" has absolute power to "cast down imaginations and every high thing that exalts itself against the knowledge of God." (2 Cor. 10:5) The righteous result is to set souls free from spiritual dungeons of doubt, fear, pride, and unbelief, all of which are specifically designed to spiritually blind, mentally cripple, and effectively deter us from becoming saved and living victorious lives. Prophecy also has the awesomely powerful ability to deliver us from sexual sins (adultery, bestiality, fornication, homosexuality, incest, and masturbation) that defile the body God has designated to be the temple of the Holy Spirit. (1 Cor. 6:19)

Speaking of prophecy, going back to that very first intercessory prayer session I had with those prophetesses in 2002, I attest to the absolute fact that each and every single prophecy they spoke has come to pass over the last thirteen years as of the writing of this book. I continued to have sessions with them, took a spiritual gifts activation class from the head prophetess in 2004, and have also been teaching classes myself in the US and Africa since 2005. It is in furtherance of this very unique and highly misunderstood ministry that I am now completing my first book on this life-and-death subject matter.

Chapter 6

TONGUES AND INTERPRETATION OF TONGUES

"And these signs will follow those who believe: In My name they… will speak with new tongues." (Mark 16:17)

Speaking in tongues is one of the most controversial of all spiritual gifts; can you imagine why? The short answer is that the enemy of man's soul does not want believers to have direct, clear, and effective communication with our Father in Heaven.

Speaking in tongues is an exceptionally important spiritual gift for two main reasons. First, the gift of tongues enables believers to pray directly to God in spirit and in truth, which fosters personal edification. When we pray in tongues, our spirit communicates with the Holy Spirit, who then joins our spirit in the same accord. When this is achieved, our natural mind is absolutely clueless as to what our divine spirit is communicating to God. The Apostle Paul confirms that "he who speaks in a tongue does not speak to men but to God, for no one understands him; however, in the spirit he speaks mysteries." He further confirms that "he who speaks in a tongue edifies himself, but he who prophesies edifies the church." (1 Cor. 14:2–4)

The second reason the gift of tongues is so important is that it has the ability to edify not only the individual speaker but also an entire church body if the tongue is interpreted. This eternal truth was also divinely revealed to mankind through the writings of the Apostle Paul, who wrote:

> I wish you all spoke with tongues, but even more that you prophesied; for he who prophesies is greater than he who speaks with tongues, unless indeed he interprets, that the church may receive edification. (1 Cor. 14:5)

Under the divine inspiration of the Holy Spirit, the Apostle Paul elevated the significance of tongues and their interpretation to the level of the greatest spiritual gift, which he declared to be prophecy.

With what we have already covered as to the awesome power and efficacy of speaking in tongues, can you now understand the reason neither Satan nor any demon under him would want any believer speaking in an unknown language? Tongues are heavenly languages that neither Satan nor his demon spirits can understand. It is for this precise reason that next to prophecy, speaking in tongues is the most controversial spiritual gift. Satan keeps a great deal of fear and confusion around tongues specifically because he knows quite well that one who can speak in tongues has direct, secret, coded communication back and forth with God that neither Satan nor his demons can understand. Accordingly, tongues are very important for self-edification, comfort, inner strength, perseverance, and many other godly virtues that protect believers from the wiles, plots, ploys, and evil schemes of Satan and his demons.

Can One Be Taught How to Speak in Tongues?
Another somewhat controversial matter along these lines is whether a Christian can learn how to speak in tongues. As revealed in 2 Corinthians 4:3–4,

Satan has blinded the minds of many people who refuse to believe one person can teach another to speak in tongues. Please allow me the liberty of tweaking the question just a little. The real question is: Can someone teach another person what the Bible says about speaking in tongues so that if they follow the Scripture, they can ultimately speak in tongues? Now doesn't this sound much more biblical, reasonable, and practical? One caveat: as a general principle, God will not violate our conscience if we absolutely do not want to speak in tongues, or if we have been placed in such a state of unreasonable, demonically driven fear that we are too afraid to speak in tongues.

Learning how to speak in tongues is simply a matter of being completely filled with love, joy, and peace, all of which come from God. These are three crucial Christian virtues that usually materialize when we completely surrender to the Lordship of Jesus. Speaking in tongues usually develops after making an earnest commitment to obey Jesus in every aspect of life. At this point in Christians' lives, we are no longer struggling with our salvation, for we know we are Heaven bound after the cessation of our physical lives here on Earth. At this point in time, we as believers have an earnest desire to please God. With such a significant objective in mind, we are willing to search for the will of God for our lives and completely fulfill our purposes for birth and existence here on Earth. At this point a true Christian's mind, will, emotions, and physical body are all aligned to accomplish God's purposes as opposed to our own selfish will.

Accordingly, the matter of speaking in tongues involves becoming completely filled with God's Holy Spirit from the soles of one's feet to the crown of one's head. When we become filled, we can then speak in tongues. The million-dollar question becomes, How can one become filled from foot to head with the Holy Spirit? Jesus says, "He who believes in Me, as the Scripture has said, out of his heart will flow rivers of living water." (John 7:38) The Apostle Peter said, "Repent, and let every one of you be baptized in the name of Jesus Christ for the remission of sins; and you shall receive the gift of the Holy Spirit." (Acts 2:38)

Both passages confirm the spiritual truth that when we believe in and obey Jesus, we will receive the Holy Spirit (Acts 2:38) and release the Holy Spirit. (John 7:38) In other words, when we obey God and confess faith in Jesus, the Holy Spirit takes up residence in our spirit. However, to the extent that we appreciate our salvation and surrender all to Jesus for having saved us from Hell and the lake of fire, we get filled with the Holy Spirit to the point that something has to flow out of our mouths. At this point, what usually flows is a heavenly prayer language genuinely worshipping, thanking, and praising God for that which He has already done for us. Simply put, speaking in tongues is a coded language that honors and reveres God to the highest extent possible. Since Satan is in the deceptive business of purloining praises that are due to God, speaking in tongues is not something demons want any Christian to practice on a regular basis.

Finally, the simplest means by which to receive the infilling presence of the Holy Spirit, the means that will surely result in your developing and being able to utilize your heavenly prayer language, is to simply ask for it. Jesus says, "If you then, being evil, know how to give good gifts to your children, how much more will your heavenly Father give the Holy Spirit to those who ask Him?" (Luke 11:13)

A Prayer for the Enablement to Speak in Tongues
Here's a very simple prayer that will help you develop your heavenly prayer language. Please speak these words out loud in complete faith in God's awesome and unlimited power:

> Lord Jesus, you are God, Lord of Lords and King of Kings. There is absolutely nothing too hard for you. It is my earnest desire to receive my heavenly prayer language so I can speak to you and hear you speak to me through the awesome and divine power of your Holy Spirit. Lord Jesus, if there is any sin in my life that is inhibiting me from surrendering 100 percent of my Mind, Heart,

Soul, Will, or Spirit, please reveal it to me so that I can renounce it, break agreement with it, and cast it away from me (in Your Righteous Name) as far as the East is from the West. Thank you, Lord Jesus, for saving me, delivering me from the powers of darkness, and blessing me with the eternality of my soul in your heavenly abode.

After having said this prayer, please go to a place where you can have some privacy for at least an hour or so. Then start thinking back over your entire life and the wonderful things God has done for you. Think of the times He blessed, delivered, and justly chastised you and the like. As you think back, open your mouth and start saying (out loud), "Thank you, Jesus, thank you, Jesus, thank you, Jesus." Please repeat these words while thinking back over the span of your life from your very first memories as a child throughout your life up to the present. Most people who earnestly undertake this spiritual exercise ultimately begin speaking in tongues. Testimonies usually range from most confirming that it happened while they were in the process of thanking Jesus to others testifying that it happened sometime thereafter.

Church Member Taught How to Speak in Tongues
Here's an actual example that's fresh off the press. Approximately two months ago (May of 2015), I was teaching about the infilling presence of the Holy Spirit during the 7:00 p.m. Wednesday night Bible study at the church where I serve as pastor. I was teaching that a person can in fact be taught how to speak in tongues, but the person must first be filled with the Holy Spirit before they will be enabled (empowered) by the spirit of God to do so. After completing the teaching, I then tried to seamlessly move into the immediate application of the principle by asking the audience if anyone wanted to be able to speak in tongues. I specifically chose to do it this way so the audience could have direct and very powerful communication with

God while we were in Bible study. There was only one lady in the entire audience who very reluctantly raised her hand. I can only imagine the demonic spirits of doubt, fear, pride, and unbelief that were attacking her mind, will, and emotions at that very moment, but she pressed and overcame them all.

I asked her to repeat after me and then proceeded to lead her through a Holy Spirit–directed prayer asking God, in the name of Jesus, to fill her from the soles of her feet to the crown of her head with the awesome anointing of His Holy Spirit so that she would be empowered to speak in tongues. After the prayer was completed, I had her thank God for having filled her with the Holy Spirit and having blessed her with the ability to speak in tongues. I informed her, and the entire audience, that sometimes the manifestation comes immediately, but it may instead come later. The point was that she needed to have faith that God had already filled her because she simply asked Him to fill her with the Holy Spirit. I asked her if she believed in her heart that she was filled despite the fact that she had yet to speak in tongues, and she said, "Yes, Pastor, I believe." It was my earnest desire and personal hope that she would start speaking in tongues right there during Bible study. I wanted the entire church to see the demonstrated power of God flowing through her, but no such outward manifestation of that which had taken place in her spirit took place at that time.

However, the next Sunday she approached me in the sanctuary with a bright smile on her face and told me she had spoken in tongues that night after she returned home from Bible study. She testified before the entire church that she was just singing a song and all of a sudden, she started speaking in tongues. She informed the church that she literally could not stop—which greatly disturbed her sister, who thought the devil was attacking her. In fact, her sister told her that if she didn't stop "speaking like that," she would put her out of the house and not let her come back until she stopped "speaking like that." What an awesome testimony she now has about speaking in tongues and how it was achieved—simply by asking God and believing that He had already filled her even before there was any evidence that she had in fact been filled.

Speaking in Tongues Greatly Angers Demons
As she was sharing her testimony, the Holy Spirit gave me a very powerful word of knowledge telling me that as this lady was speaking in tongues that night, she was speaking godly blessings over her sister's house, effectively expelling demons from the premises. That house had been under the control of demons until this lady prayed in tongues that night. The Holy Spirit specifically said she did not speak in tongues during Bible study because she was assigned to do so at her sister's residence to spiritually cleanse the place from demonic spirits that had taken up residence there. Since this lady was temporarily residing at the home with her sister's permission, she had the spiritual authority to bless or curse her sister's house. Moreover, the Holy Spirit confirmed that the reason this lady's sister was so angry with her (thinking this lady was under satanic power) was because she (the owner of the house) was in fact under satanic and demonic influence but was blinded to this by doubt, fear, pride, and unbelief.

This was very similar to the time when Jesus cast the legion of demons out of a man in Gadara, which resulted in him thereafter being both clothed and in his right mind (sane). But when the citizens witnessed the miracle, they began to plead with Jesus "to depart from their region." (Mark 5:17). Just imagine: a man who was previously insane—walking around naked, repetitively cutting himself with stones, hanging out in a cemetery, and so powerful that no chains could hold him—was now completely healed. However, the people who knew he used to be under satanic power were now deathly afraid of the person who delivered him! This speaks to the deceptive power demons can and do have over many unsuspecting souls. You would think these people would have embraced Jesus and His miraculous works. However, this was not the case because spirits of doubt, fear, pride, unbelief, and many others were controlling the minds of those who were afraid of Jesus. Simply put, the demons in them wanted Jesus to leave before He could get around to casting them out too.

Going back to this lady who was speaking in tongues in her sister's house, demonic spirits inside this lady's sister were moving her to threaten to evict the lady from the premises if she continued to speak in tongues. This was very similar to the reaction of the people in Gadara after Jesus had driven the demons out—the people wanted Him to leave their region. What was happening was spiritual warfare. As you can discern, speaking in tongues is also a matter of spiritual warfare. The question is, When will Christians gain the level of spiritual maturity to embrace speaking in tongues so God can use us mightily to defeat demons as we fight the good fight of faith?

The instructions I gave this lady are the same instructions that were given to me well over twelve years ago, and I started speaking in tongues within approximately thirty minutes of thanking Jesus. In fact, I kept on speaking for at least thirty-five to forty-five minutes thereafter because I could not stop. The Holy Spirit later confirmed that it lasted so long because I was thanking God within my spirit for each and every blessing He had bestowed upon me from my conception to that very day.

This is how awesome it is to speak in tongues, which is precisely why Satan pulls out all the stops to steal, kill, and destroy any desire we might have to worship, thank, and otherwise appreciate God. If Satan were to have his way, no one would ever praise, worship, or obey God because Satan wants all this for himself. Unfortunately, demon spirits of ignorance, doubt, fear, and unbelief keep many genuine believers from progressing to higher levels of faith and godly obedience, both of which lead to a closer relationship with God as well as ministerial excellence. The failure to achieve these two spiritual goals is most often due to a lack of accurate biblical knowledge, as so accurately confirmed by Hosea 4:6, which declares, "My people are destroyed for lack of knowledge…" It is due to a lack of knowledge that the vast majority of so-called "Bible-believing" Christians continue to live beneath their God-ordained spiritual birthright. In this regard they never enjoy the direct communication with the spirit of God that comes only through our heavenly prayer language, which is more commonly called speaking in tongues.

Speaking in Tongues Testimonies

> In the law it is written: "With men of other tongues and other lips I will speak to this people; and yet, for all that, they will not hear Me," says the Lord. Therefore, tongues are for a sign, not to those who believe but to unbelievers; but prophesying is not for unbelievers but for those who believe. (1 Corinthians 14:21–22)

Lady Confesses Faith in Jesus after Hearing Tongues
Not too long after I received my heavenly prayer language, I would often pray in tongues while driving. On one particular day, I had to drive to another city to appear in court for a client. Upon reaching the courthouse, I met a lady in the lobby who had to appear in the same courtroom. As we were both waiting for court to start, we struck up a conversation about church and faith in God. This conversation ultimately led to a very in-depth conversation about the ability to speak in tongues. Although she confirmed that she regularly attended church, she was not sure where her soul would go upon her death. As I evangelize in the marketplace, I sometimes ask people, "If you were to die right now, do you know where your soul would go?" Upon being asked this question, she could not give a definitive answer. The whole matter surrounding her uncertainty centered on the issue of speaking in tongues. She said the pastor of the church she attended taught that no one can be truly saved unless and until they can speak in tongues. With all due respect to anyone reading this book who holds the same belief, this is a false, satanic, and demonic doctrine specifically designed to send unsuspecting souls to hell. In her particular case, she was living a spiritually defeated life by going around believing she could never be saved (go to Heaven) without

first being able to speak in tongues. Now if she had placed and kept her faith in Jesus, she was in fact saved but unfortunately did not know or fully appreciate that fact. This is a classic case of the person who wakes up in heaven, shocked that she made it there. Why? Because although she believed the lie of the enemy that one has to speak in tongues to go to heaven, that's not God's standard.

Accordingly the question becomes, Why would Satan want one who is saved to believe they are not? Number one, they will live way beneath their God-given spiritual birthright, meaning a defeated life that brings little to no glory to God. Two, and most importantly, their doubt about their very own salvation effectively removes them from the battlefield such that they can't effectively evangelize and thereby help get anyone else saved—like spouses, children, grandchildren, brothers, sisters, parents, grandparents, nieces, nephews, uncles, aunts, neighbors, coworkers, employees, friends, foes, and/or strangers. Third—and quite significantly—if they think they are not saved, they may backslide into a stubborn and/or rebellious lifestyle of sin from which they don't genuinely repent, then die in their sins and wind up in Hell. Accordingly, having (or not having) a Bible-based understanding of speaking in tongues can have eternal consequences for man's soul.

Getting back to the lady, after having heard what she was taught about tongues and salvation, quite a bit of righteous indignation rose up within me toward Satan for having deceived this lady through this false doctrine. However, I simultaneously began to recall how the Holy Spirit had moved me to speak in tongues while driving to this very place to take care of some business that had nothing to do with this lady. I began to discern God's providence in that I was engaged in such a very important conversation which could have an eternal impact on the ultimate resting place of her very soul. Right then the Holy Spirit told me to explain to her that the only requirement for salvation is faith (belief plus trust) in Jesus and absolutely nothing else. Under inspiration of the Holy Spirit, I explained how Philip preached Jesus to the Ethiopian eunuch, who said, "See, here is water. What hinders me from being baptized?" Then Philip said, "If you believe with all your heart, you may." (Acts 8:36–37). I further explained to her that the Ethiopian eunuch's response was "I believe that Jesus Christ is the Son of God," after which Philip baptized him.

After hearing this biblically accurate information on how the Ethiopian, a foreigner, received salvation without any mention of a requirement to first speak in tongues, she still did not quite comprehend or spiritually grasp the fact that belief (effectively trust) in Jesus is what it takes to be genuinely saved. This was because she was so tightly bound by decades of bad doctrine that came from the mouth of a pastor in a church pulpit of all places. Having first laid a Bible-based foundation for what it takes to be saved, I was then led by the Holy Spirit to address tongues from the perspective of 1 Corinthians 14:22. I explained to her that tongues are often spoken by believers who have been filled with the Holy Spirit after they have already become saved. I explained that although it is possible for one to speak in tongues within the exact time frame they are confessing faith in Jesus and being saved, the vast majority of Christians who ultimately speak in tongues do so well after they have given their lives to the Lord. (Acts 10:44–47)

I continued to explain that this was exactly what happened to the Apostle Paul, who confessed faith in Jesus on the way to Damascus but spoke in tongues after having been "filled with the Holy Spirit," while his actual water baptism took place afterward. (Acts 9:1–6) Again I explained that the requirement for speaking in tongues is being filled with the Holy Spirit, which comes after one confesses faith in Jesus and is therefore already saved. However, there are many (if not the vast majority of genuinely saved Christians) who have never spoken in tongues—but they are just as saved as those who speak in tongues.

The Gift of Speaking in Tongues

I then gently moved on, explaining how some people can speak in tongues only when they are moved by the Holy Spirit to do so, while others have the gift of tongues. (1 Corinthians 12:10) I explained that those with the gift of tongues can speak in tongues both when moved by the Holy Spirit and also when they simply wish to pray in tongues, which is also called praying in the spirit. I could tell by her facial expression that this matter of one having a gift of tongues was very interesting to her. I then confessed to her that I have the gift of tongues and can speak in tongues at will. I told her words to this effect: "It's kind of funny we're having this conversation, because I actually prayed in tongues in my car all the way here from Jacksonville." Her facial expression changed to one of great doubt and outright unbelief, which is really sinful. However, this was simply reflective of just how much negative influence the demonic spirits of doubt and unbelief had over her faith in God. With great skepticism, she then asked if I could prove to her that I could speak in tongues at will. I prayed silently in spirit, asking God to reveal Himself to this lady as I prayed in tongues. I then began to pray in tongues, and her facial expression changed again to one of joy and peace. Less than two minutes after that, she gladly accepted the invitation I extended for her to confess faith in Jesus Christ. After she confessed faith in Jesus, I again asked, "If you were to die right now, do you know where your soul would go?"

This time she emphatically replied, "Yes."

"Where?" I asked.

"Heaven!" she emphatically replied, This all happened over the span of fifteen to twenty minutes (tops) in a courthouse.

The encounter with this lady proved the doctrinal accuracy of these words from the Holy Spirit as delivered through the Apostle Paul: "Therefore tongues are for a sign, not to those who believe but to unbelievers; but prophesying is not for unbelievers but for those who believe." (1 Cor. 14:22) Just as surely as Almighty God allowed the sun to shine this morning, this blessed lady relented and gave or rededicated her life to Christ. This providential event developed after the Holy Spirit miraculously removed deceiving scales from her eyes specifically related to the false and very confusing doctrinal belief that one can't be saved unless and until they speak in tongues. Unfortunately at least one entire denomination has been created in such error. In this particular scenario, speaking in tongues was a sign and a wonder to her, which arrested her attention and showed to her God's eternal truth that salvation comes exclusively through faith in Jesus and faith in Him alone, whether one can speak in tongues or not.

How God Helped Me Avoid a Deadly Car Crash
"He who speaks in a tongue edifies himself…" (1 Cor. 14:4)

Another fascinating aspect about speaking in tongues is that it personally edifies the speaker not only in the things of God but also in every aspect of our daily lives. God created mankind to revere, worship, praise, honor, and obey Him, so our Heavenly Father has a vested interest in our longevity here on earth to fulfill the callings He has upon our lives. (Ps. 11:9, KJV) Accordingly God often protects us from known and unknown harm, danger, and even death through natural and supernatural means.

When I first started speaking in tongues, I would sometimes get up about an hour earlier than normal just to put in some time praying in tongues. I would often have a general sense of the subject matter about which I was speaking, but for the most part it would completely escape my natural mind. Later that same day or week, however, something would happen that would immediately bring to my memory a particular time that I had been praying in tongues.

While driving home from work one night, I distinctly recall my foot easing up off the accelerator seemingly of its own volition. The car began to travel at a much slower speed, which caused me to start pushing back down on the accelerator so the car would go faster. However, just as I began to press down, a thought came to my mind—a still, small voice that said,

"Don't."

I immediately stopped pressing down on the accelerator. I recall thinking to myself, "Well, it's going to take quite a while to get home now." As I was approaching a car that was traveling in the opposite lane, the driver, who had to have been intoxicated, suddenly made a left turn directly across my path of travel without any warning whatsoever. In a split second—and before my mind could consciously think about it—my foot immediately hit the brakes. I was blessed to avoid the crash by what seemed like less than an inch. With adrenaline pumping in my veins, I was quite angry with the driver, but this quickly subsided when I heard the Holy Spirit speak these words to my mind: "This is what you were praying about in tongues this morning. You were praying in the spirit that you would obey me when I would reduce your speed of travel on the way home tonight."

All of a sudden, what had been anger and frustration with the other driver (who almost killed me) turned into a very loud praise party in my car. I was so overwhelmed with thanksgiving in my heart for what the Holy Spirit had done that I started thanking and praising God, not only for saving my life but also for having spoken to me that morning while I prayed in tongues and for having blessed me with the interpretation of my own tongue. As you can imagine, I was so full of joy that I kept thanking God for each and every thing that came to my mind that night. This scenario was proof positive that speaking in tongues is a very important spiritual gift for the personal edification of believers.

Interpretation of Tongues

> I wish you all spoke with tongues, but even more that you prophesied; for he who prophesies is greater than he who speaks with tongues, unless indeed he interprets, that the church may receive edification. (1 Cor. 14:5)

As I have said previously, speaking forth the oracles of God, better known as prophecy or preaching, is arguably the most important manifestation of the Holy Spirit in the lives of believers. This is because speaking forth that which God declares in His Holy Word can set souls free from the deceptive and soul-damning power of Satan and his legions of demons.

The Apostle Paul further declares that one who has the spiritual gifting or Holy Spirit enablement to interpret tongues is very valuable in the church. This is the case because when one speaks in tongues, their human spirit has a direct connection with the Holy Spirit of Christ Jesus, creating a direct connection between the earthly realm and the heavenly realm. Please remember this very important spiritual truth that Jesus bequeathed to mankind: "Whatever you bind on earth will be bound in heaven, and whatever you loose on earth will be loosed in heaven." (Matt. 18:18)

Christians love to quote this passage of Scripture, but I spiritually discern that far too many of us fail to fully grasp the spiritual potency of this eternal truth. When we combine this promise with one person's ability to pray in tongues and another person's ability to interpret, God has the ability to edify every person within the sound of the live or recorded voice of the interpreter. The revelation of the substance of the tongue being spoken and/or the back-and-forth exchange between the speaker and the Holy Spirit edifies those who hear (comprehend) and have faith in (believe and trust) the delivered message. This usually fosters stronger faith in God specifically because the hearers are being edified and God is being glorified. This makes for very powerful encounters with the risen savior Jesus, "the author and finisher of our faith." (Heb. 12:2)

Such powerful messages from God through speaking in tongues and the interpretation of tongues have the ultimate purpose of defeating the wiles, plots, and wicked schemes of Satan. The ultimate result is that formerly lost souls can get saved and thereby escape the lake of fire.

However, there is an infinite number of other benefits in the natural and supernatural realms. The word "salvation" in the New Testament is the

Greek word *sozo*, which is by no means exclusively limited to one going to Heaven after the cessation of natural life here on Earth. Sozo has a far more expansive meaning that includes ultimate deliverance from Satan and his demons on all fronts. Sozo means we have been saved from the ultimate penalty of sin, which is spiritual death or the eternal separation from God in Hell and the lake of fire after the second coming of Jesus. In addition, sozo means we are currently being saved from the destructive powers and influences of Satan who comes "to steal, and to kill, and to destroy" the lives God plans for us to live out in faith and obedience to Him. (John 10:10) Finally, sozo includes the ultimate deliverance from the very presence of sin, Satan, and his demonic emissaries. The following account is a testimony of tongues being spoken and interpreted in a secular setting which produced sozo or deliverance from criminal penalties in a court of law.

Courtroom Testimony

As this book is being completed in 2015 with the aid, guidance, and counsel of the Holy Spirit, I am both a full-time pastor and an attorney and counselor-at-law operating my own law firm, as ordained by God Himself. I have been a trial attorney for the past thirty years with licenses to practice law in two states. Presently I am also in my fourth year of serving as pastor of a nondenominational church, having been a minister of the Gospel for the past fourteen years. The following miraculous event happened well over a decade ago while I was at the Duval County courthouse in Jacksonville, Florida, preparing to try a case involving a young man who was being prosecuted on his second charge of possession of illegal narcotics. It was actually this young man's father who taught me how to be empowered by the Holy Spirit to start speaking in tongues. It was he who taught me to obey the Scriptures by simply asking for the ability to speak in tongues and then getting into seclusion and solemnly thanking and praising God for that which He had already done in my life.

Fighting in Faith

About half an hour before the trial, I asked my client and his parents to sit down with me in a lawyers' conference room that was just across the hall from the courtroom. I wanted us to discuss a few last-minute particulars about the trial, go over my client's testimony, and then pray before proceeding to trial. The father, mother, and son were each endued with the Holy Spirit enablement to speak in tongues at will. Additionally, my client's father also had the Holy Spirit enablement to interpret tongues. After I finished going over the young man's testimony, I was moved in spirit to ask if we could all pray in tongues before we went into the courtroom. We stood up, joined hands in a circle, and started praying in the spirit, which lasted five or ten minutes.

After the prayer, I noticed my client's father looking at me very intently. I said, "What's wrong?" I could tell he was seriously contemplating something.

After ten or twenty seconds had elapsed, he said, "Do you know what you said when you were praying?"

"No," I replied. "I can't interpret tongues."

He then said, "Do you want to know what you said?" When I said yeah, he told me, "You said, 'My God, my God, You are a mighty God, my God, my God, You fight my battles, my God, my God, you will fight this battle for me, my God, my God, let's go into battle.'"

I was awestruck and thereby physically, spiritually, emotionally, and psychologically charged up after hearing the interpretation of my own tongues. In other words, I was edified, strengthened, and encouraged just prior to going into a court of law to try a case before a judge who had the power to either acquit (which is synonymous with *justify*) my client and release him or adjudicate him delinquent (which is the equivalent of *guilty* for juveniles) and lock him up.

Needless to say, I had a great deal of confidence when I walked into that courtroom. I would even say I had a little pep in my step and a glide in my proverbial stride, for I knew God was with me. Juvenile cases are not tried by a jury. Unlike adult criminal cases, juvenile cases are tried exclusively by the presiding judge, who serves as both the finder of fact (jury) and the one who pronounces sentence if the person is found delinquent or guilty. After the trial ended, the judge looked at me and started sharply criticizing me about how he disagreed with me on this, how he disagreed with me on that, how I did not do this right, and on and on. I was shocked, thinking to myself, "This can't be happening after all of my preparation for this trial, the prayers, the tongues, and the awesome interpretation. How can this be?"

As the judge continued to disparage my courtroom performance, I started packing my briefcase, thinking, "Well, I just lost this one."

All of a sudden, I heard the judge say, "But I find for your client!"

I stopped in my tracks and looked at the two prosecutors, who had deer-in-the-headlights looks on their faces. I then looked at the bailiff, who was rolling his eyes in what looked like confusion; I looked at the court clerk, who was rolling her eyes incredulously; and then I looked up at the judge, who was now completely silent. The judge had a look on his face that I shall never ever forget as long as I live on God's green Earth. His facial expression looked as if he was pondering, "Why or how did I say what just came out of my mouth? How did I find for this kid after that performance by Mr. Barlow?"

At that very moment, the Holy Spirit reminded me of the prayer I had prayed in tongues and its interpretation. He very gently reminded me that the gist of the interpretation was that God is mighty and God fights my battles. Most importantly this reminder also fulfilled this promise from Jesus: "The Helper, the Holy Spirit, whom the Father will send in My name, He will teach you all things, and bring to your remembrance all things that I said to you." (John 14:26)

At this point, my mind was illuminated to comprehend that God had at least three objectives in mind with this courtroom victory. First and foremost, He wanted me and my clients to fully comprehend that God had won the trial. Second, God wanted me to appreciate that despite my having tried the case below the judge's expectations, God was still powerful enough to ordain the victory, even when everyone in that courtroom, especially the judge, knew that judgment was about to be pronounced against my client. Third and finally, God won the case in such a miraculous way that I could take not one iota of credit for the victory.

In other words, God knows me very well. He knows how He providentially delivered and continues to deliver me from the very strong demon of pride. God is so powerful, wonderful, and merciful that He knew that if He did not humble me through the means by which the case had been won, there would be a serious risk of Satan seducing me with the demon spirit of pride. In his awesome grace, mercy, providence, and omnipotence, God won the case by such miraculous means that I could in no way be enticed with pride to take any credit whatsoever for the win. This is just one of the many reasons that I love God with all my heart and earnestly try to serve him with my entire being. God loves us more than we are even capable of loving ourselves and proves it time and time again. The question is, Do we even realize that some of the great things "we" have done were in fact done by God through us?

Without any doubt whatsoever, this was one of the most powerful and life-changing experiences I have ever witnessed or about which I have ever heard concerning tongues and their interpretation. Can you now comprehend why Satan pulls out every stop he possibly can to push people as far as possible away from speaking in tongues and interpreting tongues? I've heard just about every excuse one can possibly imagine as to why Holy Bible–believing Christians should not speak in or interpret tongues. All of them are nothing more than poor excuses delivered to these people's hearts through demonic spirits of doubt, fear, pride, or outright unbelief in what the Holy Bible declares about speaking in tongues.

Think about it this way: Just how important was it for me to receive the interpretation of the tongue I spoke before the trial? It made all the difference in the world to me, for it showed me that in my subconscious mind and spirit, I know without any doubt, fear, pride, or unbelief that my God is mighty and my God fights my battles—regardless of whether I get credit for the wins or not. What I did not know at the time was that there would be many, many more courtroom victories in the future that would be won under some of the most insurmountable circumstances. Many of these victories would be akin to the battles fought by David (who defeated a nine-foot-tall giant) and Gideon and his ragtag army of three hundred men, who defeated a Midianite and Amalekite army that covered the earth "like grasshoppers," for their multitude was without number. (Judg. 7:7–12)

Fortunately, I have been (and am still being) used by God similarly to the way in which He used King David, and I thank Him for having humbled me in such merciful ways. God has allowed me to receive some credit for a few of the victories that continue to come forth since that fateful day in court between 2002 and 2003. Many of the same will be shared in books to come that will have a primary focus on how God works through believers and our spiritual gifts in the legal system in both civil and criminal defense litigation.

Chapter 7

POWER MINISTRY PART 1: A BIBLICAL FOUNDATION

And I, brethren, when I came to you, did not come with excellence of speech or of wisdom declaring to you the testimony of God. For I determined not to know anything among you except Jesus Christ and Him crucified. I was with you in weakness, in fear, and in much trembling. And my speech and my preaching were not with persuasive words of human wisdom, but in demonstration of the Spirit and of power, that your faith should not be in the wisdom of men but in the power of God. (1 Cor. 2:1–5)

Having dealt with prophecy, tongues, and the interpretation of tongues, the time has come to address power ministry, which is more commonly called working miracles or healing and deliverance ministry. Prophecy, tongues, and the interpretation of tongues are called speaking gifts, primarily because the chief delivery mode of whatever blessing God bestows through the person operating the spiritual gift generally comes through articulation. With respect to the power ministry, although speaking can be employed as a vehicle to deliver blessings, miracles, healings, and deliverances, the same can also take place without a single spoken word. However, most of the time speaking, declaring, or decreeing is coupled with some other means by which the Holy Spirit channels divine power through someone to manifest healing, deliverance, or the working of a specific miracle.

Channeling Divine Power

I am fully cognizant that some will take issue with the use of the word *channel*, because Satan utilizes demons to channel evil through those who are under his wicked power structure. In reality, though, the word *channel* in and of itself is a completely neutral term. When people are under the inspiration of the Holy Spirit of Christ Jesus, they can be moved by God to speak and carry out righteous acts. Conversely, when people are under the influence of satanic or demonic forces, they say and do sinful and unrighteous acts. What's so unfathomable and outright scary is that a single person can be used by both God and Satan within the exact same time frame. God can motivate a person to say and do one thing, and the next minute—or even within the next breath—Satan can motivate or channel unrighteousness through that same person.

A classic example of this is when the Apostle Peter first came under Holy Spirit inspiration to confess to Jesus, "You are the Christ, the Son of the living God." (Matt. 16:16) In terms of godly spiritual matters, you can't be more in God's perfect will than to hear from God Himself in the person of the Holy Spirit confirming that you are in the presence of God Himself in the person of God the Son! No doubt the Apostle Peter hit a grand slam in the spirit realm. Jesus Himself confirmed the magnitude of Peter's bold confession with these very words: "Blessed are you, Simon Bar-Jonah, for flesh and blood has not revealed this to you, but My Father who is in heaven." (Matt.16:17) Jesus goes on to make a declaration of spiritual war against Satan and his demons by saying these eternal words:

And I also say to you that you are Peter, and on this rock, I will build My church, and the gates of Hades shall not prevail against it. And I will give you the keys of the kingdom of heaven, and whatever you bind on earth will be bound in heaven, and whatever you loose on earth will be loosed in heaven. (Matt. 16:18–19)

Most of us tend to focus on the fact that Peter finally got something right, which causes us to ignore that Jesus makes a war declaration against the forces of darkness. This plays right into Satan's plans to make and keep us as ignorant as possible of the fact that Jesus has declared spiritual war against the Devil and his fallen angels, better known as demons.

Afterward Jesus informs the apostles about His necessary death by crucifixion, which causes Satan to launch a ferocious spiritual attack on Peter's mind, will, and emotions. Under the evil inspiration of Satan, Peter "took Him aside and began to rebuke Him, saying, far be it from You, Lord; this shall not happen to You." (Matt. 16:22) Unbeknownst to Peter, Satan had just channeled demonic spirits of doubt, fear, pride, unbelief, and selfishness right through his soul. This very subtle yet effective satanic attack quickly caused Peter to reverse course and rebuke the very person he had just previously confessed was the Son of God, the very Messiah of the entire world.

Knowing full well that the rebuke came not from Peter but from Satan through Peter, Jesus "turned and said to Peter, get behind Me, Satan: you are an offense to Me, for you are not mindful of the things of God, but the things of men." (Matt. 16:23)

The question is, To whom was Jesus speaking: Peter or Satan? The answer is yes, for He was speaking to Satan through the channel that Satan was using to speak to Jesus, which was Peter.

Without any doubt, this has to be one of the most mind-boggling scenarios in the entire Bible. How can Peter be so inspired by God one minute but then become so spiritually deceived that he becomes a spokesman for Satan the next minute? The answer lies in how well we exercise our

God-given but very fragile and feckless free will. Do we knowingly exercise it to the glory of God the Father, God the Son, and God the Holy Spirit, or do we ignorantly, negligently, or knowingly exercise it for Satan and his demons? The Apostle Paul hit a grand slam with these words:

> Do you not know that to whom you present yourselves slaves to obey, you are that one's slaves whom you obey, whether of sin leading to death, or of obedience leading to righteousness? (Rom. 6:16)

If you accept the complete inerrancy of the Holy Bible, this passage of Scripture proves that genuine believers in Jesus can unwittingly allow themselves to be used by Satan and demons. Accordingly if a person can ignorantly authorize Satan and demons to channel evil power and authority through her or his body, then those who worship Satan and demons can knowingly and intentionally do likewise.

These passages of Scripture solidly confirm that human beings can be used as conduits to channel divine (spiritual) power and influence from both godly and ungodly sources. Channeling is similar to how an electrical cord is used to direct electricity from a source to an appliance. The electrical cord is not the source, nor is it the instrument that needs the electricity. You can have all the electrical appliances you wish, but they will be good for absolutely nothing if no working electrical cords are attached and subsequently plugged into a source or electricity (which means power).

Accordingly you and I are conduits—spiritual electrical cords that can be used either for God's righteous spiritual power or Satan's evil power to flow to and through. God graciously gave us the free will to choose whom we will serve: the God of the Universe, Adonai, Jehovah, El, El Elyon, Jesus—or the little *g* god of this world, who is Satan. The manner in which we exercise our God-given free will dictates which power source we allow to be channeled through us. The level of our knowledge, faith, endurance/perseverance, and willingness to obey God will dictate who or what we will ultimately serve.

However, please know with certainty that you will be forced to choose one or the other. The unchangeable reason is because God specifically created mankind to worship Him. However, in so doing He liberally gave us the option—the free will—to worship someone or something else, which is called idolatry. The punishment for idolatry is spiritual death, which is the eternal separation of man's soul and spirit from God in the lake of fire. Accordingly you and I are going to worship something, whether we do with our full knowledge or in complete ignorance.

Unfortunately many people try to ignore evil, Satan, and his demons. Unbeknownst to them, such willful lack of knowledge will be to their personal detriment and ultimate destruction if they fail to repent. The greatest problem I have witnessed is a spirit of willful ignorance that rests upon far too many people, many of whom genuinely proclaim to be Christians. Are you familiar with spiritual ostrich syndrome? It fosters the false demonic doctrine that says, "I'm not going to mess around with demons. If I leave them alone, they'll leave me alone too." This is some very dangerous ignorance that only inures to Satan's benefit. Stubbornly or ignorantly holding onto the same is usually fatal.

The Danger of Biblical Illiteracy (Ignorance)
God warns mankind of the eternal consequences of ignorance in the Old Testament with these very familiar words: "My people are destroyed for lack of knowledge. Because you have rejected knowledge…" (Hosea 4:6) People like to say that knowledge is power, which is true. However, if knowledge is power, then the lack of knowledge, or ignorance, is certainly weakness.

Now let's relate this to the necessity of having a good command of biblical knowledge. While a lack of knowledge of things in the natural realm can cause one to lose fame, fortune, or even their natural life, ignorance in the things of God can cause many to lose their souls eternally. It is for this reason that those who claim to have faith in God are expected to know

Him and what He says in His Holy Word. God commands us to know Him with these very words: "Study to show thyself approved unto God, a workman that needeth not to be ashamed, rightly dividing the word of truth." (2 Tim. 2:15, KJV) While reading the Holy Bible is not absolutely necessary to have a deep and personal relationship with God, the more we read and therefore learn about Him, His awesome promises, and His unusual ways, the more of an opportunity we will have to live virtuous and victorious lives here on Earth.

Jesus Introduced Power Ministry
Jesus worked miracles and performed healings and deliverances through several modes. The first was through speaking: "'Go, show yourselves to the priests,' [he said], and as they went, they were cleansed." (Luke 17:14) The second was touching: "Jesus had compassion and touched their eyes. And immediately their eyes received sight..." (Matt. 20:34) The third was speaking and touching: "[T]hen Jesus, moved with compassion, stretched out His hand and touched him, and said to him, I am willing, be cleansed." (Mark 1:41) The fourth was by allowing the sick to touch Him: "Jesus said, 'Somebody touched Me, for I perceived power going out from Me.'" (Luke 8:46)

As you read this, you are probably thinking, "Sure, He could do all these wonderful things because He's God." If such a thought came to your mind, it was generated by the enemy of man's soul, who sent the demon spirit of doubt to try to dissuade you from receiving that which God has ordained for every believer. Please stay with me in this chapter by keeping an open mind and employing a little mustard-seed faith. Please articulate this prayer out loud right now before continuing to read this chapter:

> Father God, in the name of Jesus and in the power of your Holy Spirit, please guard my mind, my heart, my soul, my will, and my spirit from all doubt, fear, pride, unbelief, and any other mat-

ter that will challenge my faith in Jesus. Father God, please help me to sift through this information and protect me from all wiles, schemes, plots, plans, and ploys from the enemy of man's soul. Thank you, God, for hearing and answering this prayer. In the name of Jesus, Amen.

Power Ministry Tears Down Demonic Strongholds

Of all chapters in this book, chapters seven and eight will be the most challenging for some readers, primarily because they teach genuine believers how to wage successful spiritual warfare in the name of Jesus. The editor and I experienced the most challenges with chapter seven—more than all the other chapters combined—specifically because it explains the eternal truths of spiritual warfare, which Satan does not want anyone to truly comprehend. Successful spiritual warfare tears down demonic strongholds in our lives, with two very important benefits. The most significant is soul salvation from destruction in Hell and ultimately the lake of fire. The second benefit is becoming empowered to fulfill God's divine calling in our lives to help people who are within our spheres of influence—whether we are at home, in church, in the neighborhood, in the workplace, at social gatherings, and the like—get saved and delivered. If you know the Holy Bible, you appreciate that most of Jesus's miraculous works and power ministry took place not in local synagogues or the Temple but out in the marketplaces of Judea and the surrounding towns.

One of the most important and life-altering spiritual truths that mankind ignores is that God created us to have stewardship over planet Earth and exercise dominion over His entire creation. This is evident with this declaration that first applied to Adam:

> Let Us make man in Our image, according to Our likeness; let them have dominion over the fish of the sea, over the birds of the air, and over the cattle, over all the earth and over every creeping

thing that creeps on the earth. (Gen. 1:26)

With this single sentence, we can discern that God made us to have natural power (*dunamai*), supernatural power (*dunamis*), and authority (*exousia*), which is the legal right to exercise power.

Power Defined
Under the guidance and counsel of the Holy Spirit, I have come to understand and utilize an exceptionally practical definition of the word *power*. In essence, power is the ability to effect change. For example, if a person is suffering from sickness or disease (dis-ease), when God's divine power is applied, the person becomes healed, cured, or otherwise made whole. If one is financially destitute, when godly power is applied, their financial circumstances will be changed from lack or want to being prosperous. A classic example of this is found in Acts 3, when Peter and John met a lame man at the beautiful gate of the temple as they were going in. The man was destitute due to his inability to work, which was chief because he could not walk. Instead of Peter and John giving him a handout, they allowed the Holy Spirit to channel divine power through them to change the man's inability to walk. Once he was able to walk, he would also be able to work, which would ultimately lead to a positive change in his finances.

Dunamai is "the ability to have power, whether by virtue of one's own ability and resources, or via state of mind, favorable circumstances, or by permission of law or custom." Conversely, *dunams* is defined as "miraculous power, mighty work, strength, or ability" on supernatural levels. (The New Strong's Expanded Dictionary of Bible Words, Thomas Nelson Publishers, 2001)

Dunamis "almost always points to new and higher forces that have entered and are working in this lower world of ours." (1) It is "power ability," physical or moral as residing in a person or thing; (2) It is "power in action," e.g., put forth in performing miracles. (3) It occurs 118 times in the New Testament. (4) It is sometimes used of the miracle or sign itself, the effect being put for the cause, e.g., Mk 6:5, frequently in the Gospels and Acts. (5) In 1 Corinthians 14:11, it is rendered "meaning." (Idem. Grk. #1411)

While dunams particularizes actual manifestations of spiritual power (might), *exousia* describes the lawful (legal) right to exercise dunams. Strong's defines exousia as:

> (1) "authority," "it is lawful," (2) from the meaning of "leave or permission," or liberty of doing as one pleases, (2a) "the ability or strength with which one is endued," (2b) "power of authority," the right to exercise power, e.g. Matthew 9:6, 21:23, 2 Corinthians 10:8, (2c) "the power of rule or government," the power of one whose will and command must be obeyed by others (Strong's Idem. Grk. #1849)

As you can now discern, power ministry is both the ability to exercise spiritual power and the legal right so to do. Power ministry, which includes performing miraculous signs, wonders, miracles, healings, and deliverances (casting out demons) was divinely ordained in the spirit realm before God even "formed man from the dust of the ground" and "breathed the breath of life into his nostrils," and "before man became a living soul." (Gen. 2:7) In other words, when God said, "Let us make man in our image, according to our likeness, and let them have dominion," this was the spiritual ordination of man's God-given authority (exousia) to execute God's divine power (dunamis) to subdue each and every earthly thing God spoke into existence in Genesis 1. In other words, each and everything that has been created from God is subject to man's authority, power, and influence as long as it exists on planet Earth.

Do you believe this statement? To the extent you do, you will be clothed in just enough mustard-seed faith to powerfully carry out God's ordination for you to subdue His creations, which include Satan and every one of his demons. Here are just a few of the demons which I have had the godly pleasure of having been used by the Holy Spirit to cast out of both Bible-believing Christians and nonbelievers over the past decade or so: addictions (alcohol, drugs, sex, and many others), anger, anxiety, arrogance, bitterness, deception, double mindedness (schizophrenia and other schizoaffective disorders), doubt, curses, envy, fear (of death, man, Satan, demons, God, failure, success), generational curses, male and female homosexuality, jealousy, larceny, licentiousness, lying spirit (a.k.a. spirit of untruth), mental illness, mind-blinding spirit, murder (manifesting in abortion, deep-seated hatred, and unforgiveness for past wrongs), "psycho" (crazy) spirit manifesting in psychotic episodes and mental derangement, pride, rape, sexual battery, silliness, soul ties, unbelief, unforgiveness, waywardness, and many others. Some of these are addressed in chapter fifteen, which includes actual testimonies of deliverances.

The Advent of Spiritual War
Isaiah 14:12–17 and Ezekiel 28:1–19 record how and why Lucifer was dethroned from his abode in the heavenly realm as eternal punishment for his rebellion against God. The central reason God defrocked Lucifer from his very high position was iniquity, which is total wickedness. The two greatest sins found in him were covetousness, which is lust and pride. These were generated in Lucifer as he allowed both his beauty and his workmanship (that came from God) to fill him with sinful pride, which led him to lust for that which God will share with absolutely no one: glory. "I am the King of Glory," declares God Himself in Psalm 24, and He means just that. God said Lucifer was "perfect in all his ways…until iniquity was found in him." (Ezek. 28:15). A very significant part of his punishment was being "…cut down to the ground," which references Earth. (Ezekiel 28:12) With this revelation from God, it is quite easy to discern that Lucifer was dethroned from his heavenly abode and thereby became Satan, the devil and mankind's

archenemy. Temporally speaking, it is widely accepted by theologians that this took place after God had already created man and planet Earth.

Why would God put a very powerful and wicked angelic being, one who is now the devil himself, on a planet He made that's inhabited by people He created and loves very much? Why would God do such a thing, knowing full well Satan had already said in his heart, "I will ascend into heaven; I will exalt my throne above the stars of God" and "I will be like the Most High"? (Isa. 14:13–14) The answer to these questions is absolutely shocking and almost unfathomable. The answer to these questions can have you rethinking everything you have come to know in life. The answer to these questions can cause you to have the greatest love, awe, reverence, and ultimate belief and trust in the triune personality of God the Father; God the Son, Jesus (of Nazareth); and God the Holy Spirit. The answer to these questions can cause you to dedicate your life to Jesus and rely upon His majesty, dominion, and soul-saving power for the rest of your life.

Are you ready for the answer? Here's the answer: God cast Satan down to Earth so that mankind, the apple of God's eye, could (and still can) have absolute dominion over him and the legions of demons he deceived to rebel against God in a treasonous confederacy. Yes, God created planet Earth, formed man from the dust of the very ground upon which He would later cast Satan, and ordained eternal warfare between mankind, Satan, and his demons. To put it another way, God specifically created human beings as a mechanism of spiritual warfare to manifest His light of truth and spiritual righteousness to defeat Satan and his forces of untruth, lies, and deception. If you are having challenges with the substance of this book, it is because Satan wants to keep the proverbial genie in the bottle. Once you know and accept the truth, it "will make you free" from Satanic lies, deceptions, falsehoods, and innuendos that are so masterfully, albeit wickedly, used to steal, kill, and destroy lives. (John 8:32, 10:10)

Planet Earth Is a Theater for Battle

This entire planet is a war zone, a theater for battles that are initiated in the heavenly or spirit realm but carried out in the natural or earthly realm. From the first chapter in Genesis to the last chapter in Revelation, the Holy Bible is a book about spiritual warfare. God specifically created man to supernaturally rule over and execute God's judgment against Lucifer. We are commissioned by God to humble him as punishment for the pride, lust, and covetousness he harbors in his heart. Pride and lust are the original sins that caused God to eject Lucifer from his heavenly abode. However, the absolute key to being successful in our calling is genuine faith (belief plus trust) in God and earnest humility, which is the spiritual antidote to the sin that God hates most—pride, which precedes destruction.

Is it a coincidence or divine providence that lust and pride were the original sins that also caused God to cast Adam and Eve out of the Garden of Eden? God is omniscient and therefore knew Adam and Eve would fail and that this would ultimately necessitate God coming down to Earth, being born of a virgin, and walking clothed in human flesh the very Earth he created. What an awesome example of humility. His chief objective was to show us how to wage successful spiritual warfare wielding spiritual weapons (agape) and spiritual ammunition (faith) so that we could chose to love, revere, worship, and ultimately be in His awesome presence for eternity.

If you are still not convinced that God created Earth as a battleground so He could use mankind to conquer, humble, and humiliate Satan and his demons for their treasonous rebellion against Him, let's very carefully examine Ezekiel 28:17. In this revelatory verse, God lets mankind know the sentence He imposed upon Lucifer when he said, "I cast you to the ground, I laid you before kings that they might gaze at you." Without any doubt, God sent Lucifer to Earth to be gawked at by human beings whom God would clothe with power and authority to exercise dominion over Satan and his demons. The King James Version uses the word *behold*, which is rendered as *gaze* in the New King James Version. Here God is telling us that He cast Lucifer down to Earth where he can be seen for the sinful, evil spirit he has become.

God wants His royal priests, kings, prophets, and prophetesses to be able to spiritually discern wickedness, no matter how deceptively disguised it may be. He also desires for us to appreciate His goodness, grace, and mercy irrespective of what the ways of the world may be at any given time. It's God's divine plan that man would not only exercise "dominion over the fish of the sea, over the birds of the air, and over the cattle, over all the earth and over every creeping thing that creeps on the earth," but also exercise dominion over Satan and all demons who worship him.

However, we must exercise our God-given free will to "gaze" at Satan for the defeated foe he really is and thereafter obey God by exercising our spiritual authority to "submit to God" and "resist the devil" so that he will "flee from" us. (James 4:7) The problem is most people try to resist Satan and/or his demons without first having submitted to God. Our faith and trust in God open up our spiritual eyes that we may correctly discern evil through God's eyes. By contrast, when we have sin reigning in us, our spiritual eyes become blinded to the things of God but receptive to unrighteousness, sin, and evil.

Old Testament Warfare vs. New Testament Warfare

During Old Testament times, God often used natural warfare with natural weapons such as arrows, knives, swords, spears, javelins, fire, water, and many others to execute His judgment on human beings who continued to ignore His call for them to live righteously. Doctrinally speaking, from Leviticus 11:44 to 1 Peter 1:16, God's command has been, and still is: "Be ye holy for I am Holy."

Old Testament warfare heavily involved God establishing His sovereignty over that which He created. Mankind was specifically created to love, respect, worship, revere, and obey our Creator. The blessedness about this is that we were divinely endued with the free will to either accept or reject, love or hate, worship or not worship anyone or anything we choose. As you should very well know, there is a huge catch. The catch is that there is a day of reckoning when every human being will give an account to our God for our actions during our lifetime.

Moreover, those of us who reverentially love, respect, and obey God are blessed with the gift of eternal life in His presence as a reward for our love and obedience. Conversely, those who ignorantly, stubbornly, willfully, or rebelliously reject God's love will suffer the eternal separation of their souls from God in Hell and the lake of fire. Part of the age-old problem people have in accepting this truth is the mind-blinding wiles and schemes Satan and his demons employ on the human mind, will, and emotions. These evil schemes are specifically designed to generate doubt, fear, pride, unbelief, and/or unforgiveness toward man, God, and anything He desires or commands, most of which is for our own good.

During Old Testament times, God would allow people to live in sin for extended periods of time, waiting for them to repent and return to God. You may be thinking, "How can people return to God having never known Him in the first place?" Excellent question. The matter of returning to God goes all the way back to the Garden of Eden, when Adam and Eve allowed the sinful lust of the eye, the lust of the flesh, and the pride of life to cause them obey Satan by rebelling against God. Spiritually speaking, mankind consists of a single race: human. Physiologically and therefore scientifically, we are all brothers and sisters though we look, speak, and act differently. Accordingly, God is calling the crowning glory of His creation—mankind—to return to loving, worshiping, revering, obeying, and having fellowship with Him from the time He created Adam and subsequently brought from Eve from Adam.

However, each of us has a certain amount of time on God's divine clock to repent of our sins and humbly return to Him in spirit and in truth. This divine clock not only relates to individuals but also to families, cities, states, and entire nations. God has the sovereignty to create and destroy, to build up and tear down any and everything He so chooses. How do you feel about the fact that God has this kind of awesome power to do whatever pleases Him? If you have difficulty accepting this, please pray in the name of Jesus for the Holy Spirit to reveal whether there is any malevolent spirit influencing your heart regarding this matter of doctrinal or eternal truth. Satan often tries to sow seeds of stubbornness and rebellion in our hearts when we are confronted with God's omnipotence, omniscience, or omnipresence.

When time runs out on God's divine repentance clock, He ordains and initiates righteous punishment for our stubborn or rebellious refusal to obey Him. In the Old Testament, at times this often meant death by one of three divinely sanctioned punishments: famine (starvation), pestilence (disease), or the sword (warfare). Please read 2 Samuel 24 in its entirety for a clear understanding. With respect to individuals, God would often order the execution of a sinful person by the hand of a righteous person God had divinely chosen to execute His just punishment. A classic example of this is the famed battle of David versus Goliath.

David vs. Goliath

The fight between David and Goliath was actually about God executing righteous judgment against the Philistines, who were living in open rebellion against God. In classic form, God chose the least of the least—a shepherd boy—to defeat a seasoned and mighty warrior who had great *dunamai*, or natural ability. By contrast, David, the ninety-eight-pound weakling shepherd boy, represented the God-ordained dunamis, or unlimited spiritual power, that was deeply within David's soul and spirit, predicated in his faith (belief and trust) in the living God. David revealed the source of his hidden strength by declaring, "You come to me with a sword, with a spear, and with a javelin. But I come to you in the name of the Lord of hosts, the God of the armies of Israel, whom you have defied." (1 Sam. 17:45)

With these very familiar words, the little shepherd boy was declaring and decreeing on Earth the nature of the spiritual warfare that had already been ordained in the heavenly realm. David was proclaiming the spiritual authority, or exousia, God had previously bestowed upon him in 1 Samuel 16:13 to execute righteous judgment against Satan in the form of his demonically inspired puppet, Goliath of Gath. While vengeance belongs to the Lord, God sometimes divinely ordains certain people to manifest divine retribution against His enemies. In this particular case, His chosen instrument was a little shepherd boy whom everyone knew had to have had divine help from God to defeat a battle-tested warrior who stood nine feet tall.

The Execution of Prophetic and Power Ministry
The shepherd boy goes on to prophesy the exact judgment and manner of execution with which God would use him to judge and thereby kill Satan's superman. In other words, David preached Goliath's eulogy before his death, then killed him in accordance with the prophesy. Under divine inspiration, David said:

> This day the Lord will deliver you into my hand, and I will strike you and take your head from you. And this day I will give the carcasses of the camp of the Philistines to the birds of the air and the wild beasts of the earth, that all the earth may know that there is a God in Israel. Then all this assembly shall know that the Lord does not save with sword and spear; for the battle is the Lord's, and He will give you into our hands. (1 Sam. 17:46–47)

As you know, David immediately executed judgment on Goliath and fulfilled every iota of the prophecies the Holy Spirit inspired him to speak. However, I believe the vast majority of readers fail to comprehend that God was channeling His divine power and might through David. God received permission (authority) to do so when David submitted to God's directive for Samuel to anoint David to be King over the entire united nation of Israel. This spiritual ordination took place before this fateful battle with Goliath of Gath.

God grew tired of King Saul's repetitive disobedience and ordained David to take his place as God's chosen king to execute His righteous judgment. By the way, the single act that tipped the scale against Saul and caused him to lose favor with God, along with his kingship, was his failure to execute God's divine judgment against the Amalekites. The Amalekites were sworn enemies of God, and God had previously decreed that there would be warfare forever between His chosen people and the Amalekites. (Exod. 17:8–16) This was God's retribution for the Amalekites' cowardly attack on the children of Israel from behind after their exodus from four hundred years of slavery in Egypt. When King Saul's fear of the people overrode his obedience to and reverence of God and His righteous judgment, God replaced him with "a man after God's own heart." God spoke these solemn words to King Saul through the prophet Samuel as Saul was being removed as king:

> The Lord has sought for Himself a man after His own heart, and the Lord has commanded him to be commander over His people, because you have not kept what the Lord commanded you. (1 Sam. 13:14)

Sometime thereafter, God had the prophet Samuel anoint David as God's new king. 1 Samuel 16:13 reads, "Then Samuel took the horn of oil and anointed him in the midst of his brothers; and the Spirit of the Lord came upon David from that day forward."

Without any doubt whatsoever, the single most significant matter that took place here is that the Holy Spirit rested upon David from that day forward. This was a first in the Old Testament because God's Holy Spirit would normally come upon a person, channel through the person to do a miraculous or mighty work, and then leave the person until the next time a work was necessary.

Here are just a few examples where the spirit of the Lord came upon a person for a work to be accomplished and then departed:

> When the children of Israel cried out to the Lord, the Lord raised up a deliverer for the children of Israel, who delivered them: Othniel the son of Kenaz, Caleb's younger brother. The Spirit of the Lord came upon him, and he judged Israel. (Judg. 3:9–10)
>
> When the Holy Spirit came upon a very reluctant and cowardly man named Gideon, "he blew the trumpet, and the Abiezrites gathered behind him." (Judg. 6:34)
>
> The Spirit of the Lord came upon Jephthah, and he passed through Gilead and Manasseh, and passed through Mizpah of Gilead; and from Mizpah of Gilead he advanced toward the people of Ammon. (Judg. 11:29)

Concerning Samson, Judges 14:19 reflects "...the Spirit of the Lord came upon him mightily, and he went down to Ashkelon and killed thirty of their men..."

Many other Old Testament verses reflect the manner in which God used His handpicked servants to wage spiritual warfare that executed judgment calling for the deaths of individuals (such as Goliath), the deaths of scores of people and destruction of entire cities (Jericho), and the genocide of entire races of people from the face of the Earth (the Amalekites).

Old Testament warfare is waged not only with minds, wills, and emotions but also with weapons made of natural resources that are specifically designed to maim and kill the physical body. However, natural weapons of war have absolutely no power to "kill" or destroy the true essence of man: the soul and spirit. Man consists not only of the ephemeral (temporary and tangible) physical body but also the eternal (never-ending) soul and spirit.

Old Testament warfare is specifically designed to take a person off Earth's battlefield. Saved people who genuinely believe and trust God are a threat to Satan, whom the Bible refers to as "the god of this world" who blinds the minds of those who either refuse to believe or are ignorantly prevented from believing "the glorious light of the gospel of the glory of Christ, who is the image of God." (2 Cor. 4:4, KJV)

Doubtful, disobedient, stubborn, and/or rebellious people are a threat to the peace, unity, harmony, and blessings God ordains for his beloved. Old Testament–style warfare is still alive and well all over the entire world. Today's extremists employ Old Testament warfare in their religion-or-burn-to-death tactics. These tactics are carried out publicly to instill as much of the demonic spirit of fear in people as possible. The spirit of fear is quite effective at subduing minds, wills, and emotions to do Satan's will. The chief objective is for the victims to relent and succumb to satanically driven pressures to renounce their faith in the one and only true God in exchange for idol worship. Ever notice how extremists primarily target those who claim Christianity as their faith? How often do you hear about extremists persecuting any religion other than Christianity?

Accordingly Old Testament warfare primarily involves Satan trying to convert as many saved people to his side as he can, for he knows rebellion against God is obedience to himself. If and/or when they convert, they are used as instruments of war "to steal, and to kill, and to destroy" God's chosen. Conversely, it is God's perfect will that we "may have life, and that [we] may have it more abundantly"—which brings us to the next chapter on how God conducts New Testament warfare. (John 10:10)

Chapter 8

Power Ministry Part 2: Manifestations: Signs, Wonders, Miracles, and Healing and Deliverance Ministry

> The Spirit of the Lord is upon me, because He has anointed me to preach the gospel to the poor; He has sent me to heal the brokenhearted, to proclaim liberty to the captives and recovery of sight to the blind, to set at liberty those who are oppressed; to proclaim the acceptable year of the Lord. (Luke 4:18–19)

Old Testament warfare is specifically utilized to wound, torture, and kill the human body, but it has absolutely no power over the soul or spirit. Conversely, New Testament warfare is God ordained to crucify or sacrifice the body but preserve the soul and spirit. God has ordained fasting as the chief process of crucifying the flesh, which helps us to deny ourselves, take up our cross, and follow "the author and finisher of our faith." (Matt. 16:24, Heb. 12:2) Fasting is necessary for anyone who is serious about engaging in successful spiritual warfare. Fasting is significant because it trains, conditions, and subdues our flesh. Once the flesh becomes subdued, it can then, and only then, be bridled and thereafter brought under the controlling power of the human spirit.

If you have yet to experience or perform great signs, wonders, or miracles, it may be that your flesh needs to be subdued so you can become humble enough to be powerfully used by God. The more pride, arrogance, and self-sufficiency we exhibit, the less God can use us to demonstrate His awesome power. Why? Because the demon spirit of pride will entice us to take credit for that which God really performed through us. Conversely, the meeker and humbler we are, the greater stewardship God can release upon us to manifest His awesome power and therefore bring Him glory. Fasting is addressed in much greater detail in chapter 14.

Unfortunately, many people are clueless of the biblically proven fact that we are three—body, soul, and spirit. This is confirmed by these fateful words: "…may the God of peace Himself sanctify you completely; and may your whole spirit, soul, and body be preserved blameless at the coming of our Lord Jesus Christ." (2 Thess. 5:23)

Throughout the synoptic Gospels, Jesus repetitively confirms the pre-eminence of the soul above the physical body with the following and many other such exhortations and admonitions:

> Do not fear those who kill the body but cannot kill the soul. But rather fear Him who is able to destroy both soul and body in hell. (Matt. 10:28)
>
> If your right eye causes you to sin, pluck it out and cast it from you; for it is more profitable for you that one of your members perish, than for your whole body to be cast into hell. (Matt. 5:29)

Signs, Wonders, and Miracles Authenticate the Gospel

Because the New Testament is primarily concerned with the preservation of that which is completely intangible and imperceptible to any of our five natural senses, God uses divinely sanctioned signs, wonders, and miracles to authenticate His spiritually generated authority and power. However, God must strike a very delicate balance when using signs, wonders, and miracles to confirm His presence and providence. God runs the risk of having followers who will love Him exclusively because of the miracles He works of them, with them, in them, and/or through them.

Jesus also had to address this problem when he visited Earth clothed in human flesh. He was fully cognizant that most of his supposed disciples failed to receive the spiritual dynamic of His messages. To the contrary, they loved and sought him primarily because He could miraculously feed them with physical food, which caused them to ignore and therefore forfeit spiritual manna from Heaven. Discerning this very serious problem, Jesus sternly admonished His disciples back then and us today with these solemn words:

Most assuredly, I say to you, you seek Me, not because you saw the signs, but because you ate of the loaves and were filled." (John 6:26)

Jesus further instructs and admonishes:
Do no labor for the food which perishes, but for the food which endures to everlasting life, which the Son of Man will give you, because God the father has set his seal on Him. (John 6:27)

With these admonitions, Jesus confirms that the eternal objective of signs, wonders, and miracles is to bear witness to, and thereby authenticate, the gospel message. No doubt miracles, wonders, and signs bear witness that those who place (and keep/maintain) their belief and trust (faith) in Jesus will obtain everlasting life. God the Father has placed this priceless gift in the awesome, miracle-working stewardship of the Son, Jesus of Nazareth, the Messiah, and no other. (Acts 4:12) In other words, providentially generated signs, wonders, and miracles demonstrate or prove that God has both the right (exousia) and the physical power (dunamis) to save souls from Hell and the lake of fire. This is the significance and therefore overall reason God utilizes miracles. God is fully cognizant that although we are body, soul, and spirit, the fleshly body is what we see in the mirror, inordinately focus upon, love, cherish, and futilely attempt to preserve into eternity.

In His omniscience, God is fully aware that some, if not most, of us legitimately need to experience burning-bush moments to arrest our attention so we can start focusing more and more on spiritual or supernatural matters and less and less on natural or fleshly matters. As Jesus says: "It is the Spirit who gives life; the flesh profits nothing. The words that I speak to you are spirit, and they are life." (John 6:63) Jesus, who is God, visited and walked the Earth He created while wrapped in human flesh, which is clearly revealed in John 1:1–3. This is a wonder, a miracle, and a great sign in and of itself. God's chief objective is to convince our spirit to recognize God in bodily form in the person of Jesus with the single objective that we exercise our free will to allow "the light of the gospel of the glory of Christ, who is the image of God" to shine upon our hearts. (2 Cor. 4:4) When this takes place, genuine salvation is wrought in the soul and spirit. Satan intentionally blinds the minds of those who do not believe (that Jesus came in the flesh) so the eternal spiritual light of the gospel message will never shine into their hearts and deliver them from the power of darkness. This keeps his victims living in ignorance, error, and spiritual darkness, which amounts to doctrinal error. God manifests this awesome truth with the aid of signs, wonders, miracles, healings, and deliverances, all of which bear witness to the veracity of the gospel message. In contrast, Satan deploys false signs and lying wonders to deceive minds and hearts so he can steal, kill, and destroy in the lake of fire. (John 10:10)

The Gospel Message Destroys Satan's Evil Works

The eternal question is, How can God break through such satanic and demonic deception that's specifically devised to blind minds from the truth, the whole truth, and nothing but the truth that God is the one and only true god and Jesus is His express image and person? The answer is by destroying Satan's works. I once heard a preacher describe 1 John 3:8 as Jesus's calling card, and I agree, for it is the eternal answer to this very important question. It declares: "For this purpose the Son of God was manifested, that He might destroy the works of the devil." The natural follow-up question is, How does Jesus destroy Satan's works so that "the light of the gospel of the glory of Christ, who is the image of God, should shine…" upon and thereby save us from condemnation in the lake of fire? Jesus executed a systematic plan specifically devised to progressively tear down satanic strongholds limb by limb. The long-term goal of this strategy is to uproot and expose demonic deceptions, wiles, and schemes from their satanically driven and mind-blinding roots.

Jesus Wielded Divine Power to Authenticate the Message of the Gospel of the Kingdom

> Jesus went about all Galilee, teaching in their synagogues, preaching the gospel of the kingdom, and healing all kinds of sickness and all kinds of disease among the people. Then His fame went throughout all Syria; and they brought to Him all sick people who were afflicted with various diseases and torments, and those who were demon-possessed, epileptics, and paralytics; and He healed them. (Matt. 4:23–24)

Jesus demonstrated the awesome and unlimited divine power of the gospel of the kingdom by reversing the malevolent works of the devil. Many believers are clueless as to what exactly the gospel of the kingdom is. A very simple and easy-to-understand definition of the gospel of the kingdom of God is the idea that God is bigger than mankind's problems. In other words, whatever issues, obstacles, problems, sicknesses, diseases, fears, or doubts we have, God is able to subdue and conquer each and every one of them. God can and does solve natural problems.

God can and does also solve supernatural or spiritual problems. When we come to the knowledge of the truth of this fact in childlike faith, absolutely nothing will be impossible, for we will have Emmanuel, or "God with us." (Matt. 1:23, KJV) Jesus articulated this principle with these eternal declarations:

> …with God nothing will be impossible. (Luke 1:37)
> All things are possible to him who believes. (Mark 9:23)
> With God all things are possible. (Matt. 19:26)
> Assuredly, I say to you, if you have faith as a mustard seed, you will say to this mountain, "move from here to there," and it will move; and nothing will be impossible for you. (Matt. 17:20)

Jesus established an awesome spiritual foundation to destroy the works of the devil so that the gospel message of the kingdom of God could set captives free from bondage resulting from sin, unrighteousness, disobedience, stubbornness, or wicked rebellion against God.

Signs, Wonders, and Miracles Manifest Natural and Supernatural Healing, Deliverance, and Restoration

Jesus's chief objective in utilizing signs, wonders, and miracles is the restoration, healing, and deliverance of soul and spirit. The same can come into fruition only through repentance from sinful misconduct. Such sinful disobedience comes from Satan and his demons. Jesus demonstrated how power ministry can arrest a sinner's attention, delicately prick a recalcitrant heart, generate remorse for sinful misconduct, and pave the way for confession, repentance, forgiveness, and ultimately soul salvation. This process is of the highest importance, as Jesus Himself revealed through this declaration: "I say to you that likewise there will be more joy in heaven over one sinner who repents than over ninety-nine just persons who need no repentance." (Luke 17:7)

A classic example of this glorious work is revealed in the healing of the lame man at the pool of Bethesda. The fifth chapter of John's Gospel records a very familiar miraculous physical healing and spiritual deliverance of a man Scripture records "had an infirmity thirty-eight years." It further reads: "When Jesus saw him lying there, and knew that he already had been in that condition a long time, He said to him, do you want to be made well?" After listening to the man's reasoning as to why he had yet to be healed, the Messiah brought the kingdom of God to the man and his problems by speaking these words of healing and deliverance: "Rise, take up your bed and walk" and "immediately the man was made well, took up his bed, and walked." (John 5:5–9)

Many ministers stop right here while preaching and teaching about this man's miraculous physical healing. However, John's Gospel also records the most important aspect of what Jesus did for this man's body, soul, and spirit. John 5:14 (KJV) declares: "Afterward Jesus findeth him in the temple, and said unto him, Behold, thou art made whole: sin no more, lest a worse thing come unto thee." With this saying, we become cognizant that this man's former state of having been lame for thirty-eight years was tied to sin. After Jesus healed his physical ailment at the Bethesda pool, the man went to the temple. No doubt he could not have done so prior to his deliverance. The likely reason he went into the temple was to thank and praise God for his physical healing, which is also evidence of his spiritual healing as demonstrated by his very presence in God's house. With Jesus's very stern warning, we know this man's physical infirmity was chiefly due to his spiritual condition, as he was "dead in trespasses and sins" until He met Jesus.

The million-dollar question is, How was Jesus, who was human, able to physically heal and spiritually deliver this man from Satan's power? Because Jesus had been "filled with the Holy Spirit" at His baptism in the Jordan River and returned in the power of the Spirit from forty days of fasting and satanic temptations. (Luke 4:1) These two events clothed Him in both natural and supernatural power, allowing him to heal this man who had been lame for thirty-eight years. We too often neglect to appreciate that although Jesus is God, He came to Earth in human flesh to be, at all points, tempted as we are—so that He could demonstrate how we are to be empowered, guided, counseled, protected, blessed, and endued with the Holy Spirit's power to bring God's spiritual kingdom to Earth, as it is in Heaven.

The Significance of Baptism in the Holy Spirit

Can you name a miracle Jesus performed before John the Baptist baptized Him in the Jordan River? I am not referring to the fact that He had such excellent knowledge and command of Holy Scripture at a very early age that the scribes and Pharisees "were astonished at His understanding and answers" to their questions. (Luke 2:47) Did you know there is not one recorded miracle in any of the Gospels that Jesus performed before His baptism? The very first officially recognized miracle is reputed to be when Jesus turned water into wine at a wedding in Cana of Galilee, as recorded in the second chapter of John. Verse 11 declares: "This beginning of signs Jesus did in Cana of Galilee, and manifested His glory; and His disciples believed in Him."

This passage confirms two very significant matters. First, Jesus performed no signs, wonders, or miracles until after he was baptized. Second, the signs manifested His Glory, which caused His disciples to have faith in Him. Plainly stated, when Jesus miraculously changed natural water into supernaturally created wine, it arrested people's attention enough to interrupt the usual mundane matters of life. For many this would have been their very own burning-bush moment that allowed them to properly exercise their free

Fighting in Faith

will to place their trust and hope in Jesus as their personal savior.

Although the miracle of turning water into wine is widely taught as Jesus's first official sign, wonder, or miracle as Messiah, my personal relationship with the Holy Spirit coupled with well over a decade of intensely studying the entire Bible has caused me to be of a different opinion. I personally believe the first sign, wonder, or miracle was when Jesus escaped a murderous crowd in his hometown after he read from Isaiah 61 in his local synagogue and then preached his first sermon. After he preached, those who heard his message "were filled with rage and rose up and thrust Him out of the city, and they led Him to the brow of the hill on which their city was built, that they might throw him down over the cliff" to kill him. (Luke 4:28–29) However, verse 30 records that Jesus passed "through the midst of them" and "went His way…" Although the Bible does not specifically refer to this as a miracle, the very context of what transpired describes the working of a sign, wonder, or miracle. I hold to this view because He was being attacked by an enraged mob of religious zealots who had the demon spirit of murder in their hearts. In this regard, nothing short of a sign, wonder, or miracle could have delivered Him under those circumstances.

Just think about the evil that was taking place in this scenario. Jesus read and fulfilled a passage of Scripture in a place of worship. He expounded on the true meaning of the same, and the nice churchgoing attendees (please forgive the expression) became hell-bent on murdering Him for preaching that which they did not wish to hear!

Immediately after this miraculous escape from that angry crowd, Jesus went to Capernaum to teach and preach the gospel of the kingdom. The people "were astonished at His teaching, for his word was with authority" and divine power. (Luke 4:31–32) As Jesus was present, a man in the synagogue had an unclean (demonic) spirit inside of him that became startled upon recognizing Jesus. After the demonic spirit called Him Jesus of Nazareth and confessed that Jesus was "the Holy One of God," Jesus immediately cast the demon out of the man. The manifestation of the demon's departure from the man was so dramatic that it caused great wonderment among the people, such that they excitedly exclaimed, "What a word this is! For with authority and power He commands the unclean spirits, and they come out." (Luke 4:35–36)

The central point here is that none of these miraculous events occurred until after Jesus had been baptized and was "filled with the Holy Spirit and led by the Spirit into the wilderness for forty days of fasting and temptation by Satan." (Luke 4:1–2) It was not until Jesus successfully resisted the strongest devilish and demonically driven temptations to sin that he "returned in the power of the Spirit to Galilee" to begin his life's mission of manifesting soul salvation via destroying "the works of the devil." (Luke 4:14–19, 1 John 3:8)

In so doing, Jesus established a spiritual pattern for each and every believing Christian who would put their faith, belief, and trust in Him as Savior and Lord. When anyone accepts, places genuine faith in, and obeys Jesus, He bestows on them unlimited Holy Spirit power to heal, deliver, and save lost souls through the working of signs, wonders, miracles, healings, and deliverances. No formal education, degree, or seminary attendance is required whatsoever. In fact, in well over a decade of conducting power ministry to rescue people from demonic bondage and facilitate salvation of lost souls, I have found that the more people rely on intelligence and human wisdom, the weaker and less powerful they are in the supernatural ability to perform signs, wonders, and miracles in the name of Jesus. To the contrary, the more humble, obedient, and reliant we are upon God, the greater power and authority the Holy Spirit can channel through us (as spiritually cleansed vessels) to perform signs, wonders, miracles, healings, and deliverances.

Jesus's power ministry was very successful. However, because God's determinate counsel restricted the divine power Jesus wielded on Earth, He was very deliberate with regard to when, where, and how He performed power ministry with its accompanying signs, wonders, and miracles. Jesus came to Earth to usher power ministry into Earth's natural and supernatural realms. He typically worked signs, wonders, and miracles in very limited areas. This ministerial model required the enlistment of as many disciples as possible to help Jesus spread the message of the gospel of the kingdom of God and of Heaven in order to save as many people as possible.

The bottom line is that all of the signs, wonders, and miracles were designed to be the ultimate manifestation of just how much God loves His children and of how it is His perfect will that "whoever believes in Him should not perish but have eternal life." (John 3:15) Matthew 9:35 particularizes how "Jesus went about all the cities and villages, teaching in their synagogues, preaching the gospel of the kingdom, and healing every sickness and every disease among the people." The next two verses are exceptionally important because they reveal both His genuine compassion for vexed souls and His need for others to help Him save lost souls by destroying devilish works. Seeing so many lost souls and people in spiritual torment being vexed by demons moved Jesus with so much compassion that He simply had to do something about it. Matthew 9:36–38 states:

> ...when He saw the multitudes, He was moved with compassion for them, because they were weary and scattered, like sheep having no shepherd. Then He said to His disciples, The harvest truly is plentiful, but the laborers are few. Therefore, pray the Lord of the harvest to send out laborers into His harvest.

In this scenario, Jesus immediately calls an assembly of his disciples and providentially handpicks twelve. They were particularly chosen to help Him tear down Satan's strongholds on Earth by teaching the word, preaching the gospel of the kingdom, and confirming the same with accompanying signs, wonders, and miracles—which is the manifestation of power ministry.

Jesus Gave Divine Power to the Apostles

> And He went up on the mountain and called to Him those He Himself wanted. And they came to Him. Then He appointed twelve, that they might be with Him and that He might send them out to preach, and to have power to heal sicknesses and to cast out demons. (Mark 3:13–15)

After Jesus used divine authority and power to successfully uproot demonic works of evil and tear down satanic strongholds through working signs, wonders, miracles, healings, and deliverances, He then conferred those same powers on His twelve handpicked disciples. Make no mistake about it: these twelve were in actuality spiritual soldiers wielding eternal weapons of faith, doctrinal truth, knowledge of their own salvation, and a lack of fear to follow or be just like their Savior. These twelve were later identified as apostles, or special messengers. After their selection and commissioning, Jesus immediately sent them out to "preach, saying the kingdom of heaven is at hand" and commanded that they "heal the sick, cleanse the lepers, raise the dead" and "cast out demons." (Matt. 10:1–8, Mark 3:13–15, Luke 9:1–5) He then took approximately three years to teach them how to humbly utilize and perfect the same Holy Spirit–generated power, the central purpose of which was to authenticate the doctrinal message of the gospel of the kingdom. Friend, ponder this question: have you ever been taught this Holy Bible–based fact before having just read it in this book? If not, why do you think it has never been revealed to you before this very moment? I'll let the Holy Spirit of Christ Jesus answer this eternal inquiry for you.

No Waiting to Work

As one who practices and teaches power or healing and deliverance ministry as a means of demonstrating the efficacy of the gospel message to save lost souls, it is of personal significance to me that Jesus did not make His disciples sit down and watch Him for three years before sending them out to teach, preach, heal, deliver, raise the dead, or perform any other signs, wonders, and miracles. Unlike what I see today, they were immediately thrust out into the vineyard to "do the work of an evangelist and make full proof" of their ministry. (2 Tim. 4:5, KJV)

The readily apparent question is, Shouldn't we wait until we know all we need to know about how power ministry works before we go out trying to perform it? The answer is yes and no. Yes, we need to know all we need to know before we go out to teach the word, preach the word, and allow the Holy Spirit to confirm the same with accompanying signs. However, as the Apostle Paul said, all we need to know is "Jesus Christ…Him Crucified" and raised back to life in the power of the Holy Spirit. (1 Cor. 2:2) Once we know Jesus, we know the truth. We also gain a Holy Spirit–led understanding that Satan pulls out all the stops to blind minds from realizing, knowing, and/or accepting the gospel message because it eradicates spiritual blindness, which allows captives to be set free from sin.

The revealed truth is that Jesus of Nazareth is the promised Christ/Messiah of the entire world. This is the truth about which Jesus says, "You shall know the truth, and the truth shall make you free." (John 8:32) This is the qualifying requirement to boldly preach the gospel of the kingdom of God and have the same confirmed through the providentially designated signs, wonders, and miracles. Upon knowing and accepting the truth that Jesus is the promised Messiah, it then becomes an imperative and a burning desire to share this awesome revelation with as many lost souls as naturally and supernaturally possible. At least, this is my personal testimony of what transpired in me when I finally came to accept this truth. 2 Timothy 3:7 says many are "ever learning [but] never able to come to the knowledge of the truth." This is often manifested in people who have an outward "form of godliness" but live their daily lives in a way that conveys that they have no true convictions about the power God has available for those who revere, love, and humbly obey him with childlike trust. (2 Tim. 3:5),

No Formal Education Required

Contrary to popular belief, it does not take any formal education or seminary training to effectively teach, preach, or perform power ministry. Unfortunately, what I continue to experience is that the more formal education people tend to have in any field, the more they seem to be inhibited from letting go of their pride, ego, or perceived educational clout and letting the Holy Spirit lead, guide, and direct their ministerial paths.

The majority of those Jesus providentially selected to teach the word, preach the gospel of the kingdom, and perform authenticating signs, wonders, and miracles were those whom the pretentious religious leaders referred to as "unlearned and ignorant" and "uneducated and untrained" (Acts 4:13, KJV; Acts 4:13, NKJV) However, when filled with the Holy Spirit, they spoke with such authority, power, clarity, and conviction that the educated and superbly trained members of the Sanhedrin council marveled when they "realized they had been with Jesus." (Acts 4:13)

These phenomenal events occurred after Peter utilized power ministry via these very famous words to proclaim healing for the lame man who begged at the gate the temple: "Silver and gold have I none; but such as I have give I thee: In the name of Jesus Christ of Nazareth rise up and walk." (Acts 3:6, KJV) The Apostle Peter appropriated Holy Spirit–enabled divine power to heal the man who had been "lame from his mother's womb."(Acts 3:2, KJV) In simple terms, God the Holy Spirit channeled divine power through the Apostle Peter to heal the lame man so the man and the witnesses could glorify God, who is the "king of glory." (Ps. 24)

This healing was so dramatic that the people wanted to know how the lame man was healed. Accurately discerning that the manifested power of the man's healing paved the way for the gospel of God's kingdom to be preached, Peter seized the moment to deliver his second sermon, which resulted in five thousand people confessing faith in Christ Jesus. This wonderful miracle served the very purpose for which God intends signs and wonders to serve: to authenticate and bear witness to the eternal truth and divine power of the gospel to save souls from the lake of fire.

It is of note that Peter's very first message was delivered following the wonder of people from different places speaking in each other's native languages. Peter had previously utilized that particular sign centered on the advent of different people speaking in tongues to preach the gospel, which resulted in over three thousand people repenting of their sins and professing faith in Jesus as their personal savior. Accordingly, taking full advantage of these signs, wonders, and miracles, the apostle preached two messages centered on the death, burial, and resurrection of Christ Jesus, which together resulted in well over eight thousand public confessions of faith in Jesus as the Messiah.

When performing power ministry, we need to keep in mind that God most often uses those who are humble and obedient and do not think they already know everything. God loves to use the meekest and mildest people to produce the greatest spiritual results. This is because:

> God has chosen the foolish things of the world to put to shame the wise, and God has chosen the weak things of the world to put to shame the things which are mighty; and the base things of the world and the things which are despised God has chosen, and the things which are not, to bring to nothing the things that are, that no flesh should glory in His presence. (1 Cor. 1:27–29)

Here is a classic example of a person who was officially a "nobody" in terms of having clout with the religious leaders or with respect to having been appointed to any kind of spiritual office by Jesus. Luke 9 records what first appears to be a very strange scenario. It involves the Apostle John informing Jesus that he had observed someone casting out demons in Jesus's name, but John and other apostles forbade the man to do so with the articulated rationale that " he does not follow with us." (Luke 9:49) There's no doubt this person had not been called or sent out by Jesus to preach the gospel, heal, deliver, cast out demons, or anything else. The question becomes, How was this stranger able to perform such power ministry when he had not been sent out (empowered) by Jesus so to do? The answer is in the first part of verse 49, where John said, "Master, we saw someone casting out demons in Your name..." This unknown man apparently recognized the "Name which is above every name" then and utilized it to perform power ministry despite the fact that he did not have a personal relationship with Jesus as His disciples did. (Phil. 2:9)

This is both awesome and very frightening. Awesome, because it accurately demonstrates the eternal truth that God's unlimited divine power rests in Jesus's name as opposed to in degrees, wealth, political prestige, social status, religious clout, or any other natural position or circumstance. This is also scary because—although one can appropriate the awesome name of Jesus to perform signs, wonders, and miracles in execution of power ministry to bless and save others—those who wield such power are destined for Hell and the lake of fire if they neglect or rebelliously refuse to accept Jesus as their own personal savior. This scenario is one of the prime reasons Jesus said:

> Many will say to Me in that day, Lord, Lord, have we not prophesied in Your name, cast out demons in Your name, and done many wonders in Your name? And then I will declare to them, I never knew you; depart from Me, you who practice lawlessness! (Matt. 7:22–23)

Was the Apostle Paul the Last Apostle?
The Lord Jesus also called and sent educated believers. This is congruent with 1 Corinthians 1:26, which reads: "...not many wise according to the flesh, not many mighty, not many noble, are called." No doubt this truth was

demonstrated by His commissioning of both Luke the Physician before His crucifixion and the Apostle Paul on the Damascus road after His resurrection. Many incorrectly teach, preach, and proclaim that the Apostle Paul was the last of the apostles. This false and very dangerous teaching also bleeds over into the matter of spiritual gifts, which is the main target of such false and spiritually dangerous doctrine.

These same false teachers espouse the very incorrect assertion that signs, wonders, and miracles were discontinued with the martyrdom of the Apostle Paul. The New Testament has absolutely no Scripture that states or even implies that spiritual gifts, signs, wonders, or miracles were discontinued with the death of the Apostle Paul. To the contrary, there is a plethora of Scripture specifically refuting this false assertion. These are included in several of the main passages the Holy Spirit gave me years ago when I was debating a young seminarian who had been incorrectly taught that God removed all signs, wonders, and miracles with the death of the Apostle Paul, who was the last apostle. Here's the doctrinal truth of this controversial matter:

> He who descended is also the One who ascended far above all the heavens, that He might fill all things…And He Himself gave some to be apostles, some prophets, some evangelists, and some pastors and teachers, for the equipping of the saints for the work of ministry, for the edifying of the body of Christ, till we all come to the unity of the faith and of the knowledge of the Son of God, to a perfect man, to the measure of the stature of the fullness of Christ… (Eph. 4:10–13)

Without any question, Jesus appointed additional apostles, among other spiritual office holders, after his resurrection from the dead. (Eph. 4:10) Secondly, the specific purpose for which He made such supernatural appointments was to fully equip saints for the work of ministry, one such work being power ministry. The same can be carried out only with the deployment of spiritual gifting under the tutelage of the Holy Spirit. (Eph. 4:12)

Finally, and most importantly, the specific length of time we will have apostles, prophets, evangelists, teachers, and pastors is clearly specified, to wit: until "…we all come to the unity of the faith and the knowledge of the Son of God, to a perfect man, to the measure of the stature of the fullness of Christ." Accordingly the real question is, Have we all come to the unity of the faith and the knowledge that Jesus of Nazareth is the Son of the one and only true living God? If the answer is no—and it is—then according to the Holy Bible, we still have members of the fivefold ministry, including apostles, and we still have spiritual gifts in operation in the church.

My friend, if you have embraced a contrary doctrinal belief, I humbly ask you to pray and ask the Holy Spirit to reveal the truth concerning this very important subject. Most importantly I highly recommend that you acquire a "read-through-the-Bible-in-a-year" grid and read the entire Holy Bible from Genesis to Revelation, and trust Him with every fiber in your being. It is quite interesting to me that people, many of whom are ministers, feel comfortable telling others what God has done or will never do without having first consulted the full counsel of His Holy Word. In my view we should refrain from exposing ourselves to God's potential punishment for espousing such "doctrinal" positions (that are contrary to God's perfect will) without having first studied the entire Word of God.

To conclude this matter of whether the apostles died with the Apostle Paul, the Holy Spirit revealed to me a long time ago that Paul was not the last apostle but the first New Testament apostle. If you know the Holy Scriptures, you know that as Jesus walked the Earth and ministered before his crucifixion and resurrection, he was actually in Old Testament times. If this is true—and it is—the question becomes When did the New Testament start? The New Testament was actually inaugurated after Jesus's death, burial, and resurrection. Please refresh your recollection, or accept the pure gospel message is "Christ died for our sins according to the Scriptures, and that He was buried, and that He rose again the third day according to the Scriptures." (1 Cor. 15:4) If you genuinely believe this in your heart (mind, will, and emotions), you can be saved right now as you are reading this sentence. Do you believe Jesus came to Earth in the flesh, born of a virgin, lived a sinless life, was crucified, died on the cross, and was buried in a grave but arose back to life in the power of the Holy Spirit on third day? If you so believe, please continue doing so until your death and, God willing, we will meet in Heaven if I also practice that which I just preached to you!

New Testament Apostles
Now that you have been saved and have rededicated your life to God or have completely ignored God's saving grace again let's get back to Jesus appointing New Testament apostles after His resurrection and ascension back into Heaven. Since Jesus commissioned Saul of Tarsus from Heaven, it could be correctly argued that the Apostle Paul was the first New Testament apostle that Jesus called after He was crucified and resurrected in the power of the Holy Spirit. This is another one of those spiritual truths Jesus said "you will know, and [it] shall make you free." (John 8:32)

Satan has far too many Christians believing his fabricated lies about power ministry, apostles, and spiritual gifts, so many that many so-called "Christians" don't know what to believe. Unfortunately ignorance of God's eternal truths and spiritual promises typically leads to apathy and spiritual complacency. I have heard it taught that Jesus selected Saul of Tarsus to replace Judas Iscariot, which I believe to be accurate. Matthias was selected by the casting of lots. The same was initiated by Peter's well-intentioned albeit misguided and presumptuous desire to replace the missing twelfth apostle. Let's allow it sink into our spirit that only Jesus of Nazareth can call, qualify, equip, empower, and commission or send His chosen ministers. Fortunately for us all, both before and after the resurrection, Jesus did not stop with his appointment of the original twelve apostles.

Jesus Also Gave Divine Power to Seventy Believers

> After these things the Lord appointed seventy others also and sent them two by two before His face into every city and place where He Himself was about to go. (Luke 10:1)
>
> Whatever city you enter, and they receive you, eat such things as are set before you. And heal the sick there, and say to them, "The kingdom of God has come near to you." (Luke 10:8–9)

After the twelve hand-chosen apostles successfully used signs, wonders, miracles, healings, and deliverances to destroy satanic and demonic works in the people, Jesus again expanded his ministerial realm of power and authority on Earth by commissioning seventy regular believers to perform the exact same power ministry. Chapter 10 of the Gospel according to Luke provides a wonderful account of Jesus appointing and sending out at least seventy people to a city to pave the way for his arrival. In many ways this was exactly like John the Baptist paving straight spiritual paths for Jesus to tread in his footsteps thereafter. Please take careful notice that Jesus particularly commanded them to "heal the sick there, and say to them, 'The kingdom of God has come near to you.'" (Luke 10:8)

Let's take a minute to examine the nature of this command. With the instruction Jesus was specifically authorizing these regular, every day, run-of-the-mill believers (in Him) to declare and decree the coming of the kingdom of God to heal whatever sicknesses and diseases there may have been among the people. This is awesome! However, the key to the performance of such power ministry includes two things on their part: childlike or mustard-seed faith, and immediate obedience. The problem most Christians have is in believing we can do that which Jesus commands us to do. The key is understanding that whatever Jesus commands us to do, He simultaneously authorizes the Holy Spirit to endue us with the spiritual power to execute the command.

Satan is Subject to Jesus's Authority

The seventy put feet to their faith by obeying Jesus. They went out as commanded and "returned with joy, saying, Lord, even the demons are subject to us in Your name." At their return, Jesus was so pleased with their powerful ministerial acts that He said to them, "I saw Satan fall like lightning from heaven. Behold, I give you the authority to trample on serpents and scorpions, and over all the power of the enemy, and nothing shall by any means hurt you." (Luke 10:17–19)

However, as usual He calmed them down by letting them know they should not be so thrilled that they could conquer demonic powers. To the contrary, Jesus instructed, "…rejoice because your names are written in heaven." (Luke 10:20) Their immediate obedience produced such great results that Jesus did something the Bible records as a first:

> In that hour Jesus rejoiced in the Spirit and said, I thank You, Father, Lord of heaven and earth, that You have hidden these things from the wise and prudent and revealed them to babes. Even so, Father, for so it seemed good in Your sight. All things have been delivered to Me by My Father, and no one knows who the Son is except the Father, and who the Father is except the Son, and the one to whom the Son wills to reveal Him. (Luke 10:21–22)

This was a very big deal. Jesus had accomplished a significant feat in the matter of spiritual warfare. He had instructed seventy regular believers in the art of spiritual warfare, and they not only accepted His commission but also applied mustard-seed faith to their immediate obedience, which produced astronomical spiritual results. Jesus was absolutely thrilled with their success, for it bore out that it was getting close to the time for him to finish his mission and be glorified so He could return to Heaven.

However, the Lord Jesus providentially expanded His power base one more time before He ascended back into Heaven. This expansion was specifically designed to save, equip, train, and send every believer—including you—into the world's spiritual battlefield. Our specific orders are to be used by Almighty God to save lost souls by conquering Satan and his legions of demons through power ministry under the awesome tutelage of the Holy Spirit of Christ Jesus.

Chapter 9

POWER MINISTRY PART 3: THE GREAT COMMISSION

...Go into all the world and preach the gospel to every creature. He who believes and is baptized will be saved; but he who does not believe will be condemned. And these signs will follow those who believe: In My name they will cast out demons; they will speak with new tongues; they will take up serpents; and if they drink anything deadly, it will by no means hurt them; they will lay hands on the sick, and they will recover. (Mark 16:15–18)

Jesus Also Gave Divine Power to Every Bible-Believing Christian via the Great Commission

Jesus expanded His power base to the fullest extent possible just prior to returning to Heaven. The Gospels according to Matthew (28:18–20) and Mark (16:15–20) contain the most inclusive language of what is commonly known as the "Great Commission." This is when Jesus endues every believer with the unlimited authority and the inexhaustible power of the Holy Spirit to authenticate the gospel of the kingdom of God and His righteous life on Earth, death by crucifixion, burial, resurrection, and ascension back into

Heaven. The Great Commission according to Matthew, by far the most widely quoted, reads as follows:

> And Jesus came and spoke to them, saying, all authority has been given to Me in heaven and on earth. Go therefore and make disciples of all the nations, baptizing them in the name of the Father and of the Son and of the Holy Spirit, teaching them to observe all things that I have commanded you; and lo, I am with you always, even to the end of the age. Amen. (Matt. 28:18–20)

Moreover, the Great Commission according to Luke's Gospel declares:

> And He opened their understanding, that they might comprehend the Scriptures. Then He said to them, Thus it is written, and thus it was necessary for the Christ to suffer and to rise from the dead the third day, and that repentance and remission of sins should be preached in His name to all nations, beginning at Jerusalem. And you are witnesses of these things. Behold, I send the Promise of My Father upon you; but tarry in the city of Jerusalem until you are endued with power from on high. (Luke 24:45–49)

Along these same lines, Acts 1:8 proclaims "…you shall receive power when the Holy Spirit has come upon you; and you shall be witnesses to Me in Jerusalem, and in all Judea and Samaria, and to the end of the earth." Before returning to Heaven, Jesus wanted those who truly had faith in Him to know and fully understand the awesome responsibility we have in obeying His Great Commission. Such commissioning is accompanied by an anointing (empowerment) to witness to the entire world. Such witnessing entails making full proof of our belief and trust in Jesus as Messiah.

Although Matthew 20:18–20 is the most popularly quoted rendition of Jesus's Great Commission, I have come to favor the Apostle Mark's version. According to the Great Commission as particularized in Mark 16:15–20, each and every disciple of Christ Jesus is authorized and commanded to "preach (witness) the gospel…cast out demons…speak with new tongues," and "lay hands on the sick" for healing and deliverance. Do you believe this? My friend, the answer is either yes or no, for there is no middle position. This is exactly the way Jesus prefers it, because we cannot sit on the fence. We're either with Him or against Him, as is so well stated in Luke 9:49–50—in other words, those of us who obey Jesus by doing that which He instructs us to do are "with Him and for Him." Conversely, those of us who fail to carry out His directives are against Him. In other words, there is no such thing as a neutral Christian, for you are either pulling with Jesus or being pulled away from Him. Now I just wrote that there is no middle position, but what does the Holy Bible and Jesus say about this scenario? According to Luke 11:14–23:

> And He was casting out a demon, and it was mute. So it was, when the demon had gone out, that the mute spoke; and the multitudes marveled. But some of them said, "He casts out demons by Beelzebub, the ruler of the demons."
>
> Others, testing Him, sought from Him a sign from heaven. But He, knowing their thoughts, said to them: "Every kingdom divided against itself is brought to desolation, and a house divided against a house falls. If Satan also is divided against himself, how will his kingdom stand? Because you say I cast out demons by Beelzebub. And if I cast out demons by Beelzebub, by whom do your sons cast them out? Therefore, they will be your judges. But if I cast out demons with the finger of God, surely the kingdom of God has come upon you. When a strong man, fully armed, guards his own palace, his goods are in peace. But when a stronger than he comes upon him and overcomes him, he takes from him all his armor in which he trusted, and divides his spoils. He who is not with Me is

against Me, and he who does not gather with Me scatters.

Ready, Willing, and Able
If you believe Jesus's promises, you are both able and ready to manifest your anointing and in so doing fulfill another great promise Jesus made when He said, "…if you can believe, all things are possible to him who believes." (Mark 9:23) In this regard, the question becomes, Are you willing to manifest your anointing to fulfill your calling in life? Conversely, if you refuse to exercise your God-given free will and to believe Jesus has commissioned you with this divine authority, power, and influence over all of God's creation, then the very opposite is true. Namely, almost everything is extremely difficult or impossible for you. Why? Because you are using whatever "faith" you have in the negative to doubt God and His awesome promises.

Doubt is the opposite of faith. Doubt is having "faith" that one can't do that which God has specifically declared, decreed, and, in many cases, commanded can and should be done. It only takes a little doubt to trump faith. Conversely, it takes just a little mustard-seed faith to conquer a mountain of doubt. (Matt. 17:20, Luke 17:6) Doubt leads to double mindedness, which God absolutely detests.

God sends a very strong message to those who allow the unrighteous demonic spirit of doubt to make them too fearful to place their belief and trust in Him. The message is: "Let not that man suppose that he will receive anything from the Lord; he is a double-minded man, unstable in all his ways." (James 1:7) In other words, doubt cancels prayers. Can you now understand why Satan and his demons spend so much time and energy devising malevolent schemes to try to convince Christians to doubt, disbelieve, or outright ignore God's awesome promises?

Without question Jesus's prime objective in giving the entire world the Great Commission was for us to face and conquer satanic and demonic forces that come to "steal and to kill and to destroy." (John 10:10) This is the apex of spiritual warfare, which entails preaching the gospel message so that God Himself can partner with us in this wonderful service to mankind. Our part is to trust God, then open our mouths and speak God's Holy Word. God's part is to confirm, validate, and otherwise authenticate the words we speak through accompanying signs, wonders, and miracles. However, there is one more very important and necessary step that must take place before any genuine believer in Jesus can preach, or shall I say witness, the gospel message with authority, power, clarity, and conviction of heart, mind, soul, will, and spirit.

Being Filled with the Holy Spirit
It is God's perfect will that every believer be constantly and continually filled with His Holy Spirit! This is a real no-brainer because God commands that we:

> …be filled with the Spirit, speaking to one another in psalms and hymns and spiritual songs, singing and making melody in your heart to the Lord, giving thanks always for all things to God the Father in the name of our Lord Jesus Christ, submitting to one another in the fear of God. (Eph. 5:17–21)

God wants us not only to be filled but to continue being filled. The apostles were not just filled once; they received several fillings. They were initially filled on the day of Pentecost (Acts 2:4), and Peter and John received another divine filling while praying in jail after having been imprisoned for having been used by God to heal a lame man through their obedience. (Acts 3:31)

Please accept this spiritual truth: no one can be successfully used by God to powerfully preach the gospel and witness for Jesus and have the message confirmed with accompanying signs, wonders, or miracles unless and until that individual is filled with and controlled by the Holy Spirit. The reason is that there is a holy boldness to revere, worship, praise, thank, and obey God that only comes with the infilling presence of the Holy

Spirit. Without this wonderful work in the life of a Christian, demonic spirits of doubt, fear, pride, unbelief, and many others make it virtually impossible for believers to obey the promptings of the Holy Spirit. Believers are then hindered from fulfilling their life's calling to glorify God in both word and deed. Jesus's perfect will is for every believer to be filled with and controlled by the Holy Spirit so we can live righteously and submit to God and therefore be able to resist the devil in accordance with James 4:7.

An excellent example of what transpires when a believer is not yet filled with and therefore led by the Holy Spirit is found in Luke 22, where Peter infamously denied Jesus three times. This fateful and heartbreaking event took place at night and was probably witnessed by very few people. These faith-crushing denials happened before Peter had ever received his first filling of the awesome presence and power of the Holy Spirit. Before this night, Peter and the other apostles had been operating under the authority of Jesus's anointing.

However, after Peter became filled with the awesome presence and power of the Holy Spirit on the day of Pentecost, he boldly confessed faith in Jesus in the presence of several thousand people in broad daylight. How could one person be at such opposites? These two scenarios accurately represent what transpires when a Christian has yet to be filled with the Holy Spirit versus when a believer has been filled with and is being controlled by the Holy Spirit.

Devilish demons of doubt, fear, pride, and sinful unbelief take over and dominate the soul and spirit when we are not filled with God's Holy Spirit. Conversely, after we have been filled to the spiritual brim with the awesome power and comforting presence of the Holy Spirit, we receive great confidence and a holy boldness in the things of God. Such confidence allows us to be on spiritual automatic pilot, which allows God to instruct us through the Holy Spirit of Christ Jesus, and such holy boldness allows us to execute God's directives with dispatch. If you are an athlete, you can relate to this concept of being on spiritual automatic pilot, for it is akin to what's called being "in the zone" in athletics. Basketball players are often heard commenting that it was as if the basket was five feet wide, as just about every shot they put up went in. Spiritual automatic pilot plays out when we have developed a relationship of reverence (respect), faith (belief plus trust), and obedience (a genuine desire to please God). Once these three Holy Spirit–generated virtues are in a Christian's soul and spirit, God can use them mightily to bring His kingdom to Earth as it is in Heaven. Under such grace, there is a symbiotic relationship of instruction from God and obedience toward God's directives that He gives through man. In other words, you are either filled with and controlled by the Holy Spirit or you are not. If you are, you have the requisite holy boldness to witness for Jesus. If you are not filled with and controlled by the Holy Spirit of Christ Jesus, you don't have it—period.

The Apostles First Received the Indwelling Presence of the Holy Spirit Before Being Filled

The apostles first received the indwelling presence of the Holy Spirit after Jesus's resurrection. Prior to Jesus's crucifixion, He had the apostles on, for lack of a better phrase, spiritual training wheels. However, they would soon have the Holy Spirit operating not only with them but in them and through them as well. Accordingly, after His resurrection from death, Jesus took the remaining eleven disciples, "breathed on them, and said to them, Receive the Holy Spirit." (John 20:22) In Greek the word *holy* is "*hagios*" (hag'-ee-os), which is defined as "separated from sin and therefore consecrated to God; sacred." (The New Strong's Expanded Dictionary of Bible Words, 2001) This was the New Testament version of that which took place in the Old Testament when "the Lord God formed man of the dust of the ground, and breathed into his nostrils the breath of life; and man became a living soul. (Gen. 2:7, KJV) Man became alive naturally and spiritually in Genesis 2:7, then sinned and thereafter died (as forewarned by God) in Genesis 3:6 but became "alive again" in John 20:22. In my view, this is when the eleven remaining apostles became supernaturally born again as Jesus "breathed" the Holy Spirit into their nostrils. These events transpired after Jesus's resurrection from the grave. The word *spirit* itself is defined by New Strong's as "breath, wind, life-spirit." "In the beginning, God created the heavens and the earth…and the Spirit of God was hovering over the face of the waters." (Gen. 1:1–2) This same Spirit of God that created and gave life to all creation in the beginning later renewed life that was previously dead in trespasses and sins.

The apostles' receiving of the indwelling presence of the Holy Spirit was itself a miraculous event that occurred after Jesus's resurrection from the grave, the faith in which produces genuine salvation. There is no greater sign, wonder, or miracle than when the Holy Spirit moves in the heart, soul, and spirit of sinful man, convicts the conscience of its sinful rebellion against its Creator, generates remorse, and produces repentance, humility, and faith in God. All lesser signs, wonders, miracles, healings, and deliverances produced by power ministry point to the ultimate sign of salvation in Jesus as Savior and ultimately as Lord. Put another way, genuine repentance leads to confession of sin, and salvation is the ultimate sign, wonder, and miracle produced by the preached (witnessed) gospel of God's kingdom.

The Apostles Received the Baptism of the Holy Spirit, Also Known As "Being Filled"

After having breathed on the apostles the breath of the Holy Spirit, Jesus declared, "John truly baptized with water, but you shall be baptized with the Holy Spirit not many days from now." (Acts 1:5) He was specifically letting them know they would thereafter be filled with the Holy Spirit, which is also called the baptism of the Holy Spirit and would take place "when the day of Pentecost had fully come."(Acts 2:1) However, before these divinely inspired prophecies would take place, Jesus specified: "…Behold, I send the Promise of My Father upon you; but tarry in the city of Jerusalem until you are endued with power from on high." (Luke 24:49)

Although they had just received the indwelling presence of the Holy Spirit, they had not yet received (been equipped or endued with) the awesome infilling power of the Holy Spirit. This would come later and cause many to miraculously and wonderfully speak in tongues and consequently move Peter to preach his first official sermon after Jesus's resurrection. Peter's powerful preaching (in explanation of the signs, wonders, and miracles surrounding so many speaking in tongues) would result in the official start of Jesus's church with three thousand converts.

No doubt God used tongues and the interpretation of tongues to arrest people's attention and provide a multiplicity of burning-bush moments for those present. The same resulted in their genuine repentance and heartfelt confession of sins and ultimately their salvation. This powerfully demonstrates how God works with us in ministering His Holy Word, for it is His Holy Spirit that actually produces miracles. This also reveals how signs, wonders, and miracles authenticate the veracity of the gospel message. In Mark 16:17, Jesus solemnly promises "signs will follow those who believe," and not vice versa. True believers trust that the gospel message will do what God promises and are therefore not surprised when signs, wonders, and miracles are produced before, during, or after the word is preached.

Truth be told, we should be surprised if God never confirms the preached gospel message with some corresponding sign, wonder, or miracle—the greatest of which is salvation of lost souls. There is a proper balance that must be struck, because we are not to be overly concerned with signs, wonders, or miracles. On the other hand, we need to accept the truth of Jesus's promise that corresponding supernatural signs will accompany the preached word of God. The converse is just as significant: when anything other than the gospel of the kingdom of God is being preached or taught, no genuine sign, wonder, or miracle will be produced to authenticate that which was proclaimed.

The central truth here is that God endues us with Holy Spirit power to declare and decree the bringing of His kingdom to Earth as it is in Heaven.

In so doing, we are used by God in the name of Jesus and in the power of the Holy Spirit to wrest the control of demonic forces away from those who are being vexed by Satan. Under such circumstances, God's demonstrated power over demonically driven evil forces allows the rescued victim to receive and appreciate God's unconditional love. When we as believers obey God's directives, love Jesus, become filled with the Holy Spirit, and open our mouths, God will not only give us the words to speak but will also put signs, wonders, and miracles (power ministry) in our hands to work. Even before the Holy Spirit was "poured out on all flesh" in Acts 2:17–18, thereby fulfilling prophecies in Joel 2:28–29, God had already filled several of His servants with the Holy Spirit. Every one of them was used to produce some kind of sign, wonder, or miracle, either while they were being filled or after they were filled with the powerful presence of the Holy Spirit.

Some Were Filled with the Holy Spirit Before Pentecost
Here are just a few who were filled with the Holy Spirit well before the Great Commission was given. The Lord Jesus was filled with the Holy Spirit when he returned from having been baptized in the Jordan, after which He was "led by the Spirit into the wilderness" to be tempted by Satan. (Luke 1:1–2) His forerunner, John the Baptist, was "filled with the Holy Spirit, even from his mother's womb." (Luke 1:15) John the Baptist's mother, Elizabeth, was filled with the Holy Spirit as she "heard the greeting of Mary." (Luke 1:41) The unborn child's hearing, recognizing, and responding to Mary's voice by leaping in his mother's womb are all signs and wonders that were produced as Elizabeth was being filled with the Holy Spirit. It should surprise no one that God would want both of John the Baptist's parents to be filled with and controlled by the Holy Spirit. After all, their son's mission in life was to beat down a doctrinally sound and spiritually straight path for the coming of Christ Jesus. John the Baptist's father, Zacharias, was filled with the Holy Spirit, and prophesied, but only after God worked a sign, wonder, and miracle, although it was in the negative. (Luke 1:67) Zacharias's ability to speak

was completely removed from him for the duration of Elizabeth's pregnancy as divine punishment for the hard-hearted lack of faith he displayed when the Archangel Gabriel prophesied that he and his wife would produce a child in their old age. It was not until Zacharias wrote, "His name is John" on a tablet that God miraculously restored his ability to speak, after which he immediately praised God. This was a great wonder, and "fear came on all who dwelt around them" as news of these signs, wonders, and miracles were "discussed throughout all the hill country of Judea." (Luke 1:63–65)

Signs, Wonders, and Miracles Today
Have you ever read, said, or heard words to this effect: why don't we see the kinds of signs, wonders, and miracles that took place back in New Testament times? The fact is that we are living in New Testament times, and the same kinds of signs, wonders, and miracles are still being worked on Earth. In fact, even greater works are being performed in fulfillment of Jesus prophetic promises. Greater works are being performed on at least two specific fronts about which I have personal experience.

First, greater works are being carried out because there are greater numbers of believers today than there were in the first century. Second, because of the outpouring of the Holy Spirit on all flesh during Pentecost, signs, wonders, and miracles are no longer limited to one particular person in any particular place, city, territory, kingdom, province, country, nation, or hemisphere. The gospel is being simultaneously preached all over the entire globe and is producing corresponding signs, wonders, miracles, and salvations. This was certainly not the case before Pentecost.

Unfortunately, many of today's signs, wonders, and miracles are being explained away by man's natural tendency to doubt and be skeptical about supernatural or unexplainable phenomena. For example, when you read the testimony about my encounter with two angels when I received my commission to preach, did doubt or unbelief spring up in your spirit? If so, this is the same kind of skepticism that allows Satan to steal many a victory from us that God providentially orchestrates to demonstrate the awesome and unlimited power He wields. Such power serves not only to vanquish our adversaries but also to save and seal us "until the day of redemption in Christ Jesus." (Eph. 4:30) Accordingly when people doubt very obvious signs, wonders, and miracles, they do so to their own detriment and, unfortunately, for some their own eternal damnation in Hell and the lake of fire.

Speaking of signs, wonders, and miracles in today's times, I hope you are ready to learn about and receive some. Having explained my introduction into the supernatural realm of ministry and having provided a biblical basis revealing that it is God's perfect will for believers in Him to preach (witness) the gospel of the kingdom with authenticating signs, wonders, and miracles, the balance of this book will address how to obey the Great Commission in this day and age.

As genuine believers, we have all been called, sanctified in Christ Jesus, and sent out into the world's vineyard to save lost souls by conquering Satan and his demons. Holy Spirit–empowered Christians are peculiarly ordained to thwart satanically driven schemes that are specifically devised to deceive minds and destroy souls. The first question is, Do you know this to be true? Secondly, if so, what are you actively doing about it? Do you realize we sin when we know to do good but refuse to exercise our free will to actually carry it out? One of the most sobering and frightening passages for Christians in the entire Bible reads "…to him who knows to do good and does not do it, to him it is sin." (James 4:17) Please pause for a moment to meditate on the truth of this very solemn warning before continuing to read. This passage challenges many a believer on the unrighteous omission of failing to affirmatively do something we know is in God's perfect will for us to do.

Please don't allow Satan to condemn you as you ponder this very important matter. However, you will be in grave error if you fail to allow the Holy Spirit to convict you "of sin, and of righteousness, and of judgment…" concerning any stubbornness, disobedience, or rebellion that may

Fighting in Faith

be present with regard to this very significant matter. (John 16:8) Don't be complacent—get up, get equipped, and get into the battle to win lost souls for the kingdom of Heaven! After all, is this not the reason you exist—to glorify God by being fruitful and multiplying souls for the kingdom of heaven?

Chapter 10

MINISTERING TO MEN, HUSBANDS, AND FATHERS

Then God said, "Let Us make man in Our image, according to Our likeness; let them have dominion over the fish of the sea, over the birds of the air, and over the cattle, over all the earth and over every creeping thing that creeps on the earth." So God created man in His own image; in the image of God He created him; male and female He created them. Then God blessed them, and God said to them, "Be fruitful and multiply; fill the earth and subdue it; have dominion over the fish of the sea, over the birds of the air, and over every living thing that moves on the earth." (Gen. 1:26–28)

Whenever Satan deceives a man into settling for a lifestyle that is outside of God's perfect will, he will live and operate beneath his spiritual birthright until he knows who he is in Christ Jesus. Unfortunately every person under his authority will be thrown into spiritual chaos until the man takes his rightful place as priest, prophet, and king of his household. Before "God formed man of the dust of the ground, and breathed into his nostrils the breath of life; and man became a living being," He had already spoken man into existence as a spiritual being created in his own image, according to His likeness. (Gen. 2:7)

Most importantly God had also given him "dominion over the fish of the sea, over the birds of the air, and over the cattle, over all the earth and over every creeping thing that creeps on the earth." (Gen. 2:7, 1:26) These passages make it crystal clear that God first created us as spiritual beings, then subsequently formed us from the earth and breathed life into us. What's most significant with respect to spiritual warfare is that God designed man to exercise stewardship and authoritative dominion over the Earth and every living thing that lives on it. Put another way, before we were ever given a terrestrial body, God destined and ordained us to have the spiritual authority and the divine power to rule the Earth and execute God's righteous judgments on rebellious sinners. Before Adam ever existed in the flesh, God had already spiritually put him in charge of the entire Earth.

When Eve came along, Adam's first responsibilities were to serve or minister to her as priest, prophet, and king. As her priest he was obligated to pray for God to give him the wisdom to be the kind of husband God designated him to be and to intercede on her behalf. As prophet Adam was responsible for listening to and obeying God's directives with respect to how he should love, care, and provide for his wife. Finally, as King Adam was charged with the responsibility of protecting her from danger and death while also serving as the chief provider of her physical and emotional needs. God set up this spiritual model before Adam or Eve existed in mortal flesh.

Accordingly it is an eternal ordination for godly men to serve their wives in these respective capacities. Conversely, when a man is too deceived or spiritually wounded to serve in all three capacities, he will live in a state of being in which God never intended for him to exist. Brothers, don't be like Adam and let your mate talk to a snake; take spiritual charge! If Adam had spoken up for Eve, we wouldn't be in the absolute mess we are in today.

With respect to Eve, when Satan appeared in the likeness of a serpent, he tested her willingness to look to her God-given priest, prophet, and king for spiritual guidance and protection. Unfortunately she failed that test. Likewise Satan tested Adam's willingness to obey God by conquering the temptation to sin by failing to speak up and defend his wife. Adam's trust in God, over and above the bad advice of his wife, was also tested in the offer from Eve to partake of the forbidden fruit from the tree of the knowledge of good and evil.

We all know what happened: Adam disobeyed God by obeying the voice of his wife. In doing so he thereby voluntarily, albeit ignorantly, forfeited his divine authority over the entire Earth to Satan. This is exactly why Satan was able to accurately tempt Jesus by saying, "[A]ll this authority I will give You, and their glory; for this has been delivered to me, and I give it to whomever I wish." (Luke 4:6) This dominion has now been legally purchased back by the righteous, albeit murderous, death and holy resurrection of Jesus from the grave. God has now charged those who trust Jesus with the grave responsibility of enforcing that which Jesus "finished" on the cross: namely the power to execute judgment on demonic forces who come to deceive, hinder, steal, kill, and destroy our chances of being with the Father in the kingdom of Heaven. (John 19:30)

Men, husbands, and fathers play vital roles in God's master plan to fill the Earth with His righteousness, omnipotent presence, and unfathomable peace. God providentially chose males (men), to have dominion over that which He created in and upon Earth. Women, I don't know why God chose men to take the lead, but He did. I have absolutely nothing against females, girls, women. or ladies. As a matter of fact, you all have played, and still play, a great role in who I am as a man, what I do for God as a gospel minister, and all that I have become in Christ Jesus. The roles women play are just as important as the roles God designated for men to play in bringing His kingdom to Earth as it is in Heaven.

However, Satan has a full-court press and is forever trying to spiritually castrate men so we will never come to "the knowledge of the truth" of the awesome and unlimited power men can wield. (2 Tim. 3:7) Such power is wielded through God to "the pulling down of strongholds, casting down imaginations and every prideful thing that exalts itself against the Name of God and bringing into captivity every thought to the obedience of Christ." (2 Cor. 10:4–5)

Satan primarily attacks men because he knows God put His authority in the very first man, Adam, and provided him with the exousia and the dunamis to subdue and exercise dominion on Earth. If and when Satan finds it more advantageous to attack a man through a woman who has the man's affections, he will not hesitate to do so. All Satan needs is a biblically ignorant or spiritually weak man who has no clue about the power he has through God to exercise divine power to pray for, bless, protect, and provide for his family. Upon zeroing in on such a poor soul, Satan can easily usurp the man's spiritual authority by placing a worldly-wise woman in his life to manipulate him into allowing her to usurp his authority.

When this occurs the roles are reversed, and the woman then usurps and thereby wields the man's God-given authority. Under this less-than-optimal scenario, the woman starts serving natural and supernatural roles in which God originally intended for men to function. God's grace is abundantly manifested in such scenarios, as He providentially allows men and women in such less-than-perfect relationships to live in his permissive will until the man can become spiritually mature, confess his current lifestyle as sinful, repent, and take his rightful position as the spiritual head of the household.

The spiritually upside-down relationship of King Ahab and his notoriously wicked wife Jezebel in the Old Testament is a classic example of this. Ahab was a spiritually weak and biblically ignorant king who disobeyed God. One of the worst manifestations of his disobedience occurred when he married Jezebel, a pagan woman who drew his heart away from God—if it had ever really been there. He pouted like a spoiled brat about things he could not acquire through his own power, authority, or influence. He allowed his pagan wife to usurp his natural and supernatural authority in order to serve Satan rather than being the righteous king God intended for him to be. Ahab and Jezebel both ended up being righteously judged by God, who had them killed for the sinful misconduct that was produced through their spiritually upside-down relationship.

In today's times, the average household in the United States of America is occupied by women who have a deeper connection to God than the man of the house. This is readily evident in the average church, many of which have membership consisting of at least two-thirds women and children. Where are the men God providentially ordained to be the priests, prophets, and kings over their families? Satan and his demons have taken them off the spiritual battlefield in at least one of three scenarios that Jesus so well explained in the parable of the sower. This parable is so important that Jesus said this about it: "[I]f you can't understand the meaning of this parable, how will you understand all the other parables?" (Mark 4:13, New Living Translation)

First, some men hear the word of God, but the "wicked one comes and snatches away that which was sown in" their spirit before it is comprehended. (Matt. 10:19) Second, other men joyfully receive the word but endure only for a while and later fall away due to the trials and tribulations that come specifically because they accepted the word of God. According to Jesus, the primary reason hearers suffer defeat is that they have no spiritual roots. (Matt. 10:21) The third and final category of men Satan strategically attacks and removes from their God-given place of power and authority are those who allow "the cares of this world, the deceitfulness of riches" to "choke the word," which correspondingly renders them "unfruitful." (Mark 4:19)

No doubt Satan and his legions of demons are behind such potentially devastating schemes. Such devilish wiles are wickedly employed against men to keep us in spiritual darkness. The prime purpose of such evil is to prevent men from ever coming to the full knowledge, understanding, and truth of the awesome divine power we have been authorized to wield to exercise dominion over God's creation.

Who is the Spiritual Head of the Household?

Many Christians—and most people—are clueless as to just how powerful a man can be in the spirit realm when he takes his rightful place in his household. While men should serve as the natural provider, serving and operating as the spiritual head of the household has far greater significance than the provider role. Please understand that serving as the spiritual head has more to do with being a protector and a very strong spiritual warrior for the family.

In my years of performing healing and deliverance ministry, I have often assisted men who were living in the deepest demonic deception because they were the breadwinners or the natural providers, yet they were eighty-eight- (not even ninety-eight-) pound weaklings in things concerning the spirit realm. In my years of hands-on experience in taking people through deliverance and watching their enhanced spiritual maturity thereafter, I have come to three Holy Spirit–led conclusions with respect to this matter:

> A man who has no personal relationship with God is spiritually weak.
>
> A man who never consults the Holy Word of God for inner strength is spiritually weak.
>
> A man who is so devoid of God's spirit within himself that he's too afraid to lead his family in prayer, take the lead in praying over a family meal, or pray out loud in public is spiritually weak.

Please don't think I'm being insensitive concerning these matters, because I'm not. To the contrary, conclusions one, two, and three are actually personal confessions of what used to be me!

I thank God for having sent my wife, Cassandra Salter Barlow, a saved and godly woman who helped me take my rightful position as the spiritual head of the household. I surmise this is what God had in mind when he called woman to be man's helper as opposed to her being used by Satan to usurp man's rightful place as the spiritual leader. Shortly after God blessed me to take my rightful place as the spiritual head of our household, the Holy Spirit showed me how to recognize men who have not quite yet achieved this very difficult task that Satan never wants any man to accomplish. It was as if I was looking deeply into a mirror, seeing a reflection of my "old" man who was morally bankrupt, spiritually weak, and completely incapable of taking my rightful place to serve my family as priest, prophet, or king.

The Test
When couples and families visit churches and the time comes to recognize visitors, pay close attention to who speaks up to introduce the family. Does the wife, woman, or girlfriend do all the talking, or does the husband, man, or boyfriend speak? With few exceptions, whoever naturally and without fear takes the lead is the spiritual head of that particular household. I've been there, my friend, so I'm merely speaking the truth in love. When men come to know our God-given place of spiritual authority, power, and dominion in the world, we are virtually untouchable by Satan. Being cognizant of such important knowledge allows men to start living in accordance with God's perfect will for our lives. Actively wielding such godly wisdom and knowledge allows men to exercise our free will to take our rightful place as priest, prophet, and king. Men, it's time to take our rightful place as the spiritual heads of our households, in Jesus's name.

Deliverance Prayer
If the Holy Spirit has convicted your heart of living beneath your God-given spiritual birthright or otherwise failing to step up to the spiritual plate and take your rightful place as the spiritual head of the household, why not reverse the curse right now in prayer? Let's appropriate the truth of an eternal

promise Jesus spoke into the spirit realm over two thousand years ago, which is still actively bearing fruit today. Jesus said:

> Assuredly, I say to you, whatever you bind on earth will be bound in heaven, and whatever you loose on earth will be loosed in heaven. Again, I say to you that if two of you agree on earth concerning anything that they ask, it will be done for them by My Father in heaven. For where two or three are gathered together in My name, I am there in the midst of them. (Matt. 18:18–19)

If you are a man and the Holy Spirit is convicting your heart of living beneath your God-given spiritual birthright but you want to change, please agree with me in prayer (for your deliverance) by speaking these words out loud:

> Father God, in the name of Jesus of Nazareth, the Christ of the entire world, I confess that I have not been living up to the potential you have already given me to take authority, power, and dominion here on Earth. I further confess that I have neither loved you with all of my heart, mind, soul, and strength nor diligently pursued a very intimate and personal relationship with you. In the name of Jesus, I renounce any doubt, fear, pride, unbelief, unforgiveness, stubbornness, rebellion, and all other unrighteousness in my life that has hindered me from having an intimate and meaningful relationship with you. Holy Spirit, please fill me from the soles of my feet to the crown of my head with godly wisdom, godly knowledge, and a godly understanding of the rightful place I am to occupy as the head of my household. Thank you, God; thank you, Jesus; thank you, Holy Spirit, for delivering me from Satan, his demons, and the powers of Hell, death, and the grave. Amen.

Chapter 11

MINISTERING TO WOMEN, WIVES, AND MOTHERS

> They served their idols, which became a snare to them. They even sacrificed their sons and their daughters to demons, and shed innocent blood, the blood of their sons and daughters, whom they sacrificed to the idols of Canaan; and the land was polluted with blood. (Ps. 106:36–38)

Having examined how God can use you to minister to men, now let's examine how God can use you to minister to women. Whereas man was created to have dominion over God's creation, woman was specifically created to complement and help man fulfill his calling. In fact women fulfill their life's calling when they help men take their rightful place as protector and provider. I am fully cognizant that in today's times, Satan has so severely twisted the truth of God's plans and purposes for women's lives that it's almost offensive to hold to what modernists call "old-fashioned" virtues. However, look at today's broken marriages, skyrocketing divorce rates, out-of-wedlock pregnancies, proliferating abortions, and gender confusion issues, and you will begin to see how much disaster comes from rejecting God's master plan.

These anomalies are all outside of God's perfect will. They are all chiefly instituted by Satan and his demons to pervert the master plan God has for the family. Here's the bottom line: God gave mankind free will to accept or reject His perfect will. However, he also warns us of the consequences of rejecting it. Namely it will be well with us if we obey but it will not be well with us if we rebel. The phrase "that it may be well with you" is listed eight times verbatim in the New King James Version of the Holy Bible and 980 times by topic.

God specifically created, designed, and ordained woman to be a blessing and a complement to man. However, Satan has so sullied and defiled this original plan that many women have been deceived into believing they can do everything a man can do. Conversely, some men likewise ignorantly believe they can do everything a woman can do. "God created man in his own image, in his own image created he him; male and female created he them." (Gen. 1:27) This means He differentiated between them in the spirit realm before he ever formed the physical body from the dust of the Earth and breathed life's breath into Adam.

God divinely wired men one way and women another way. This is specifically why men and women naturally—or shall I say, supernaturally—gravitate in opposite directions, which moves them to like and dislike different things. Unfortunately, Satan can cause much confusion, acrimony, and outright chaos when men and women lack contentment in being who God created them to be and fulfilling the specific life purposes which He created them to fulfill.

To the contrary, when men and women are respectively content in their God-given places, they enjoy very blessed, peaceful, and prosperous lives, although not totally free from devilish temptations to sin. Their God-enabled spirit of contentment with their state in life insulates them from being overcome by the normal trials of life, many of which are deceptive and therefore demonic in origin.

God ordained men and women to serve distinct roles, each of which glorifies God when carried out in the spirit of thanksgiving and obedience that God deserves. Although men and women serve different roles, both receive the exact same accolades, rewards, and blessings from our Heavenly Father when they humbly submit to His divine will and therefore operate in the manner they were created to operate. While men were created to serve as priests, prophets, and kings, women were created to complement men in that capacity and produce male and female children who would replicate their respective roles in life.

Since it is God's perfect will for women to produce children who will be raised up to praise, worship, glorify, and obey Him, one of Satan's oldest schemes is to thwart this divine plan. Satan's chief objective in so doing is to deceive unsuspecting victims into worshiping him instead of God. Satan often accomplishes this wicked scheme by convincing women to abort an existing pregnancy. This is especially the case when an abortion is undergone primarily for selfish or sinful desires.

Ministering to Women Who Have Had Abortions
The killing of an unborn child is murder! Murder is biblically defined as the taking of innocent life. Abortion is a very touchy subject but one that is absolutely necessary to address when covering how to conduct successful spiritual warfare. God is the Creator, and He put the spirit of creation (procreation) in man and woman. One of the most normal and therefore supernaturally driven desires is to reproduce. God hardwired men and women this way when He declared and decreed, "Be fruitful and multiply; fill the earth and subdue it…" (Gen. 1:28) Since it is God's perfect will for us to be fruitful by producing children, Satan wants the very opposite. In an attempt to hurt God and thwart His perfect will, Satan devises evil schemes to deceptively convince both men and women to destroy unborn children. He does this by having us place inordinate focus on our own selfish desires, worldly ambitions, fears, or failures. When a woman carries a baby in an unwanted pregnancy, the demonic spirit of rejection attacks

the unborn fetus at the moment the mother gives serious contemplation to aborting and/or not wanting her baby in any way whatsoever, which includes putting the baby up for adoption. Demons gain authority to launch such attacks through the mother's ungodly contemplation about getting rid of her baby.

Please allow me to go just a little deeper with this. The sixth commandment in the New King James Version reads, "You shall not murder." (Exod. 20:13, Deut. 5:17) Jesus went much further, declaring that murder starts in the heart (mind, will, and emotions) a long time before it makes it to our hands to commit the sin that has been conceived in our hearts. (Matt. 5:21–22) Accordingly giving serious consideration to taking the innocent life of an unborn child is the most serious kind of murder to contemplate, pay for, facilitate, or otherwise carry out. This is very wicked because the unborn baby that's naturally tethered to the mother is also spiritually, emotionally, and psychologically connected to the mother. When a pregnant woman willingly or ignorantly allows demonically driven thoughts to captivate her mind to give serious contemplation to having an abortion, it is a sin of the heart. Her deliverance from the supernaturally imposed guilty conscience that will ultimately come for having contemplated such sinful misconduct could come quickly if and when she agrees with God that it is a sin of the mind, will, and emotions by confessing, repenting, and asking for forgiveness. When a man or a woman pays for an abortion, it is akin to, but much worse than, funding a contract killing of a completely innocent person. When a mother, a doctor, or a physician's assistant carries out or facilitates an abortion procedure, it is worse than actively pulling the trigger of a gun to kill an innocent adult human being.

Whenever Satan deceives a woman into murdering her unborn child, he convinces her to insult her creator in one of the most disrespectful, hurtful, and ungrateful ways imaginable. Please understand that this language is not employed with the intention of condemnation if you are in any way guilty of wanting an abortion or having had, paid for, carried out, or facilitated the carrying out of an abortion. It is, however, to soberly inform you of the mind, will and heart of the Lord our God on the deceptive and satanically driven practice of rebellion called abortion.

Law Office Testimony: Deliverance Ministry
Sometime between 2002 and 2005, I met with a prospective law client about a civil case she wanted me to handle. We sat down in the conference room to discuss her case. I was seated at the head of the conference table, and she was seated to my immediate right. As she was articulating the facts of her case, the Holy Spirit started moving in me to get my attention. When this happens, it usually means that this will not be a run-of-the-mill law office appointment but a Holy Spirit–generated divine appointment. This being the case, past experiences demonstrate that the spiritual impact of such encounters is of far greater significance than the legal matter being discussed.

As she was speaking, I heard this still, small voice in the back of my mind saying these unforgettable words: "Ask her if she's ever had a pregnancy that did not make it to full term."

I specifically remember answering in my mind, saying, "God, I'm not asking this lady that question; she may slap me in my face."

Again I heard the Holy Spirit in the back of my mind saying, "Didn't you say you would do whatever I asked you to do?"

To which I said, "Yes, I did, but this lady will probably get offended and slap me."

The Holy Spirit for the third time said, "Ask her if she's ever had a pregnancy that did not make it to full term."

At the third request, I very sheepishly said, "Excuse me, ma'am, but I have a question to ask that you may find a little odd under the circumstances." As I leaned back at a distance that was out of her reach and looked down, I said, "Have you ever failed to carry a pregnancy to full term?"

There was complete silence in the room. I slowly lifted my head and looked into her eyes to see what was transpiring. I noticed her lips trembling, and tears welled in her eyes and slowly rolled down both sides of her face. I recall thinking, "What in the world have I done?" I hurriedly got some tissue for her while asking, "What's wrong?"

After a few minutes (that seemed like an eternity), she regained her composure, looked at me, and said, "I've had five abortions; how did you know that, and why did you ask me that question?"

I told her the Holy Spirit told me to ask it, which caused even more tears to come down her face. I proceeded to explain to her that what man cleverly calls "a woman's right to choose" God calls the taking of innocent life, which is, by definition, murder.

Under the very delicate guidance of the Holy Spirit, I further explained that although man has renamed it something that's socially acceptable, God has been convicting her heart of sinful misconduct. I went on to inform her that such misbehavior requires acknowledgment that it is wrong (confession) and complete renunciation (repentance) for forgiveness to take place. I then explained that if and when she agrees with God that she took five innocent lives, renounces such misconduct as sin, and asks God to forgive her for the same, then and only then would He forgive and release her from the very heavy guilt in her conscience about those abortions.

After explaining this process, she agreed to let me to walk her through deliverance ministry, after which she said it felt like a thousand pounds had been lifted off her spirit. This was the correct response because when true deliverance takes place, the very heavy spiritual burden of guilt from the sinful misconduct is completely lifted from the mind, will, and emotions (the very soul of mankind). It is the overwhelmingly vexing guilt from having been devilishly enticed into committing the sin that Satan and his demons seek. Demons are fully aware that the more a person feels guilty, the more they are susceptible to self-condemnation for their sinful misconduct, which opens up the door for self-destruction via suicide.

Suicide is the ultimate goal demons seek in the lives of unsuspecting souls because it leaves absolutely no room for repentance or salvation. Just in case you are wondering, there is no way for one who committed suicide to be eternally saved, because they committed the sin of self-murder. Demons entice unsuspecting women into having abortions, then bombard their minds with condemnation for having succumbed to the very temptations that motivated them to have the abortion in the first place. Only the Holy Spirit of Christ Jesus can divinely orchestrate situations and circumstances, like the foregoing example, that allow both women and men to be convicted, confess such misbehavior as sin, repent from it, receive forgiveness for it, and experience physical, mental, emotional, and psychological restoration. Needless to say, this lady was exceptionally happy at the conclusion of her deliverance session that transpired in a law office conference room. Only God would be so bold, unpredictable, loving, and merciful as to do something so wonderful for a woman who came looking for something she wanted but left with that which she genuinely needed.

Deliverance Prayer
Friend, have you ever given serious contemplation to having an abortion, actually had one, or paid for, conducted, assisted, or in any way facilitated the carrying out of an abortion? If the honest answer is yes to any of these inquiries but you have yet to own up to the same as sin in the eyes of God, you need deliverance! If the Holy Spirit has ever pricked your heart about that which you either actively did or passively allowed to transpire with respect to any of the above, this is confirmation that God wants to set you free from demonic powers you may not even be aware of that are weighing on your spirit. If you are willing to receive God's forgiveness and restoration, please say this prayer out loud:

> Dear Heavenly Father, I humbly come to you in the precious name of Jesus. Lord Jesus, I have sinned in that I have (had, paid for, performed, assisted, facilitated) the murder of the unborn, which is commonly called abortion. I renounce each and every sinful act

on my part in the taking of innocent life. I break all agreements between my heart, soul, will, and spirit and every unholy spiritual influence in my life.

Father God, please forgive me for my sins and help me to manifest true heartfelt repentance for my sinful misconduct. Holy Spirit of Christ Jesus, please comfort, counsel, and help me to be true to my calling in life. From this day forward, it is my will and heartfelt desire to obey you, God, in that which I say and do. Thank you, God, for delivering me from the powers of darkness and for having placed your divine seal of approval upon me until the day of redemption in Christ Jesus. Amen!

Please take three to five very deep breaths by closing your mouth, inhaling in through your nostrils until your lungs are completely filled with air, and then exhaling through your mouth. Please be sure not to neglect reading chapter on maintaining deliverance. If you have never aborted a pregnancy, do you know at least one person who either had one, paid for one, counseled someone to receive one, or in any away facilitated the carrying out of an abortion? If yes, please pray, asking the Holy Spirit to let you know if, when, and how you should share this lifesaving information. I can assure you that God will richly bless your obedience in ways you might not be able to fathom.

There are many other ways Satan uses demons to disrupt the unity and harmony God has ordained for women to enjoy with men in general and their husbands in particular. Quite frankly they are too numerous to attempt to cover within the confines of this book. However, in general Satan does not want women to fulfill their calling to be godly while single, married, or raising children. Satan often moves many women to teach children to disrespect their father, which is unwise and spiritually dangerous.

If wives fail to properly teach children to respect authority in general and male authority in particular, they will raise children who have a natural tendency to rebel against man, which leads to rebellion against God. Accordingly if Satan can't deceive men and women into dishonoring God by aborting the child(ren) God ordained for them to birth into the world, demons will try to convince them to fail to raise up children in the way they should. (Prov. 22:6)

Ministering to Mothers Whose Children Have Died
While there are women who succumb to satanic temptations to abort their pregnancy, I believe the vast majority embrace their God-given instinct to carry their pregnancies to full term. Such women tend to be very eager to adhere to their natural inclination toward motherhood and are very happy to fulfill God's ordination for them to "be fruitful and multiply" (Gen. 1:28) Unfortunately, even when a woman resists the satanic temptation to abort a pregnancy, gives birth, and goes about loving, nurturing, and training her child(ren), what happens if the child(ren) precede(s) the mother in death?

Although the same question could be reasonably directed toward fathers, there tends to be a stronger bond between mothers and the children they carry inside of them for nine months. There is quite a bit of bonding between mothers and their children during the gestation period, to which no man could naturally relate. This fact makes the death of a child that much more difficult to handle for a mother who persevered through all of the natural trials and tribulations of successfully birthing a child into the world.

In direct response to Eve's disobedience concerning her consumption of the forbidden fruit from the tree of the knowledge of good and of evil, God specifically said, "I will greatly multiply your sorrow and your conception; in pain you shall bring forth children…" (Gen. 3:16) In accordance with this just punishment for her disobedience, all women experience such tribulation during the gestation period of each pregnancy. With this eternal chastisement in place, although there are exceptions, women tend to have a much closer bond and therefore relationship with the children they have carried and birthed into the world.

Accordingly Satan can try to gain an unfair and potentially dangerous advantage over mothers whose children precede them in death. I have had the very solemn opportunity to minister to both fathers and mothers whose children have preceded them in death, and the matter is always a bit more difficult for mothers to handle than fathers. In so ministering I have seen one particular circumstance that appears to be quite common and that makes it more difficult for some mothers to get past such an unfortunate occurrence.

When Mothers Idolize Children
That circumstance exists if and when a mother has poured too much of her life into her children so that they become "idols." I surrounded the word "idols" in quotations because when this happens it tends to be so gradual or incremental that it is imperceptible to the mother who is really being victimized by demons. A practical definition of idolatry is holding a person, place, or thing in higher esteem in one's mind, will, or emotions than God occupies. If and when this occurs, an inordinate (ungodly) amount of a mother's time, talent, and treasure will be expended on her child(ren) over and above just about everything else, including her God-given priest, prophet, and king—her husband. This is especially so if she somehow feels less attractive to her husband after she has given birth.

When this scenario occurs, Satan can attack God's preordained family structure by having a wife put all of her eggs in one basket—her child(ren). This scenario will reverberate in the natural and supernatural realms, thereby throwing a previously well-settled household into a spiritual tailspin that sometimes can only be corrected through confession, repentance, prayer, and sometimes fasting.

If and when a child dies, it will heavily impact a mother who has invested so much of her personal life (mind, body, will, and emotions) in the child's birth, life, nurturing, and training. If the child is idolized, the pain of the loss is much harder on the mother. This is often the case because in her view all that she placed her hope upon has been lost. I have ministered to mothers who ultimately confessed that they had idolized the child that preceded them in death. However, this confession did not take place until they received and confirmed the accuracy of a word of knowledge that such was the case. Upon acknowledging the same, the usual remedy is found in 1 John 1:9, where God declares, "If we confess our sins, He is faithful and just to forgive us our sins and to cleanse us from all unrighteousness." The very next verse says, "If we say that we have not sinned, we make Him a liar, and His word is not in us." (1 John 1:10)

While ministering to women who are having an inordinately difficult time coming to grips with the death of a child (whether the child was carried through birth or adopted), the Holy Spirit usually moves me to try to determine whether any kind of idolatry is afoot. As you can imagine, this is a very, very delicate conversation to conduct, as the mother is already in deep grief for the loss. The good news, however, is that the deeper the pain cuts into the mother's heart for the loss of her child(ren), the more freedom she will be able to experience upon admitting to God that she held her child(ren) in a place of higher esteem in her heart (mind, will, and emotions) than she did her Heavenly Father. When a mother can acknowledge such a scenario as idolatry, she can then (and only then) be set free from any bondages of sinful thoughts, regrets, self-condemnation, and/or all other unrighteousness that may exist in her heart surrounding the death of her child(ren).

Deliverance Prayer

Here's a prayer that can bring emotional relief and deliverance, in the name of Jesus:

> Dear Heavenly Father, I humbly come to you in the precious name of Jesus. Lord Jesus, I have sinned by_____.

(Specify each and every shortcoming the Holy Spirit leads you to confess. For example, "having held my child(ren) in a place of esteem that comes too close to what God means to me or having placed my child(ren) before my husband.")

Please forgive me for such misconduct, cleanse me from all iniquity that resulted from my mind, will, emotions, and conduct. Father God, please create in me a clean heart and clear conscience about the death of _____. (Call the actual name.)

Father God, in childlike faith I believe and trust you to deliver me from all guilt I have experienced due to the death of _____. (Call the actual name.)

Thank You, God; thank You, Jesus; and thank You, Holy Spirit for my complete deliverance.

Unfortunately, if and when a mother idolizes her child(ren), she tends to be the very last to know. In this regard, it takes something very drastic to shock the mother's conscience into the reality of her true condition that could be hindering her from experiencing the fullness of God's presence in her life. This scenario can also play out in the lives of grieving fathers but most often involves grieving mothers. Accordingly God providentially orchestrates burning-bush moments to convict such grieving parents into a state of repentance for having allowed their child(ren) to occupy a place in the heart that is specifically reserved for God. Jesus taught this principle in one of the most radical means one could ever imagine when He declared, "He who loves father or mother more than Me is not worthy of Me. And he who loves son or daughter more than Me is not worthy of Me." (Matt. 10:37) With these very strong words, Jesus makes it crystal clear that parents, especially mothers, can idolize children and children can idolize parents to their own personal detriment. Such detriment can ultimately lead to God rejecting them. In Greek, *dokimos* means "accepted or approved" while *adokimos* means "unapproved, rejected, reprobate, or castaway." (Strong's Expanded Dictionary of Bible Words, 2001)

Accordingly if and when a parent can't seem to ever find solace after the death of a child, there is a possibility, however slight, that Satan may have gained a foothold in the victim's mind, will, and emotions regarding the child's death. In this regard, it would behoove the person to pray for a word of knowledge as to the possible existence of some unrighteousness in them with regard to their unresolved grief and pray for a word of wisdom as to whether confession, repentance, and/or forgiveness are in order.

Grieving Mothers Who Have Not Idolized Children
Obviously there are many who have not idolized their children and therefore should not allow the enemy of our souls to move them to false condemnation while experiencing natural grief for the loss of their child(ren). Death is a natural part of the normal course of life here on Earth. With only a couple of documented exceptions in the Holy Bible—Enoch in Genesis 5:24 and Elijah in 2 Kings 2:1, whose miraculous departures from Earth were signs of the coming Rapture—we all must taste natural death before we can experience eternal life with God in the bliss of Heaven.

Unfortunately, it takes the death of a very dear loved one for many of us to be shocked into having a practical understanding of how awesomely loving and merciful God can be to us as His children. When a child dies, the mother who carried, birthed, nurtured, loved, educated and cared for that child will naturally experience some of the deepest grief one could ever imagine. No matter what family, friends, associates, coworkers, or even gospel ministers say or do to try to bring comfort, the truth is that God is the only one who can bring solace to that grieving mother. However, such comfort must be received in the spirit of reverence, humility, and obedience. Demons often try to move us to being angry with God for the death of our loved ones. When this wicked scheme is effective, a grieving mother will become angry, blame God, and live in misery until she ultimately repents for her such insolence or irreverence toward our Heavenly Father.

However, what we sometime fail to fathom is that God often calls the dead to be with Him in the bliss of Heaven after the purposes for which He allowed them to visit Earth have been accomplished. At this point we are to lovingly release them to God and patiently await our turn for God to reunite us with our beloved who are with Him. In the words of the Apostle Paul: "We are confident, yes, well pleased rather to be absent from the body and to be present with the Lord." (2 Cor. 5:8) Obviously this would not be the case if either the deceased or the grieving parent is not genuinely saved. Under such undesirable circumstance, there will be no reunion in Heaven, for one of the twain would never make it there.

It is for this very reason that God wants parents to provide children with not only natural blessings but also supernatural blessings. One of the best blessings parents can bestow upon their children is to lovingly lead, guide, and direct them to appreciate God and the death, burial, resurrection, and ascension (back to Heaven) of Jesus of Nazareth, the Christ, and to receive the infilling power of the Holy Spirit. Unfortunately too many parents do a fine job providing for their children in the natural realm but woefully fail on the supernatural side of life. Accordingly if you have lost a child, ask yourself this question: did I do all I reasonably could to introduce my child(ren) to God and His righteousness? If in good conscience your answer is "yes, please take comfort in the fact that God is well pleased with the stewardship you exercised with His child(ren) who were really on loan to you for the span of that child's life here on Earth. Too many times parents forget that we are all God's children, and our natural children are only on loan to us from God. At the appointed time, God will call each and every one of us "home."

Unfortunately home is not where many think it is for them. There's an old cliché that's right on point with respect to this subject. The cliché goes: "Home is where the heart is." This is very accurate to some people's eternal benefit and to other people's eternal detriment. Home is Heaven for those who retain God in the mind, will, and emotions and thereby earnestly try to obey Jesus. Home is Hell and ultimately the lake of fire for those who refuse to retain God in their consciences and thereby rebel against God and refuse to accept Jesus.

If you have lost a child but believe you did not do all you reasonably could have done to help that child come to know and revere God, please allow the Holy Spirit to tenderly convict your heart, then confess (your shortcomings) and ask God (in Jesus's name) to forgive you. Upon so doing, God will give you a peace that surpasses all mankind's exceptionally limited understanding. This is the only true remedy when the Holy Spirit convicts us of having fallen short of God's requirements in any area of our lives, especially while grieving and feeling helpless after the death of a loved one.

With such eternal truths in mind, it matters not that a parent provided natural blessings to their child(ren) if the same were not ultimately utilized in attempts to help their children come to know, revere, and obey God. To the contrary, parents who spend quality time exercising proper stewardship over their God-given time, talent, and treasure to help their children accept God should take comfort when God calls their child(ren) home to eternally reside with Him in the awesome bliss of Heaven. As a minister of the gospel of peace, I can assure you that God is well pleased with such parents.

Ministering to Women Who Have Spiritually Weak Men

Is a good woman God's shoehorn for a good man? God has a custom-made shoehorn for every man! In Genesis 2:18 (New Living Translation), the Lord God said, "It is not good for the man to be alone. I will make a helper who is just right for him." After having done so, God then commanded: "Therefore a man shall leave his father and mother and be joined to his wife, and they shall become one flesh." (Gen. 2:24, New Living Translation) With these two passages of Scripture, God makes eternal declarations that He custom made woman to be a "just right" (perfect) helper for man, and the two are supposed to become as one, forsaking all others, starting with their own mothers and fathers. Rendering obedience to this directive alone could save countless marriages today.

In my short lifetime, I have come to greatly appreciate the eternal accuracy of these two passages of Scripture. Furthermore God has metaphorically shown me the efficacy of the same via comparing the functionality of a common shoehorn. A shoehorn is a tool that's customized to facilitate the process of putting human feet into shoes while simultaneously reducing stress on the shoe by keeping the back of the shoe open while the foot slides in. The operative words in this definition are the following:

> Tool
> Facilitates
> Process
> Putting on
> Reduces stress
> Keep
> Open
> Slides into

Likewise God has a particular woman for every man whose life's ministry is to help her husband/man "slide into" the holy calling God has for his life!

According to the Bible, men are naturally supposed to serve as priest, prophet, and king in the household. Unfortunately, in what seems like the vast majority of households, wives or unmarried women occupy such roles. While it is commendable that women are doing so, the fact remains that they are operating under God's permissive will rather than His perfect will. Any godly woman who wants to please God knows quite well that God will tremendously bless her over and above her current state if/when her husband/man takes his rightful place as priest, prophet, and king.

One of the most recurring requests for prayer I receive as a pastor is from women who want their men to take their rightful place as the spiritual head of the family and household. They testify that they have tried everything but nothing seems to work. However, upon being asked, "Have you lived a righteous life before your man in complete submission to God?" the answer is usually no.

As a man who used to live beneath my spiritual birthright, I testify that one of the most important purposes (ministries) in life that God has given to woman is to help man (the one for whom God made her) "slide into" the purpose for which God made him. There is absolutely no doubt in my mind that God uses godly, submissive, and obedient women as spiritual shoehorns to facilitate the process of helping men slide into their calling in life and in so doing reduce the stress of the trials and the tribulations that the world, the flesh, and the devil will send before the process is completed.

I am a living witness that a man's wife is supposed to be his spiritual shoehorn to help him smoothly transition (slide) into the custom-made ministries God called him to fulfill in life, the first of which is to serve his wife and family as priest, prophet, and king. I thank God for my blessed wife and custom-made spiritual shoehorn, Lady Cassandra D. Barlow, whose obedience to God helped me to receive that which God had ordained from before the foundations of the world. No doubt this is what a "just right" helper is supposed to do for her husband.

Accordingly, to my beloved sisters (all women on Earth) who earnestly yearn for your man/husband to rise up to the place where God wants him to be, please read, meditate on, pray over, and obey 1 Peter 3:1–6. God used these very powerful passages of Holy Scripture to bless my wife to facilitate the process of helping me easily transition from having been a heathen to a man of God. Her faithfulness to God substantially assisted me in sliding into my custom-made ministry with less stress, thereby keeping me open to God's plans and purposes for my life while I underwent trials and tribulations the enemy sent trying to keep me from serving as priest, prophet, and king.

These very powerful words are the key: "[You wives must accept the authority of your husbands. Then, even if some refuse to obey the Good News, your godly lives will speak to them without any words. They will be won over observing your pure and reverent lives." 1 Peter 3:1(NLT)

In other words, ladies, living like the world lives will never lead a man to God: only living right in God's sight can do that!

Chapter 12

MINISTERING TO CHILDREN

Train up a child in the way he should go,
And when he is old he will not depart from it. (Prov. 22:6)
"A tree grows in the direction the wind blows."
(The Holy Spirit, 7:45 a.m., July 4, 2015)

As I was on a thirty-mile ride on my bicycle in July of 2015, the Holy Spirit spoke to me about this chapter, which covers deliverance ministry for children. The message I received was: "A tree grows in the direction the wind blows!" It immediately arrested my attention, so I repeated it several times in my mind to retain it in my memory. As the spiritual significance was resonating with me, I envisioned how strong winds blow against trees. While the leaves, limbs, and branches yield to the direction of the wind, the trunk usually remains in place unless the roots are shallow, the ground becomes too wet for the tree to hold itself in place, or the tree has some type of hidden decay or damage from fungus or insects eating it from within.

We live in Florida, which has many beaches. The trees along the shoreline typically lean away from the ocean toward the land. It is easy to discern that the constant gusts of wind from the ocean toward the land force the trees to lean away from the ocean. With respect to children, there are only two ways they can be taught, nurtured, and raised to adulthood—through godly or ungodly means.

God has a tender and special place in His heart for children. While preaching I often warn that if you want to get on the wrong side of God, hurt a child. When it comes to children, even the twelve apostles angered Jesus enough to warn them of hellfire for rebuking a child who wanted to come to Him. Jesus said:

> …whoever causes one of these little ones who believe in Me to sin, it would be better for him if a millstone were hung around his neck, and he were drowned in the depth of the sea. (Matt. 18:6)

Knowing this to be the unadulterated truth, Satan has special plans for children. He therefore assigns demons to entice unsuspecting, stubborn, outright rebellious adults to injure, maim, sexually molest, and even murder children. Satan so moves against us for he very well knows God will punish even His very own elect who harm children. I don't care how close you think you are to God, if you harm a child—even your own—you will stir up God's just wrath against yourself.

Attacks at Conception and in the Womb

What is absolutely mind-boggling and almost inconceivable is that satanic attacks upon children occur as early as conception. When children are conceived in sinful acts of adultery, fornication, prostitution, rape, or other sinful circumstances of lust (or any kind of sexual immorality), demons can gain authority to start tormenting them while they are still in the womb. Sadly if the mother fails to renounce the sinful circumstance that led to the pregnancy, her child can be born needing deliverance ministry.

I am fully cognizant that it is very difficult to fathom these statements, but they just happen to be accurate. Unborn babies feed off their mothers both naturally and supernaturally. When a mother is happy, her unborn baby is happy; when she's sad, her baby is sad; when she's in fear, her unborn baby is in fear too.

Here's a testimony of an occurrence that I personally witnessed back in 2000. When my wife was pregnant, her doctor recommended she undergo amniocentesis, which involves sticking a very long needle through the abdomen and into the amniotic sac to take a fluid sample for analysis. Neither of us wanted her to undergo the procedure, but it was highly recommended because of my wife's age at that time. My wife was fearful of the procedure and therefore very reluctantly agreed to have it performed. I was with her the entire time for encouragement and emotional support.

Prior to the start of the procedure, we watched our unborn child on an ultrasound monitor. As the doctor proceeded to insert that very long needle into my wife's abdomen, we could see that it slowly touched the fetal sac. As the needle touched the sac and attempted to penetrate it, the doctor, my wife, and I were amazed at what we saw on the monitor. When the sac bent in toward the baby, our unborn child quickly moved away from the area where the needle was trying to penetrate the sac! I literally had to blink several times to make sure my eyes were not deceiving me. The doctor tried a second time to penetrate the sac; the sac bent in toward the baby, and she backed away from that spot again.

I was in complete awe on two fronts. First, I was blown away that our unborn baby girl was fearful of whatever that foreign object was that she somehow knew was dangerous. Second, I was awestruck that the needle could not penetrate that sac, although the doctor was trying to force it in to take a fluid sample. It was a sign, wonder, and miracle from God that this procedure was not to take place. After the third attempt, we all agreed that the procedure should be stopped. If I ever had any doubts about the natural and supernatural connectivity between a mother and her unborn baby, they were erased after having witnessed that miraculous event.

As I pen this book, our daughter is now fifteen years of (2015), and her greatest challenge is fear. We take her through deliverance, and she does fine for a while, but the process has to be repeated every so often. Could this fear have been generated from the womb when her mother underwent amniocentesis? God only knows, but I suspect this is the case because my wife was quite fearful of the procedure due to the serious risk to our child. Had I known back then what I now know about deliverance ministry and how demons can (and do) attach to children even while still in the womb, I would have discussed taking my wife through deliverance to cast out any spirit of doubt, fear, or confusion surrounding that amniocentesis procedure.

The Effects on Fetuses of Drug Use by Pregnant Women
Many children I have ministered to over the last decade have been those who have been officially diagnosed with some form of hyperactivity or attention deficit disorder. It is widely speculated that such conditions are due to overwhelmingly large numbers of pregnant women who are on some kind of prescription drug to manage anxiety, sleep disorders, headaches, mood swings, and sundry other emotional and psychological anomalies. One scheme demons have been known to use is to orchestrate stressful situations to ultimately entice people to rely on any kind of chemical substance to ameliorate their less-than-desirable moods or conditions. Demons are notorious for generating confusion and chaos so their victims can seek relief from a drug dealer, a pharmacy, a liquor store, a tarot card reader, a psychic, religiously consulting horoscope readings, or just about any source other than God.

Unfortunately the fix they receive is short lived. They therefore need another one almost as quickly as the last fix dissipated. What's most unfortunate is that these people are unknowingly searching for the peace of God, which is the only thing that can bring everlasting comfort of soul and spirit.

There are many demons that specialize in enticing expectant mothers into such great fear that they are willing to ingest almost any chemical substance that promises them an escape from their perceived misery. Unfortunately what they fail to realize is that the true targets are their unborn babies. Scientific studies have pinpointed many birth defects from which children suffer to be directly related to chemical substances that were regularly ingested during pregnancy. However, what is less conclusive on the medical side is the connectivity between drug use and abuse during pregnancy and the antisocial behaviors that have become so common in today's children and young adults.

> An article from *Merck Manuals* notes:
> More than 50% of pregnant women take prescription or nonprescription (over-the-counter) drugs or use social drugs (such as tobacco and alcohol) or illicit drugs at some time during pregnancy, and use of drugs during pregnancy is increasing. (Gunatilake and Patil 2015)

With respect to alcohol consumption, studies further show:
> …drinking alcohol during pregnancy is the leading known cause of birth defects. Because the amount of alcohol required to cause fetal alcohol syndrome is unknown, pregnant women are advised to abstain from drinking any alcohol regularly or on binges. Avoiding alcohol altogether is even safer." (Ibid.)

Concerning illicit drugs, the article continues:
> Opioids, such as heroin, methadone, and morphine, readily cross the placenta. Consequently, the fetus may become addicted to them and may have withdrawal symptoms 6 hours to 8 days after birth. Hallucinogens may, depending on the drug, increase the risk of spontaneous miscarriage, premature delivery, or withdrawal syndrome in the fetus or newborn. (Ibid.)

Postpartum depression in women may also be an avenue for demons to invade the spirit of a newborn child. According to Gunatilake and Patil, "Postpartum depression is a feeling of extreme sadness and related psychologic disturbances during the first few weeks or months after delivery." (Ibid.) When and if this happens, it causes a domino effect within the entire household.

> Women may not bond with their baby…As a result, the child may have emotional, social, and cognitive problems later. In postpartum psychosis, depression may be combined with suicidal or violent thoughts, hallucinations, or bizarre behavior. Sometimes postpartum psychosis includes a desire to harm the baby. Finally, fathers may also become depressed, and marital stress may increase." (Ibid.)

As you can discern, deliverance ministry can play a key role under such circumstances. Depression is a spirit that's specifically designed to cause its victim to lose the very thing the gospel message is designed to give lost souls: hope. Any time demons can convince people to render harm to themselves or another, especially a child, the person can benefit from deliverance. When a mother becomes detached, cold, or indifferent toward her own child, this is a very significant sign that demonic activity is present. I am by no means suggesting that every single anomaly, issue, problem, negative situation, or circumstance is generated by Satan or demons. However, I am acknowledging that had Lucifer not been successful in enticing Eve, who was used like a customized tool to entice her husband, neither sin nor death would have been introduced into God's creation.

Now we have a trifecta of an enemy in the world, the flesh, and the devil himself. The course of the world runs diametrically opposite to God's perfect will for his creation. Like an ocean current going in the wrong direction, the world consists of popular culture, peer pressure, peer influence, and the "keeping up with the Joneses" spirit. The flesh is the inward fallen nature of mankind that has a natural tendency to think wrong thoughts first, which move us to do the immoral rather than the moral. Finally the devil attacks us by sending strategically selected enticements that he already knows our natural appetites are predisposed to accept. This is usually the case because of the negative influences he and his demons have had in our family lines for generations. Please refer to the self-deliverance practicum module at the end of this book for specific instructions on breaking generational curses.

Children with Autism—The Natural (Medical) Side
Over the past year or so, God has been slowly and progressively ushering me into ministering to children who have been diagnosed with autism.

> Autism – more formally known as autism spectrum disorder (ASD) – is a neurological disorder that is characterized by impaired social interaction, such as having difficulty communicating: restricted, repetitive behavior and a lack of empathy. Children with ASD have trouble understanding social cues like facial expressions or tone of voice. (Llamas 2013)

There have been many scientific studies within the past decade whose results confirm a strong connection between prescription drug use and the explosive increase in cases of autism in children. The results of a Swedish scientific study found that "the use of antidepressants during pregnancy increases the risk of autism spectrum disorders in children." Studies have also found that exposure to selective serotonin reuptake inhibitors (SSRIs) "especially during the first trimester, may modestly increase the risk of autism spectrum disorders (ASD)." (Ibid.) The most commonly prescribed SSRIs during pregnancy are Prozac and Zoloft. Finally a "Danish study published in the Journal of the American Medical Association found that mothers who took Depakote (valproate), an antiseizure drug that is used to treat bipolar disorder and migraines, were five times more likely to have children born with autism, Asperger syndrome and other developmental disorders." (Ibid.)

Unfortunately, expectant mothers who suffer from depression during pregnancy may have unwittingly subjected their unborn babies to autism from the usage of prescription drugs taken to relieve depression, which I have come to realize can be caused and/or aggravated by demonic influence. The most controversial matter, however, is the question of whether there is a connection between vaccinations and autism spectrum disorders. Due to such fears, many parents have decided to completely forgo all vaccinations. No doubt there is something terribly wrong in that there have been so many new diagnoses of autism over the past thirty years.

"There is concern in the medical community and the public because the incidence rate of autism in the United States jumped from 1 in 5,000 in 1975 to 1 in 50 in 2013." (Ibid.)

This is very tragic. The important question is, Why such a drastic increase? Is it natural (organic) or supernatural/ spiritual?

Children with Autism—The Supernatural Side

> My people are destroyed for lack of knowledge: because you have rejected knowledge, I also will reject you from being priest for Me; because you have forgotten the law of your God, I also will forget your children. (Hosea 4:6)

I will be the first to unequivocally state that I don't know whether autism and any other birth anomalies are of natural or supernatural origin. However, I am quite confident that it is highly probable that it is a combination of both. I am also confident that if the same are the results of sin, malevolent spirits of doubt, fear, pride, and unbelief will pull out all stops to blind the minds of people so they will never seek the one and only solution—namely a healthy faith in Father God, through the Son Jesus, in the power of the Holy Spirit.

With respect to the supernatural side of this issue, we must first examine the underlying sinful misconduct that could possibly lead to the reliance on legal or illicit drugs. What makes people lean toward relying on drugs, alcohol, and chemical substances? Such substances are usually taken as a means of escaping some type of sickness, disease, or painful or uncomfortable situation. The utilization of chemical substances generates some kind of temporary relief—but at what cost? Unfortunately the impact such actions have on unborn children can far outweigh the temporary relief that often comes.

It is of utmost importance that we examine what God says about drug or alcohol use. Believers are strictly warned:

> [D]o not be drunk with wine, in which is dissipation; but be filled with the Spirit, speaking to one another in psalms and hymns and spiritual songs, singing and making melody in your heart to the Lord, giving thanks always for all things to God the Father in the name of our Lord Jesus Christ, submitting to one another in the fear of God. (Eph. 5:18)

Here we are specifically cautioned against being under any temporary euphoric escape from reality due to the ingesting of any chemical substance. To the contrary we are specifically instructed to be spiritually uplifted and enlightened via the awesome and unlimited power of the Holy Spirit. This type of supernatural euphoria leaves no hangover, side effects for expectant mothers, or birth defects in their unborn babies.

The word *sorcery* is used several times throughout the Bible. Depending upon the specific context, sorcery relates to enchantment, magic, magicians (Jer. 27:9); witchcraft (Rev. 21:8) acting covertly (Isa. 57:3); and/or *phar-*

makeia (Rev. 22:15), from which we get the word *pharmacy*. The formal definition of *pharmakeia* specifically relates to the use of medicine, drugs, spells, and poisoning. The expanded definition specifies sorcery as "the use of drugs…accompanied by incantations and appeals to occult powers…" (Strong 2001) Accordingly sorcery is rooted in the occult, which is the pursuit of spiritual knowledge from ungodly sources such as the devil or his demons. This is specifically why those who adhere to occult practices very seldom do so without the abuse of some type of mind-altering drug to help them tap into the dark, demonic side of the spirit realm.

In today's times we live in an instant-grits, microwave-oven world that is overmedicated with instant "cure-all" drugs. Large multinational corporations have commercialized over-the-counter and prescription drugs. This billion-dollar-per-year industry has saturated the human psyche to such a great extent that people now think popping a pill can solve any sickness, disease, issue, problem, or social ill. This problem is so bad that prescription drugs are marketed directly to the consumer. In times past, pharmaceutical companies marketed new drugs to doctors, hospitals, and pharmacies. Today television, radio, and internet advertisements directly target the consumer. You are probably familiar with these ubiquitous words: "Ask your doctor about _____" or "If you're suffering from _____, ask your doctor if _____ is right for you."

Spiritually speaking this kind of commercialization of prescription drugs can be said to have bewitched some to rely upon prescription drugs for that which only a believing relationship with the Lord Jesus can bring: peace of mind. To rely upon anyone or anything other than God for peace of mind is the sin of idolatry, which is what the spirit of sorcery is specifically designed to foster under the deceitful guise of prescription medicine. The Bible has a very stern warning for those who engage in sorcery and especially those who allow it to dominate or negatively impact their lives, even when it's done in ignorance. God specifically warns from Heaven that:

the cowardly, unbelieving, abominable, murderers, sexually immoral, sorcerers, idolaters, and all liars shall have their part in the lake which burns with fire and brimstone, which is the second death. (Rev. 21:8)

I am not referring to those who are legitimately using prescription drugs to ameliorate injuries, diseases, and anomalies that have been duly diagnosed and treated by licensed physicians. To the contrary, lest Satan gain a deceptive advantage over your comprehension, please understand that I am referring to the abuse of legal drugs and the use of illegal drugs as a "cure-all" for matters the Holy Bible says can be addressed through faith in and a personal relationship with Jesus. Could this be why He is known as the Great Physician, who never lost a patient?

You may be asking, How in the world does this relate to ministering to children? Here's the answer to such a legitimate question. If expectant mothers are relying on prescription drugs for relief from anxiety (which is the spirit of fear) or depression, which is rooted in the spirit of hopelessness or despair, this is idolatry in its basic form. Idolatry is simply placing one's belief, trust, faith, expectations, or heartfelt reliance on anyone or anything but God. Put another way, idolatry is relying on that which was created instead of relying upon the One who created it.

Throughout the entire Holy Bible, no sin generated as much righteous indignation or severe judgment from God as idolatry. Idolatry has always led to the suffering and destruction of children. In the Old Testament, Satan deceived God's people into adopting pagan customs that called for the worship of the Ammonite little-*g* (and therefore false) god of fire called Molech. The only proper means by which to worship this idol, or demonic spirit masquerading as a god, was to burn your child alive. In today's times we frown upon such a "barbaric" practice while ignorantly sacrificing our unborn children on the modern-day altar more commonly called "a woman's right to choose." Choose what? Whether to murder an innocent infant or let it live to the glory of God?

Unfortunately the spirit of sorcery has very deceptively infiltrated our psyche to the point that we reach for a prescription drug before we search for a relevant Scripture (or as I like to say, "prescripture") in God's Holy Word. We ask for pain medication before asking, seeking, and knocking in prayer to our Heavenly Father through the Son Jesus in the unlimited and awesome power of the Holy Spirit. (Matt. 7:7–8)

Autistic Children Have Heightened Spiritual Discernment

As this book is being completed, I am actively ministering to several autistic children from different families. Through a very specific word of knowledge from the Holy Spirit in 2014, I was enlightened that autistic children are highly gifted in ways most nonautistic people are not. In particular the Holy Spirit revealed that some autistic children tend to have a supernatural ability to accurately perceive the spirit realm.

For lack of a better phrase, human beings are born with a spiritual "veil" over our supernatural senses. This veil protects us from perceiving the spirit realm with any of the natural five senses. This veil produces results that are positive in some respects but negative in others.

The Positive Side of Spiritual Blindness

This supernatural veil blinds our hearts from perceiving (seeing, hearing, tasting, touching, or smelling) things that have dual existence in the natural and supernatural realms. Satan and demons are real, yet most human beings have difficulty accepting this fact as absolute truth, chiefly because we cannot perceive or "see" the spirit realm. The word *Satan* is used forty-nine times in the King James Version and fifty-four times in the New King James Version of the Holy Bible. *Devil* is used 106 times in King James and 34 times in New King James. *Demon* is used a total of eighty-three times between these two versions of the Holy Bible. Yet far too many people on planet Earth have active doubts in their minds as to whether Satan or any of his demons

Fighting in Faith

(fallen angels) are real. This is astounding!

Even the average person who loosely claims to be a Christian doubts the actual existence of Satan and demons. If you don't believe this, please try this experiment. Randomly ask someone, "Do you believe God is real? What about angels? Do you believe Satan is real? What about demons, are they real?" The prevailing answer to the first and second questions is yes. However, the usual response to the third and fourth is "No," "I'm not sure," or "I don't know," which is scary. Such responses reveal the very subtle, deceptive, and blinding influence Satan can have over the mind, will, and emotions. This is specifically why Jesus sent the Holy Spirit as a gift to teach us all things and to "bring to our remembrance all things" that He taught. (John 14:26) It is also the Holy Spirit's responsibility to "convict the world of sin and of righteousness and of judgment." (John 16:8)

It is sinful to exercise the free will God so graciously gave us to refuse to believe that which He reveals in his Holy Word. Sadly, sinful unbelief is the chief reason Isaiah 5:14 (KJV) declares, "[H]ell hath enlarged herself, and opened her mouth without measure: and their glory, and their multitude, and their pomp, and he that rejoiceth, shall descend into it." This is also why the sin of unbelief is second only to fear on the list of sinful misconduct that causes its unsuspecting victims' souls to wind up in the lake of fire. As stated in Revelation 21:8 (KJV):

> [T]he fearful, and unbelieving, and the abominable, and murderers, and whoremongers, and sorcerers, and idolaters, and all liars, shall have their part in the lake which burneth with fire and brimstone: which is the second death.

An analogy of how demons operate is akin to how we accept that air is real despite the fact that we cannot actually see it. Is it not peculiar that spirit is translated as "breath or wind," the very thing we cannot see but whose presence and existence we can perceive because of the effects it has on trees and other matter upon which it moves when it blows. Demons operate in a very similar fashion. People with the gift of "Discerning of Spirits" can perceive the actual presence of demons. (1 Cor. 12:10) Fortunately, or unfortunately, the rest of us must rely upon the natural effects that demons cause in order to be cognizant of their presence. For example, when one has a negative, unethical, immoral, or illegal habit that seems to have no natural remedy no matter how hard the person tries to ameliorate it, more than likely the issue has some origin in the spirit realm. In such cases the same will only be eradicated through spiritual means such as deliverance ministry.

We have issues accepting the reality of the spirit realm chiefly because we cannot perceive angelic beings with our natural senses. Even if we could accurately perceive, Satan deceives us with demons of skepticism, doubt, or unbelief that reject the veracity of the perception as nonsense. Think about the word *nonsense*, which means something that doesn't make sense. Put another way, it means the mind either cannot accurately understand that which has been delivered to it by any of the senses or it refuses to do so.

While conducting electronic research for this topic, I ran across a reply from a writer who read and took issue with a post from a Christian who was relating the genesis of autism spectrum disorders to demonic activity. This particular writer took such sharp issue that they wrote a response titled "Religious Moron Believes Autism Caused by Demons." Without ever even considering that there may be a possibility of truth in that autistic behaviors can possibly be caused, influenced, or aggravated by malevolent spirits, this person summarily dismissed the entire concept as nonsense. To make matters worse, the person continued by insulting the Christian's beliefs. This is a classic example how demons of doubt, fear, pride, skepticism, and unbelief blind the mind to dismiss things of the spirit realm as utter nonsense. When this happens Satan and demons continue to have uninhibited and unfettered opportunities "to steal and to kill and to destroy." (John 10:10) What's so unfortunate is that in all probability this skeptical person is already under the power of demons that have blinded his mind from accepting the possibility that autistic people can be susceptible to demonic influence just like every other human being.

Demons are so grotesque that accurately perceiving them in their actual spiritual state of being would petrify the average person. Such great fear could result in a fatal heart attack, which the Bible identifies as "astonishment of heart." (Deut. 28:28, KJV) In this regard it is a blessing that we cannot accurately behold the actual visages of demons and their unseen activities in the spirit realm. God has provided such divine protection for us, but the converse of this is that our inability to see that which would harm us can cause us to doubt its existence, which is why faith (belief plus trust) in God is so important to Him and so invaluable to us. We literally cannot see God with the natural eye, yet many of us believe He is real. Likewise we should also accept as true and believe that which God in His Holy Word explains to us about the reality of both Satan and his fallen angels, who are better known as demons.

The Negative Side of Spiritual Blindness
Conversely, at least one negative side of spiritual blindness is that the doctrinal (eternal) truth of the gospel message is also veiled, as the Apostle Paul so very well stated in 1 Corinthians 4:3–4. This side of spiritual blindness allows Satan to disguise or transform "himself as an angel of light" for the specific purpose of deceiving those who are unable to accurately see, discern, or otherwise perceive who he is. (2 Cor. 11:14) The gospel message is vitally important because it rips the spiritual veil from our minds (hearts) so we can accurately discern the reality of the spirit realm. Once we can accurately discern the reality of Satan and demons, we can also perceive their malevolent plans for mankind. Upon perceiving their reality, we can then gladly receive and rely upon Jesus, who is the only one who can save us from such unfathomable evil forces of darkness, torment, and death (eternal separation from God).

Some autistic children appear to be born without a spiritual veil over their minds, allowing them to see accurately and quite deeply into the spirit realm. If you either have an autistic child or work with one on a regular basis who can communicate in some way, you may have noticed they do so about things of a spiritual nature such as God, Jesus, Satan, demons, spirits, and the like.

Since it was discovered that autistic children communicate very well through typing on computers and tablets, we now know that they are not "retarded" as many previously believed. To the contrary, the advent of typing reveals that many autistic children are very intelligent both academically and spiritually. Typing has opened up a whole new world both for those with autism and for their families, educators, and ministers. Autistic children often describe things they witness in the spirit realm that many of us are too doubtful, fearful, prideful, or skeptical to accept, believe, or receive. Could it possibly be that God is trying to use autistic people to communicate with us about the things that transpire in the spirit realm, but we are unwittingly ignoring them to our own detriment? I am slowly but surely coming to this conclusion. I am discerning that God has gifted at least some of these children to help us recognize matters that are of spiritual origin that we are otherwise completely ignoring or explaining away. From my limited experiences ministering to autistic children thus far, I am highly impressed with their ability to discern both benevolent and malevolent spirits.

It is not uncommon for some autistic children to regularly communicate about things the average person hardly ever discusses, such as the presence and activity of demons. When we hear such things, our blinded minds immediately stir up skepticism, doubt, and fear, which lead us to rebuke the children specifically because we can't discern or perceive what they can. Accordingly many autistic children are exceptionally frustrated because their parents, loved ones, and educators seldom take them seriously when they try to communicate about that which they are witnessing in the supernatural realm.

Satan Can Appear as Himself or Through Someone Else

If you are a believer, you accept the biblically revealed fact that Satan appeared to Jesus both directly and indirectly on several occasions. He first appeared to Jesus while He was fasting for forty days in the desert after John the Baptist baptized Him in the Jordan River. (Luke 4:1–13) Christians accept that Jesus lived in a fleshly body as he walked the Earth. In particular this means Jesus was able to perceive Satan's spiritual presence while He was in his fleshly body.

However, when Satan appeared again through the prideful selfishness of Peter after his confession of faith in Jesus as Messiah, apparently no one except Jesus accurately perceived that it was Satan motivating Peter to rebuke Jesus about His desire to be crucified but raised again on the third day thereafter. (Matt. 16:23) The point is that just as Jesus could recognize Satan and demons while his disciples could not, there are autistic children who have somehow been blessed (and somewhat cursed) with the ability to accurately discern and otherwise deeply see into the spirit realm, unlike the majority of us who are not autistic. One day the Holy Spirit revealed to me the phenomenal inner strength possessed by the average autistic child with words to this effect:

> Autistic children can see things in the spirit realm (and continue to live) that would cause the average person to instantaneously die from a heart attack generated by great fear. (Word of knowledge from the Holy Spirit, based upon 1 Cor. 12:8)

Accordingly if you have or work with an autistic child who continues to communicate about having seen, heard, or otherwise experienced happenings concerning God, Jesus, the Holy Spirit, angels, or demons, please do not summarily dismiss the same as being off the wall, odd, or worse yet, unbelievable. This will only add to frustrations that naturally result from an autistic child's unique inabilities to communicate in ways the vast majority of nonautistic people communicate.

Frankly speaking I am finding it a little easier to minister to autistic children than the average nonautistic person because they tend to be already aware of the existence of both angels and demons. When ministering to the average person (even a so-called Christian) who is not autistic, I often have to take time to bring them up to speed on the reality of Satan and demons. Not so with those who are autistic. The autistic children with whom I have been blessed to serve all receive ministry without fear and are even able to confirm when certain demons leave them after having been commanded to come out in the name of Jesus. While the average person who has been delivered from the presence and power of demons can sense or realize when the demon has departed from their spirit, autistic children can further identify the exact demon, when it left, how it looked, and even the emotional state it was in (angry/sad) when it left.

Parental Involvement with Autistic Children
One particular day I met with two autistic children at separate times for ministry. The first session included the child along with his mother and father. This was my second time ministering to this particular child, whose mother was present during the first session but not the father. The first time we met, the child was very active, walking around the church, going into the audiovisual room, trying to leave out the front door, and refusing to sit down for ministry, nor would he allow me to anoint him with prayer oil or even touch him. At one point he started screaming out while walking around the church. The Holy Spirit then moved me to repeat these words immediately after saying his first name, "_____, God loves you. _____, God loves you." Hearing it for the very first time stopped him in his tracks. He stood still to hear it over and over again. After I repeated this divinely provided phrase well over fifteen or twenty times, he returned to his seat,

allowed me to touch him, anointed himself with my prayer oil, and gladly received ministry. It was of particular significance to me that his father was not there. This was kind of rough for his mother, for she was miserable until her son became calm, sat down, and allowed me to be used by the Holy Spirit to cast out several demons, none of which wanted him to submit. That day the Holy Spirit revealed to me the significance of a father's involvement not only in a deliverance ministry session but also in the child's daily life.

Months later I met with this child a second time. Both parents were present at this deliverance session. Although my purpose was to minister to the child, as soon as we sat down and prayed, the Holy Spirit immediately directed my attention to the child's father. As I ministered, we came to the conclusion that the father was unsure of his own salvation, which was having a great negative impact on his autistic son. Accordingly I went over Romans 10:9–11, and he confessed his sins and asked Jesus to save his soul from eternal separation from God in Hell and the lake of fire. As I ministered to the father, the son was completely calm and relaxed. As his father was submitting to God's perfect will by accepting salvation and rededicating his life to the Lord, his son started dancing with glee.

The Holy Spirit gave me a word of knowledge that spirits of doubt and confusion were present in the father. Both he and his wife confirmed that one of his biggest struggles was with doubt, as he constantly doubted his own abilities. Accordingly he submitted to deliverance ministry, during which we cast out doubt and confusion. The child was as calm as he had been after having submitted to deliverance ministry the very first time we met. It was clear that the spiritual work his father was receiving was having a very positive impact upon him. I was therefore able to conclude that the peace and joy his father's soul was receiving in Jesus was being experienced by his son. The bottom line is that this child was delivered from demonic influence as part and parcel of his father's salvation and deliverance experiences. This scenario shows just how significant the roles are that parents, especially fathers, play in their children's natural and supernatural maturation.

Chapter 13
MINISTERING TO HOMOSEXUALS

> Do you not know that the unrighteous will not inherit the kingdom of God? Do not be deceived. Neither fornicators, nor idolaters, nor adulterers, nor homosexuals, nor sodomites, nor thieves, nor covetous, nor drunkards, nor revilers, nor extortioners will inherit the kingdom of God. And such were some of you. But you were washed, but you were sanctified, but you were justified in the name of the Lord Jesus and by the Spirit of our God. (1 Cor. 6:9–11)

The Special Case of Homosexuality
Homosexuality is unlike just about every other sin such as masturbation, heterosexual perversion (adultery, fornication, incest), bestiality, assault, battery, murder, rape, robbery, burglary, theft, idolatry, and all other sinful unrighteousness. The primary reason is that this sin is based upon a strong combination of two very stubborn demons: pride and idolatry, manifesting as the worship of self. The haughty spirit of homosexuality is not satisfied with just having a few victims—it flaunts and promotes itself in concerted efforts to deceive, de-evangelize, pervert, and spiritually defile as many others as

possible, especially the genuinely righteous. Such efforts are generally undertaken to get as many souls as possible to join ranks with its current victims.

Yes, these people are victims of Satan and his demons just like drug addicts are addicted to their drug of (don't miss this word) choice. Ask any meth or heroin addict if they can stop using any time they choose, and they'll say, "Absolutely not," because they genuinely—but falsely—believe they can't. Guess what? They truly can't! The question is, Why? The answer to this legitimate question is contained within the eternal (never changing) pages of Holy Scripture, one of which proclaims that as a man "thinks in his heart, so is he." (Prov. 23:7)

In other words, we are exactly what and who we think (genuinely believe) we are. Satan and all demons know this is the gospel truth, but "supremely intelligent" man continues to discount this as silly folklore contained with the pages of an "irrelevant," "outdated" book called the Holy Bible that's full of "self-righteous," "bigoted," "racist," and "mean-spirited lies." To our own detriment, legions of demons continue to custom fit (prepare) unsuspecting souls for hellfire by falsely convincing them to believe one of the biggest lies of all time: namely that homosexuality is natural and therefore God made them that way. On the other hand, Christians hold to the Bible-based belief that homosexuality is of supernatural origin and facilitation.

Homosexuality: Is It by Nature or by Nurture?

A great number of practicing homosexuals genuinely believe they were born homosexual, while the prevailing biblical worldview is that it is a choice. In accordance with the staunch belief that same-sex preference is genetic, most, if not close to all, homosexuals operate in the spirit of "This is how God made me, so it must be right." Once this idea is accepted, the person's mind starts thinking against their soul's best interests, which starts a domino effect. Supernaturally the person's body thereafter starts to receive, act, and feel exactly as the mind thinks.

What such victims fail to spiritually discern is that in so thinking and actively doing, they are rejecting God and His righteous ways. It therefore goes without saying that Satan's false doctrine is being swallowed hook, line, and sinker. Unfortunately, if such misconduct continues, God providentially turns them over to Satan's will to do the very things God forbids of mankind. In this regard they can be fairly punished for rejecting God's love through their willful rebellion or stubborn disobedience. Accordingly God does not send them to Hell—they ignorantly or otherwise knowingly fight tooth and nail to get there after having rejected God's eternal truth by accepting and embracing Satan's lies.

There is an old cliché that says, "You are what you eat," specifically referring to types of food that are eaten and therefore taken into the physical body. However, we are three in one—body, soul, and spirit. (1 Thess. 5:23) Accordingly, on the soul and spirit side, we are what and who we think we are. Put another way, as we think in our hearts, so are we, which spiritually means our behavior is a product of the substance of who we are on the inside in spirit and in truth. (Prov. 23:7)

Under this scriptural scenario, the more an individual is convinced that he or she is a homosexual, bisexual, or heterosexual, the more the individual's body will act like their mind thinks. For example, I have heard many testimonies from transformed former heterosexual male adulterers and fornicators who were convinced that no single woman could ever satisfy their sexual appetite—until they traded masters. The day they allowed Jesus to become the Lord of their lives, they began a long journey that ended with them finally having the godly wisdom, knowledge, and understanding that they had been believing satanically driven lies and therefore living demonically driven lives. These same falsehoods (formerly) stimulated their sexual appetites to mindlessly pursue woman after woman, only to feel like miserable failures after the euphoria they pursued in false hopes of satisfaction slowly dissipated.

This is also true for homosexuals who have been duped into believing the lie of the enemy that this is just the way they are, and no one can change it. It is for this reason the Holy Bible says:

> Therefore, God also gave them up to uncleanness, in the lusts of their hearts, to dishonor their bodies among themselves, who exchanged the truth of God for the lie, and worshiped and served the creature rather than the Creator, who is blessed forever. Amen. (Rom. 1:24–25)

"Gave them up" can be reasonably translated as "turned them over"—but to whom? Satan!

God's Righteous Punishment is Just

The first chapter of Romans reveals that God justly punishes sinful misconduct. Such punishment is by no means exclusively reserved for unrepentant homosexuals. God repetitively warns everyone that all sinful misconduct and unrighteousness will suffer His just wrath on Judgment Day if we fail to repent. The fact is that homosexuals—even those who earnestly, albeit mistakenly, believe their condition is by birth—are no exception to this just rule. Accordingly it is incumbent upon us who know the truth to mercifully witness and minister (render godly service) to those who have been swept away into living a wayward lifestyle that is completely against God's will.

God never intended for men to have sexual intercourse with men, or women with women. The ideas, lusts, and passions behind such unrighteousness were all generated by Satan and carried out by his demons in evil attempts to pervert God's perfect will for men and women. It is God's will for men and women to be in passionate love with each other in monogamous marital relationships that produce children who can then be trained in the right ways to replicate the God-pleasing lifestyles their parents modeled before them.

To the contrary Satan has devised a master plan to introduce the lie that "God made men to desire other men and women to desire other women." Once this lie is accepted, it tends to generate anger, bitterness, and distrust in the mind of the homosexual toward God for having "made me this way." This is precisely what Satan wants, because such a mindset makes it quite difficult for God's love to penetrate, since the heart or spirit becomes hardened and therefore resistant to the gospel of peace.

For the purposes of this book and my Holy Spirit–led attempts to minister to homosexuals, let's presume they are all born that way. Now what? Does this mean evangelical Christians should do what Satan convinces homosexuals to do and just give up on trying to save them from a trajectory to Hell? Should we make homosexuals comfortable in a lifestyle the Holy Bible says will not allow human beings to "inherit the Kingdom of God"? (Rev. 6:10) Should we completely ignore the plethora of doctrine that warns us about God's hot judgment that surely awaits those who continue to ignore His call for confession and repentance that is manifested by living a righteous life thereafter?

Lest we get too complacent or prideful and forget, the exact same judgment they face awaits those of us who know to do good by trying to help unrepentant sinners yet fail so to do. In this scenario God clearly warns us all via James 4:17, which declares, "To him who knows to do good and does not do it, to him it is sin." I am highly concerned that Satan has deceived many well-intentioned, so-called Christians into disliking homosexuals and gay, lesbian, bisexual, and transgender people. We must never, ever forget that Satan and demons are our real enemies and that they spend a great deal of time trying to turn Christians against each other and against nonbelievers. If and when they succeed, it causes us to circle our own wagons and spiritually cannibalize each other.

Ministering Deliverance to Homosexuals
I am blessed to have been used by the Holy Spirit to minister to several people who were living in open homosexuality when we met. I found each

to be normal in just about every area of life with the specific exception of their sexual preference. Each person was totally convinced they were born with natural tendencies to prefer intimacy with those of the same gender. Not only did each believe this, but they strongly believed it to the extent that it angered them when anyone doubted, questioned, or challenged their belief (faith) that they were naturally homosexual. So how do we as Christians minister God's genuine love, compassion, and desire in order to forgive, heal, and save them from Hell and the lake of fire? In other words, how can we be like Jesus and love the sinner (the person) but hate the sin (ungodly lifestyle) being produced in the person?

As it relates to ministering to homosexuals, sometime between 2003 and 2005, God focused my attention on the account in John 9:1 of Jesus having healed a man who had been blind from birth. The Holy Spirit impressed upon me that this account of Jesus having the power to heal a man who had been blind from birth is a powerful means by which to minister to those who are earnestly (albeit erroneously) convinced that their issue came from birth. When Jesus and His disciples came upon the man who had never seen anything with his natural eyes for the span of his entire life, the disciples asked Jesus, "Master, who did sin, this man or his parents, that he was born blind?" (John 9:2)

Jesus replied, "Neither this man sinned, nor his parents: but that the works of God should be made manifest in him." (John 9:3)

In reality Jesus could have accurately taken this scenario all the way back to the Garden of Eden when Adam and Eve allowed sin to enter into the world through "the lust of eyes, the lust of the flesh and the pride of life." (John 2:16) Jesus could have explained that we live in a fallen world that has been placed under the curse God pronounced in Genesis 3:14–19. Jesus could have accurately said that mankind's original parents were enticed to rebel against God's commandment to refrain from eating fruit from the tree of the knowledge of good and evil. He could have correctly explained that Adam and Eve's sinful disobedience caused the course of the entire world to be changed from a natural tendency of humble obedience to God to a natural tendency of disobedience, doubt, fear, pride, rebellion, stubbornness, and unbelief. Each and every one of these negatives was authored by Satan. In other words, we live in a fallen world where faith in and obedience to God are no longer the rule but the exception.

However, Jesus bypassed this and cut to the chase by telling them that which was (and is still) most important: namely that God providentially allows anomalies to happen in our lives so His awesome, delivering, healing, merciful, mind-boggling, and eternally saving power can be manifested with us, in us, and through us. Applying this concept to homosexuality completely removes the satanically driven issue of whether homosexuals were born that way or chose that lifestyle. When we apply Jesus's explanation that some are born a certain way that the works of God should be made manifest in them, it neutralizes Satan's trap that causes such confusion among well-intentioned people on both sides of this very important issue.

Jesus's explanation of why some people are born a certain way presents a faith problem for the average homosexual. For the sake of argument, let's presume people who practice homosexuality were in fact born that way. So what? For the purposes of deliverance ministry, this "fact" would not prevent them from being transformed—that is, if they genuinely want to live a heterosexual lifestyle. Conversely, if they exercise their God-given free will to choose to continue in behavior the Holy Bible declares to be sinful, they will remain in that state until they repent or otherwise die in a state of not having been forgiven by God for their sins, which leads to Hell and ultimately the lake of fire. God's awesome and limitless power can deliver them if they simply have faith that He can. I fully realize the spirit of doubt may have you thinking, "Well, they would need to muster a great deal of faith for God to deliver them from having lived a lifestyle of homosexuality predicated upon believing they were that way from birth." To the contrary, it only takes mustard-seed faith.

Mustard-Seed Faith

We often hear Christians referencing mustard-seed faith specifically based upon Jesus having said, "[I]f you have faith as a mustard seed, you will say to this mountain, 'Move from here to there', and it will move; and nothing will be impossible for you." (Matt. 17:20) We love to quote this, but have you ever stopped in your tracks, meditated upon it, and asked the Holy Spirit to reveal to you what it really means or how we can practically apply it to our daily lives? On a completely unsolicited basis, the Holy Spirit revealed to me that we apply it by immediate obedience.

Mustard-seed faith is simply childlike trust in God. It relates to having a willing heart and an obedient spirit whose first thought is yes to that which God says, promises, instructs, or forbids. To the contrary, those without mustard-seed or childlike faith tend to doubt first and obey second (if at all). These are doubters who have a very difficult time being actively and affirmatively used by God. The reason is specifically because "…without faith, it is impossible to please Him, for he who comes to God must believe that He is, and that He is a rewarder of those who diligently seek Him." (Heb. 11:6) Accordingly, those with mustard-seed faith tend to obey God first and ask questions later, not vice-versa. Is this not what caused Abram to become Abraham and therefore the proverbial "Father of Faith?"

Now let's allow the Holy Bible to actively demonstrate how mustard-seed faith in Jesus can produce mind-blowing signs, wonders, miracles, and most importantly soul salvation. Let us go back to the man Jesus met who was born blind. By the way, unlike with the issue of whether homosexuality is by nature or nurture, there was no question that this man was born blind. Everyone in his hometown knew and had known this for a very long time, as this man was an adult when he met Jesus. The Bible clearly states:

> When He had said these things, He spat on the ground and made clay with the saliva; and He anointed the eyes of the blind man

Fighting in Faith

with the clay. And He said to him, "Go, wash in the pool of Siloam" (which is translated, Sent). So he went and washed, and came back seeing. (John 9:6–7)

First of all, Jesus did something that many would consider to be nonsense. He spat on the ground, mixed the saliva with the earth (which must have been quite a bit of saliva), made clay, and rubbed it on the blind man's eyelids. There is no question that if we were to witness something like this, spirits of doubt and unbelief would rise up in us so fast that we would laugh at something like this with scorn. However, the actions of one with mustard-seed faith would be quite different.

Let's proceed to the next step in this man's miraculous deliverance from "natural" blindness. After Jesus rubbed dirt and spit on his eyelids, He told the blind man, "Go, wash in the pool of Siloam." (John 9:7) It is of interest to me that there is no record of Jesus or any of the disciples escorting this blind man to the pool so he could rinse the dirt (clay) from his eyes. Neither is there any record of the man asking Jesus or anyone else for help in this regard. Apparently Jesus gave him the opportunity to exercise his free will to ask for assistance in getting to the pool. However, what's most important is that the man went to the pool immediately after Jesus told him what to do.

Let's now examine exactly what Jesus said. The first word Jesus said was *go*, which was succeeded by *wash* and "in the pool of Siloam." Accordingly these seven words consist of three specific commands Jesus gave to the blind man without any promise. Notice there is no statement whatsoever by Jesus that this man would be able to see if and when he obeyed those specific instructions. The man simply appropriated childlike (mustard-seed) faith and obeyed that which he was instructed to do. He somehow found his way to the pool and obeyed to the letter each and every instruction Jesus gave him without doubt, questioning, or complaining. By the way, the things Jesus instructs us to do are those things which are physically possible for us to accomplish, while He takes care of that which is naturally considered to be "impossible." In reality, as the formerly blind man discovered, "all things are possible to him who believes." (Mark 9:23) This is one of many eternal truths Satan spends great time, energy, and effort trying to block human beings from believing and therefore acting upon.

The Holy Bible records that the man "went," "washed" (as instructed), and "came back seeing." (John 9:7) This is textbook mustard-seed faith, which only takes immediate obedience without doubt, confusion, or complaint. Accordingly, if it only took mustard-seed faith in Jesus's instructions for a man who had been legitimately born blind to receive sight for the very first time in his entire life, can the same result be applied to homosexuals who were "born" that way?

Put another way, John chapter 9 is a real excuse eliminator! It effectively cuts to the jugular vein of satanic lies and innuendos that homosexuality is a natural circumstance deriving from birth as opposed to being a matter of choice. In the spirit realm, it matters not whether homosexuality is by nature or by nurture. The reason it does not matter is that God's omnipotence is powerful enough to deliver one from homosexuality no matter the genuine source of this very controversial lifestyle, which the Bible declares to be sinful and therefore not pleasing to our Father in Heaven. (Matthew 6:8)

Finally, and most importantly, this man who had been born blind ultimately gave his life to Jesus and became saved after his run-in with the unbelieving, scornful, and jealous Pharisees. His testimony was so powerful that the Pharisees excommunicated him from the synagogue. Not only were this man's physical eyes opened, but God providentially used this as a sign, a wonder, and a miracle to authenticate the gospel and Jesus's ministry, which was and still is "to seek and save that which was lost." (Luke 19:10) By the way, each time I have witnessed a former homosexual's deliverance from satanic darkness into God's marvelous light, they were subsequently and summarily rejected (excommunicated) from the ranks and associations of their homosexual comrades.

This formerly blind man's salvation is recorded as follows:

> Jesus heard that they had cast him out; and when He had found him, He said to him, "Do you believe in the Son of God?" He answered and said, "Who is He, Lord, that I may believe in Him?" And Jesus said to him, "You have both seen Him and it is He who is talking with you." Then he said, "Lord, I believe!" And he worshiped Him. (John 9:35–38)

This man's salvation, the eternality of this man's soul in the bliss of Heaven, was the chief goal all along, as opposed to just giving him physical sight that would only be a temporary benefit while he lived on Earth. This brings us back to the fact that God loves all people and all sinners, including homosexuals. However, it is God's perfect will for all sinners to admit (confess) their sins, turn (repent) from such unrighteousness, and rely upon Him to heal them, deliver them, and set them free from satanic bondage that's specifically designed to lead them to the lake of fire.

Deliverance from Homosexuality
After the Holy Spirit providentially focused my attention on how this blind man's mustard-seed faith allowed God to give him his sight, I was moved to employ John chapter 9 when ministering to homosexuals, especially those who were convinced they were so from birth. Each time God has blessed to me minister His awesome, merciful, unlimited love to a homosexual, the results have been awesome. The outcomes have ranged from seeds being planted in hearts to people being completely delivered from years of living in open homosexuality and now leading peaceful and spiritually prosperous heterosexual lifestyles. With respect to the former, the implanted spiritual seeds fostered godly truth that homosexuality is a spirit and that faith in God can bring deliverance irrespective of whether homosexuality is by nature or

by nurture. Just accepting the possibility that God is able to deliver a person from a homosexual lifestyle is a huge accomplishment in and of itself. This is chiefly because it destroys Satan's insidious and spiritually defiling lie that nothing can be done about homosexuality because it's "natural."

The first time I utilized John chapter 9 was with a young man whom I initially met as a legal client about a decade ago. He first popped in unannounced, asking if I could help him on a criminal matter for which he was being prosecuted. I confess that upon first laying eyes on him, I judged him for the lifestyle that he was apparently living and immediately referred him to another lawyer. Within about two hours, he returned to my office saying he did not like or feel comfortable with the other lawyer and imploring me to represent him. At his insistence the Holy Spirit moved me to accept his case, which I did not want to do. I admit that initially I did not want to handle his case primarily because I had not had too many dealings with openly gay men before this time. However, having promised God that I would do whatever He asked of me, I reluctantly accepted his case.

While representing him in the legal matters, I was moved to share Christ with him, which he initially rejected. He ultimately wound up having to serve a short term of prison time, during which we communicated in writing. Although we discussed matters of everyday life, I made it a point to relate just about everything we touched on back to God, His goodness and mercy, and ultimate salvation. While he was incarcerated, he was having various medical problems related to being HIV positive, which had resulted from his promiscuous homosexual lifestyle. He wrote asking for prayer, and I prayed for him in this regard, after which I discerned that the prayers softened his heart and made him just a little less resistant to the gospel.

"I Hate Women"

Upon his release from prison, we communicated regularly via telephone. He ultimately confessed Christ and started trying to live a righteous life. However, the demonic spirit of homosexuality was still present and hindering the sanctification process. The fact that he was saved yet still having issues with the spirit of homosexuality is proof positive that once we become genuinely saved, we can still be plagued by demons and therefore need deliverance ministry to facilitate sanctification after salvation. In other words, we need to stop telling people that once they confess faith in Jesus, all vestiges of their former sinful lifestyles will be immediately eradicated.

After a while he consulted me about going through deliverance ministry to have the spirit of homosexuality cast out of him. He was so serious and determined that he traveled a very long distance from another state to submit to deliverance ministry, which actually took place in my law office conference room on a Saturday afternoon. I vividly recall that the ruling prince demonic spirit that had him bound in decades of homosexuality identified itself as "I hate women." Demons operate in a hierarchical structure, with higher- and lower-ranking demons giving orders and obeying orders respectively. One who lacks sufficient biblical knowledge is cognitively blinded to the eternal veracity that "we do not wrestle against flesh and blood, but against principalities, against powers, against the rulers of the darkness of this age, against spiritual hosts of wickedness in the heavenly places." (Eph. 6:12) Demons that are of the highest order are commonly referred to as ruling prince demons because they rule lower-ranking demons with a proverbial iron fist.

If you are familiar with deliverance ministry, you already understand that demons take on odd names that can be nouns, verbs, adverbs, adjectives, and the like. This demon's identity was revealed when we began having a discussion about the man's childhood and the relationships he had had with his mother and father. His relationship with his mother was very strained, and there was no relationship whatsoever with his father.

As I ministered to him, this spirit spoke through his vocal chords, repetitively saying, "I hate women, I hate women, I hate women." This happened every time I spoke to him about the necessity of forgiving his parents, especially his mother, whom he felt had failed to protect and adequately provide for him when he was a helpless minor. Having been conceived and born outside of wedlock, he had no knowledge of or relationship with his father. These two anomalies played heavily into Satan's ability to convince him to harbor hatred in his heart toward women. This allowed the spirit of homosexuality to disguise itself as "I hate women," thereby capturing and enslaving his soul to accept, adopt, and unwittingly embrace a lifestyle that would dishonor his Creator, God, and place his soul in jeopardy of spending eternity in the lake of fire.

The Spirit of Unforgiveness
However, the underlying problem was that he had unforgiveness toward both of parents deeply imbedded within his heart. Unforgiveness is a demonic spirit whose chief goal is to insulate a person from receiving love from anyone—especially the author of love, which is God, "for God is love." (1 John 4:8) Accordingly this young man was being plagued by twin demons: homosexuality, masking itself as "I hate women," and unforgiveness, which served as the lock holding homosexuality in place. Under this circumstance, his deliverance and ultimate freedom called for him to genuinely forgive both of his parents from the heart. Accomplishing this would allow his soul (mind, will, and emotions) to be set free from the spirit of unforgiveness, which would then allow the spirit of homosexuality to be cast out.

The problem was that the demons had him convinced that he had a right to be angry about how his mother had treated him as a child and therefore to continue to hold her in a spirit of unforgiveness for the same. In other words, logic was trumping faith in God and His will for us to forgive. As all should know, it is God's perfect will for us to forgive others with the same ease and sincerity that God forgives us. God is so serious about forgiveness that He threatens His own children with eternal punishment for refusing to forgive our fellow man as He freely forgives us when we earnestly pray for it. One of the best examples of this, and perhaps the most famous, is when Jesus Himself warns, "[I]f you forgive men their trespasses, your heavenly Father will also forgive you. But if you do not forgive men their trespasses, neither will your Father forgive your trespasses." (Matthew 6:14–15)

I have found that allowing a person to read the Lord's model prayer coupled with these two verses that immediately follow tends to loosen demonic strongholds on the mind, will, and emotions. I also employ the parable of the wicked servant from Matthew 18:21–35, where Jesus deals with the evil consequences of one stubbornly refusing to freely forgive others as God has already forgiven us. These passages of Scripture paint a very vivid picture of what transpires in the supernatural realm after one sinfully holds another in a spirit of unforgiveness that proceeds from stubborn hard-heartedness. The climax of this parable is contained in verses 32 through 35, where the servant's master says to him:

> "You wicked servant! I forgave you all that debt because you begged me. Should you not also have had compassion on your fellow servant, just as I had pity on you?" And his master was angry, and delivered him to the torturers until he should pay all that was due to him. So My heavenly Father also will do to you if each of you, from his heart, does not forgive his brother his trespasses.

This is what was transpiring in this young man's life. His sinful and stubborn refusal to forgive his parents (his mother in particular) authorized God to turn him over to the "torturers until he should pay all that was due to" God—namely forgiving his parents as God was willing to forgive him. In his particular case, the torturers were the demon spirits that were motivating him to live a lifestyle that was wayward, unnatural, and very displeasing in the eyes of God. Although this young man had confessed faith in Jesus as his personal savior, he had yet to allow Jesus to become the absolute Lord of his entire life, which is the gradual sanctification process.

In this regard the greatest lie that's unwittingly believed and therefore spoken by Christians is "my Lord and Savior Jesus Christ." While Jesus is most people's savior, unless and until we learn to obey him, and with a quickness, He is by absolutely no means our Lord!

Once this young man heard the awesome, terrible, and uncut truth of the Holy Bible, he genuinely repented of his unforgiveness toward both of his parents. He verbally confessed to having been ensnared by unforgiveness and the demon spirit of homosexuality masking itself as the idea of "I hate women." He then allowed me to lead him in a prayer blessing his mother and father, thereby fulfilling Jesus's commandment to "bless those who curse you, do good to those who hate you, and pray for those who spitefully use you and persecute you, that you may be sons of your Father in heaven…" (Matt. 5:43–45)

Within seconds of completing the confession of the aforementioned sins and praying in the name of Jesus for God to bless his mother and father, he said, "I feel different." He further explained that his body felt different from the way it had before. Although he could not quite comprehend what this meant that day, he later came to realize that what was transpiring in him was that he was developing a natural attraction to women. This made complete sense specifically due to the fact that the spirit of homosexuality had deceived his mind so long that his body had come to obey the urges of the mind to passionately crave same-sex relationships with men. After confession and repentance, however, his body started the gradual process of obeying the renewed mind that had been restored to its supernatural state, which is to be attracted to and stimulated by members of the opposite sex, to the glory of God.

As of today, which is now well over ten years since I took him through deliverance, he is still living a celibate, heterosexual lifestyle, having completely renounced and given up homosexuality. He has also attended theological school and is well versed in the entire Holy Bible, having committed himself to God's directives contained in 2 Timothy 2:15. He and

I still communicate although we live in different states. I told him about this book and asked if he would consider sharing his testimony, and he graciously agreed. Please receive his testimony in the spirit in which he delivered it—agape.

Testimony: "My Conversion"

> I was twenty-eight years old, and for my entire life I was a heathen, having no real relationship with God. I was involved in illegal activity, homosexuality, drug use, and basically I was living as an active member of the world.
>
> Unfortunately I had gotten arrested in Florida for drug possession, and I was already on probation. Based on a recommendation by my probation officer, I hired Attorney Barlow to represent me. During the case Minister Barlow witnessed Christ to me. For the first time in my life, I listened for real. Minister Barlow told me to totally turn my life over to God and to turn myself in, in reference to being in violation of my probation. I listened and received Christ.
>
> My life has been totally turned around for the better. I am a Christian, heterosexual, not a drug user, and a witness now for the Lord. Minister Barlow did an excellent job of witnessing Christ to me. People in the past have told me about the Lord, and I have been to church in my youth, but I never found out about God for myself until Minister Barlow witnessed Christ to me.

This is his testimony of how God rescued him eternally by snatching his soul from Satan's plan to usher it into the lake of fire. In chapter 15, you will read how God later delivered him from physical death after doctors told him he had only a short time to live due to his HIV diagnosis and a myriad of other conditions that were being aggravated by the same.

Chapter 14

MAINTAINING DELIVERANCE

> When an unclean spirit goes out of a man, he goes through dry places, seeking rest; and finding none, he says, "I will return to my house from which I came." And when he comes, he finds it swept and put in order. Then he goes and takes with him seven other spirits more wicked than himself, and they enter and dwell there; and the last state of that man is worse than the first. (Luke 11:24–26)

If you have ever been taken through deliverance or ministered in this area for any extended period of time, you already know the veracity of the aforesaid Scripture, which is paralleled in Matthew 12:43–45. Over the past decade, I have witnessed churches and ministries that do an excellent job of extracting demons out of people and setting them completely free from the bondages of sinful misconduct. However, too often the freedoms experienced seemed to be short lived, and those who were previously delivered subsequently wound up in much worse conditions than they were before they underwent deliverance ministry. This is primarily because there were insufficient warnings and inadequate instructional emphasis placed upon the necessity of living as righteously as possible afterward. The only way this can be achieved is by humbly submitting to God through Bible study, prayer, fasting, and fellowship with like-minded believers who earnestly desire to live holy lives before God and man.

Many who revert to living sinful lifestyles after having been set free from demonic bondage do so out of ignorance, stubborn disobedience, or plain old rebellion. (Hosea 4:6, 1 Sam. 15:22–23) The degree of their reversion or relapse back into sin will dictate the level of divine punishment God will providentially allow to overtake them in their sins, issues, and shortcomings. (Lev. 26, Deut. 11:26–28, 28)

After having read the first thirteen chapters, you should now know that signs, wonders, and miracles follow believers and not the other way around. You should therefore also be fully cognizant that being used by God to heal a sick person or work a miracle by casting a demon from one's soul is relatively easy. Problems often come, however, in maintaining freedom after healing or deliverance ministry has been deployed and successfully received.

Just because you have been delivered from a demon does not mean that demon will never try to reunite with you again. Not only will that demon try to re-enter you, but it will try to come back with reinforcements that will make your life more of a living Hell on Earth than it was before you were initially delivered. Even Jesus Himself was not free from temptations when He walked the Earth in the flesh, for Scripture says He "was in all points tempted as we are, yet without sin" and that "when the devil had ended every temptation, he departed from Him until an opportune time." (Heb. 4:15, Luke 4:13) Although we don't like to accept it, as long as we are in earthly tabernacles called human bodies, we will be subjected to temptations to sin against our Father and Creator in Heaven. How we react to the same will determine the level of freedom and victory or bondage and defeat we will continue to experience throughout our lives here on Earth. In this regard deliverance from the presence, power, and/or influence of fallen angels is mutually exclusive from the state of being saved from Hell and the lake of fire. One can be saved yet under the negative influence of demons.

Very early on in my training, God moved me to place great emphasis on instructing people in Bible-based means to maintain the deliverance that Jesus shed His righteous blood on calvary's rugged cross for us all to receive and enjoy. Unfortunately too many people neglect to take deliverance ministry seriously enough to take the necessary precautions to maintain their freedom after demons have been miraculously expelled from the mind, will, and emotions or psyche.

Testimony: One Who Took Deliverance Ministry Lightly
I was introduced to Pastor Barlow through a common connection who happens to hold a doctorate degree in Christian counseling. She thought I needed more of a deliverance experience over a shoulder to cry on. She was correct. Pastor Barlow asked me about my relationships, as far back as I could remember, and he began to teach me about soul-ties and how these women, the ones of my past, are still very much a part of my present and future. Sex creates a bond; we become one with each sex partner, not only physically, but in the spiritual realm. They own a part of us, and we own a part of them as well. It transfers into the heart and stays with us. I could especially see this in my life, so he decided to take me through deliverance and assist Jesus in cutting me free from the soul-ties. Each woman, each relationship discussed we prayed about.

Afterward, I felt lightness and freedom I hadn't experienced in some time. It was a beautiful feeling. I walked in that freedom for a couple weeks. However, my desire for the married woman I had been seeing for a while didn't die easy. Temptation isn't a sin, but sin happens when we allow ourselves to be enticed and the desire begins to grow within us. This is what happened to me, and I opened the door to sin and allowed it back into my life. Pastor Barlow had sternly warned me to resist temptation. He basically said, now that I have been delivered, Satan will try his best to place temptations in my path that will cause me to fall. Pastor Barlow also warned that if I did fall, the demons I was delivered from would return seven times stronger. Well, he was correct.

I can't give you an exact count, but I can say that I have experienced confusion, depression, lust, insecurities, idolatry, financial hardship, and a few others. I cannot seem to let go of this woman because in my heart, I think I'm in love. The problem I was having is this: I wasn't committed to following God's path for my life. I thought I knew what I wanted, who I loved, and what I believed and I needed to do to obtain it. The relationship delivered me into heartbreak after heartbreak, broken promises after broken promises, and my spiritual life was spiraling out of control. Pastor Barlow and I counseled multiple times during this relationship I was in, and he even assisted me in deliverance a second time. Same freedom and lightness, I am witnessing the power of God, but my same sinful tendencies and idolatry of the same woman had me open the door to my sin again, and the same devastation followed.

If "the wages of sin is death," I was beginning to experience some in my reality. It's funny how old ways begin to take their hold of you, and the freedom you experienced from God's liberation is transferred into bondage and self-mutilation to suppress my own pain. I thought I was trying to change my life for someone, even though the woman was completely unavailable. I took it personal and began to question my own worth in the eyes of women. Well, why won't she see me for who I am and choose me? Well, I needed to know I still had it.

With this in my spirit, I began to seek and have as many relationships with women as possible to show myself I was desirable. I began to run into all sorts of women, and before long I was involved in five different sexual relationships, all simultaneously. The funny thing is, I'd hear from the married woman here and there, drop all of the others to be available to her, and when she had her fill of me, she'd drop me…I'd become enraged and pick up right where I left off with the other five. I was jealous and suspicious.

I'd stalk the married woman. I was spending all sorts of money to entertain the other five, lie, and then just forget all about God.

It's very peculiar how we don't even realize at times how we create weakness in our mind, soul, body, and our surroundings. When we chase sin, we become what we seek, but when we decide to trust in God and seek our Savior, it's amazing how He saves and somehow makes things right. I understand that my choices have caused me to experience "death." Maybe I broke a heart or two, even my own. While living in such sin, I couldn't concentrate on my daily tasks (work) so I lost a few opportunities due to my depression. I also lost time and distance. Jesus has the ability to cause all things to work together for the good, for those who love Him. I have experienced this firsthand and pray my desires to please Him with my life become the ultimate path I walk.

As for my deliverance, I have proven to be a poor recipient of the freedom offered through Christ, and for the fear of additional demonic activity in numbers. I am learning to manage my sinfulness, resist the demons that have plagued my life, and rely on Christ for all of my requirements. Jesus has been extremely patient and tender with me. Pastor Barlow had a word from God for me, and it was to go on a forty-day fast from relationships. Jesus said some demons can only be cast out by prayer and fasting…and for me a forty-day minimum fast must take place with no relationship activity. I am currently walking that path and experiencing some freedom. I've definitely had some temptation. It's not easy, but with His help, I haven't opened that door. I've severed all of my relationships, and I'm currently avoiding any and all invitations and dialogue.

"Take the long path," Pastor Barlow told me… God wants you to walk the long way for once. I thought about it for a couple days and felt like God opened my mind to understand this: we see the long path as some overwhelming task, so we find shortcuts along the way, and in our mind we believe we will arrive sooner by taking them. The problem is this: those shortcuts always find a way of pushing us back further, further past the original starting line. For me, the shortcuts were other relationships I thought were good for me, but they ended up doing more damage than good, and the time it took me to recover and start over was far longer than a forty-day commitment.

So to the eyes that see and the ears that hear, take the long path. It's the shortest distance.

Kevin.

As you can discern by the foregoing testimony, the most important question after deliverance from malevolent spiritual forces has been effectuated is, How do I maintain my deliverance when often sinful proclivities generated by demonic strongholds in family lines (a.k.a. generational curses) are afoot? In these regards, demons have been very comfortable in the spiritual abode of their particular victims for extended periods of time that can cover several generations. Accordingly, even when expelled they will attempt to return through a different door in sinful thought, ungodly attitude, unrighteous disposition, or stubborn or rebellious misconduct. Matthew 12:43–45 and Luke 11:24–26 contain very stern warnings from Jesus Himself about the consequences of allowing unclean spirits to return to our spiritual house, which is the soul or mind, will, and emotions.

The unfortunate result is that not only does each expelled demon return, but each one brings a total of at least seven along with it! As you can easily discern, this can be exceptionally problematic for well-intentioned yet biblically ignorant Christians who love Jesus and earnestly believe they are saved and on their way to heaven yet cannot seem to live out victorious lives here on Earth. A victorious life is one in which we can be a light for others to be drawn to a saving knowledge of Jesus. This is what God wants for every true believer. Genuine Christians are light (eternal truth) bearers. Unfortunately, Satan and his demons want the exact opposite and will pull out all the stops to contest, block, hinder, disrupt, and prevent this from happening—that is, if we negligently or willingly authorize it. Too many people fail to do the bare minimum that is required to maintain the precious deliverance from the power of sin that Jesus purchased with his own blood.

Jesus voluntarily allowed himself to be murdered through the torturous process of crucifixion so we could spiritually apply his holy blood and broken body for our deliverance from sin on three separate and distinct fronts. First, we are delivered from the penalty of sin, for the wages of sin are death, which is scripturally defined as eternal or permanent separation of soul and spirit from God in Hell and ultimately the lake of fire. (Rom. 6:23) Second, we are delivered from the power of sin through the process of power or deliverance ministry, where the Holy Spirit defangs the serpent's deadly influences over the mind, will, emotions, and conduct. Finally, upon dying in faith, we are ultimately delivered from the very presence of sin, as our final place of peace and rest is with our Father in Heaven.

Kept by God

Accordingly once we have providentially received our miraculous healing or deliverance from God—irrespective of whether it was effectuated through our own prayer or the ministry of a third party or divinely delivered by God Himself—we are obligated to obey God if we earnestly wish to continue in our newfound freedom. The question then becomes how and what to obey. Jesus said, "If you love me, keep my commandments." (John 14:15) He then explains that those who truly love him are only those who "keep" His commandments. (John 15:21) He reiterated and expounded on these declarations by promising:

> If anyone loves Me, he will keep My word; and My Father will love him, and We will come to him and make Our home with him. He who does not love Me does not keep My words; and the word which you hear is not Mine but the Father's who sent Me. (John 23:24)

The true essence of these passages is obedience. If and when we mature to the level of having a mind to obey God first and everything else second, we will be insulated from the wiles and evil schemes of Satan that are specifically designed to steal our belief in God, kill our trust in God, and destroy our souls in the lake of fire. The exclusive remedy to avoid these undesirable results is to develop and maintain strong faith in God through Jesus in the power of the Holy Spirit. In this regard we must know beyond a shadow of any doubt the following:

> …God and Father of our Lord Jesus Christ, who according to His abundant mercy has begotten us again to a living hope through the resurrection of Jesus Christ from the dead, to an inheritance incorruptible and undefiled and that does not fade away, reserved in heaven for you, who are kept by the power of God through faith for salvation ready to be revealed in the last time. (1 Pet. 1:3–5)

Having operated in deliverance ministry for an extended period of time, I have seen many who were able to maintain their deliverance as well as many who reverted to even more sinful lifestyles after having first been set free. Unfortunately I have even heard of at least one person whose penalty was literal death. The question becomes, Why do some people progress on to spiritual excellence while others return to the pigpen to wallow in the mud of sinful disobedience, stubbornness, or rebellion? I have personally observed three chinks in the armor that lead people to fall back into sin. Unfortunately these individuals can ultimately wind up in the fires of Hell if they continue in their rebellion. The chinks relate to failures regarding Bible study, prayer, and fasting.

Bible Study

"Study to shew thyself approved unto God, a workman that needeth not to be ashamed, rightly dividing the word of truth." (2 Tim. 2:15, KJV)

Fighting in Faith

The central problem across the entire world today is pervasive biblical ignorance. God commands us to study the Holy Scriptures so our spiritual eyes can be opened both to God's unfathomable mercy, love, and forgiveness and to the dark forces of the spirit realm that wish to devour mankind. The chief woe caused by biblical ignorance is the lack of a healthy respect or reverence for God. When one fails to revere God, there is a lack of spiritual comprehension of the awesome power and dreadful judgment He wields. Reading through the entire Bible with an open mind is the best means of (to borrow a phrase from national radio broadcaster and pastor Paul Sheppard) "rendering permanent damage to ignorance."

With this truth in mind, upon having taken a person through deliverance ministry for the casting out of demons or the pronouncement of healing of sickness or disease, I often provide them with a grid for reading through the entire Holy Bible in a year. I also inform them that this has been a practice of mine since circa 2004, and I do it every other year. I encourage the congregants of the church where I pastor to do it too. We even give out Bible completion award certificates. In fact this year I finished within in six months and then started writing this book. I have found that a healthy, habitual practice of Bible study is one of the best means to maintain one's healing, deliverance, or breakthrough from the relentless attempts by demons to return to their former place of spiritual abode. Additionally, having a healthy command of Scripture energizes, enhances, and greatly impacts one's ability to pray, which is another very powerful means of maintaining deliverance.

Prayer

> Watch and pray, lest you enter into temptation. The spirit indeed is willing, but the flesh is weak. (Mark 14:38)
>
> Is anyone among you sick? Let him call for the elders of the church, and let them pray over him, anointing him with oil in the

name of the Lord. And the prayer of faith will save the sick, and the Lord will raise him up. And if he has committed sins, he will be forgiven. (James 5:14–15)

Of all the weapons of spiritual warfare at our disposal, in my experience prayer is the most powerful. God has providentially ordained prayer to be the means for us to bombard the heavenly realm. The forces of evil make every attempt possible to hinder and prevent believers from engaging in prayer. The chief reason is that prayer is God's chosen method for His children to summon Him in Heaven to address, resolve, and conquer every problem we may encounter here on Earth. Demonic forces also pull out all the stops to keep Christians from coming into agreement in prayer concerning situations, issues, or problems. Unlike many of us, demons know the truth and potency of the fact that when we seek God's face and favor in prayer, one of us can "chase a thousand" and two of us together can "put ten thousand" of God's enemies to flight. (Deut. 32:30) Unfortunately, far too many believers never develop a proficient or powerful prayer life, chiefly due to a lack of knowledge concerning just how effective prayer can be. Just think about this for a second: what happens just about every time you are alone and try to pray? It is not uncommon for demons to try to distract or dissuade us with drowsiness (spirits of sleep and slumber); interruptions by people, children, or pets; and on down the line. Most people are clueless that such phenomena are the works of demons warring against the soul and spirit to ultimately impact the physical body.

Sinful Procrastination
One the most effective hindrances to cultivating a healthy prayer life is the demonic spirit called procrastination, which deceives people into putting off until tomorrow that which God is moving in them to accomplish today. Or as one situation comedian once said, "Why put off until tomorrow what could be put off until the day after tomorrow?"—which is even worse. God

hates the sin of procrastination chiefly because it deceives people into believing that time is on their side when in fact it's not, for the Scripture says:

> Therefore, as the Holy Spirit says: "Today, if you will hear His voice, do not harden your hearts as in the rebellion, in the day of trial in the wilderness, where your fathers tested Me, tried Me, and saw My works forty years. Therefore I was angry with that generation, and said, 'They always go astray in their heart, and they have not known My ways.' So I swore in My wrath, 'They shall not enter My rest.'" (Heb. 3:7–11)

The spirit of procrastination moves its victim to presume they can do something whenever they feel like it, which is often not the case under God's divine providence. When God instructs us to do a particular thing now, it is sinful and stubborn disobedience to do it even five minutes later.

Friend, did you know that God has a sense of humor? I have personally witnessed God responding to my prayers in the exact same way that I responded to some of His directives. I can recall a few times when God specifically asked me to do something, and I took my time (which is really His time on loan to me) to do it when I felt like it, which in reality is disobedience. The very next time I prayed asking Him to do something for me, He let me know that it would be done when He felt like it! Needless to say, I have learned the value of immediate obedience when the Holy Spirit moves me to do something. This is especially true when I don't like what I am being told to do, I don't particularly feel like doing it, or I don't understand why He wants me to do it.

Powerful Ways to Pray: Asking, Seeking, and Knocking Prayer

> Ask, and it will be given to you; seek, and you will find; knock, and it will be opened to you. For everyone who asks receives, and he

who seeks finds, and to him who knocks it will be opened. (Matt. 7:7–8)

Asking Prayer

While there is a plethora of ways to pray, I am limiting this segment to just two that are specifically relevant and applicable to spiritual warfare. First, asking, seeking, and knocking prayer. Second, power and authority or command prayer, which is really not prayer but implementing God's divine power to command that which we have the *exousia* (right) and *denumis* (ability) to perform. One of the most effective ways to pray is knowing what God promises in His Holy Word, meeting his specific conditions to receive the promises, and then reminding Him of that which He solemnly promised. This is commonly called asking, seeking, and knocking prayer.

An excellent movie just premiered a few weeks ago called *War Room*. The movie delves into the awesome power of prayer as manifested by two of the lead characters' faith and routine practice of seclusion in their prayer closets (war rooms) to pray, asking, seeking, and knocking on Heaven's doors for God to answer their prayers. The entire movie centers on asking, seeking, and knocking prayer. However, there are two segments of the movie where two of the leading characters employ power and command prayer to stop a robber in his tracks and to cast Satan out of a marital home. Power and command prayer is the second means by which to pray and will be covered shortly.

God promises to give us wisdom if we ask in faith with absolute confidence (no doubting) that He will give it to us. (James 1:5) Wisdom is crucial in God's divine providence because giving Him reverence "is the beginning of wisdom and the knowledge of the holy is understanding." (Prov. 9:10) This form of prayer can be substantially enhanced and made exponentially even more powerful when people come into agreement, asking for the same things on one accord. Jesus promised:

...if two of you agree on Earth concerning anything that they ask, it will be done for them by My Father in heaven. For where two or three are gathered together in My name, I am there in the midst of them. (Matt. 18:19)

How awesome is this to know? If we pray alone, it is effective, but when we have at least one other person to agree with us on the exact same subject matter, Jesus then gets involved to supercharge our prayers to make sure they get answered! Wielding such knowledge and having solid belief and trust in the same is awesome for a Christian.

Here's an example of an asking prayer that I penned and first prayed on July 5, 2004, that has had exponential returns in my life: "Lord God, in the Name of Jesus Christ and in the power of the Holy Spirit, I pray that you strengthen my inner man according to the riches of your glory." This prayer was gleaned from my reading of Ephesians 3:16. This is a spiritual prayer that is completely devoid of anything material. I have come to learn that these are the kinds of prayers that really excite God on and move Him to respond with great dispatch.

Seeking Prayer
A meaningful personal relationship with God comes through humbly submitting to His Word, His Will, and His Ways. God promises to "lift [us] up" only after we "humble ourselves in the sight of the Lord." (James 4:10) This is something that does not haphazardly materialize. To the contrary we must earnestly seek it in spirit and in truth. Pride alienates us from God, while humility draws God's grace, mercy, and forgiveness, all of which are very important in being able to persevere through trials authorized by God and temptations from the devil himself. (Prov. 6:17–19, 15:33)

Having been personally delivered from a former lifestyle of arrogance and pride, this is a very important promise to me. It is particularly significant for those of us who have been formerly made captive by demons that enslave people into foolishly thinking more highly of themselves than they "ought to think." To the contrary the Bible instructs us to "think soberly, as God has dealt to each one a measure of faith." (Rom. 12:3) God further warns, "Pride goes before destruction, and a haughty spirit before a fall." (Prov. 16:18)

Accordingly those who have been delivered from former sinful attitudes and dispositions of the heart concerning pride can consult the relevant promises from God (which they have discovered from regular Bible study) and pray them back to God for continued protection from the enemy. This is just one of many examples of how implementing Scripture in our prayers can allow God to help us to maintain our deliverance from demonic powers and undue influences in our daily lives.

As I study the Bible, I look for how the saints of old overcame trials and tribulations in their efforts to live out their lives here on Earth. While I was reading through the entire Bible about eleven years ago, the Holy Spirit focused my attention on how the apostles prayed and the specific requests for which they petitioned God. I was immediately struck by the fact that they prayed for more Holy Spirit power to boldly witness, teach, and preach the gospel. Here's an example of a prayer I was led to adopt from the apostles in Acts 4:29–30 and from the Apostle Paul in Ephesians 6:19:

Prayer for Boldness to Witness

> Lord God, please give me Holy Spirit boldness to witness (speak) about the Gospel of Salvation, by stretching forth your mighty hand to Heal, Deliver, and perform Signs, Wonders, and Miracles through the name of your Holy, Righteous, and only begotten Son, Jesus of Nazareth, the Christ, in the omnipotent power of your Holy Spirit!

This is a seeking prayer in that it is requesting God to provide something to or for me as opposed to me utilizing God's supernatural powers to "command" something to come into fruition, which will be addressed shortly.

Knocking Prayer
Knocking prayer specifically relates to bombarding the heavenly realm for the release of benefits or blessings that will have a direct impact here on Earth. Knocking can relate specifically to sending up prayers to unblock paths, unlock doors, and open up pathways for us to be successful in specific endeavors. What happens on Earth is but a shadowy reflection of what takes place in Heaven. Although there are exceptions, the spirit realm influences, dictates, dominates, and otherwise controls what happens on Earth. Jesus explained it to his disciples back then and explains it to us today like this: "Assuredly, I say to you, whatever you bind on earth will be bound in heaven, and whatever you loose on earth will be loosed in heaven." (Matt. 18:18)

With this eternal truth in mind, it is vitally important that we understand the direct connection between what's transpiring on Earth and in Heaven. Having been heavily involved in deliverance ministry for so many years, I have seen patterns of mistakes that allow people to either go into bondage or wind up back in bondage after having been successfully delivered from evil. Such mistakes involve negative professions or declarations of doubt. For instance, there's an old cliché that says "I can't win for losing." Harboring such thoughts in one's mind will eventually cause them to proceed out of the mouth. Once such negative professions of doubt or unbelief escape the vocal cords and are released out into the spirit realm, they can negatively impact the declarant's life. Once such negativity has been released or "loosed," it will have whatever devastating impact Satan has prescribed for that individual and everyone under that person's authority. As you can discern, what we say has a positive or negative impact in both the natural and supernatural realms.

Approximately fifteen years ago, I read about a situation that was a classic but very unfortunate example of the negative powers that can be brought upon us by negative professions. There was a man who had a daughter who was deathly ill and dying. The father repeated several times that he would die if his daughter could live. In other words, his expressed desire was to take her place. If I correctly recall, afterward he was either struck by lightning and killed or was killed by other means, but his child wound up surviving and continued to live.

Power and Authority (Command) Prayer

> Jesus answered and said to them, "Have faith in God. For assuredly, I say to you, whoever says to this mountain, 'Be removed and be cast into the sea,' and does not doubt in his heart, but believes that those things he says will be done, he will have whatever he says. '"
> (Mark 11:22–23)

The second kind of prayer is power and authority prayer, which is really not praying but commanding that which we have been given permission to bring into fruition. Whereas asking, seeking, and knocking prayer solicits God to do something for us, power and authority (command) prayer is a "prayer" in which we implement the authority we have through the shed blood, death, burial, resurrection, and ascension of Jesus to do something for God. The two types of prayer fit hand in glove, for when we ask God to reveal our spiritual gifts and empower us to use them in faith, we can then manifest the truth of our answered prayers with power and authority (command) prayer.

If you pay very close attention to the Holy Bible, it is replete with symbiotic happenings between the natural realm involving mankind and the supernatural realm with the Father, Son, and Holy Spirit. God asks man to perform only that which is naturally possible, while God takes care of everything that would be impossible for mankind in the natural course of life.

For instance, God asked Moses to "stand still and see the salvation of the Lord" at the Red Sea, "hold up the staff," and speak. God's part was to miraculously force nature to obey the commands that Moses spoke in Exodus 14:15–18. All Moses was required to do was obey God's instructions. God said, "Lift up your rod, and stretch out your hand over the sea." God's part of this supernatural partnership was to "divide it." (Ibid.) God commanded Moses to "strike the rock" and "speak to the rock," but it was God who literally made the water come from each rock. (Exod. 17:6, Num. 20:8)

Likewise, with the miraculous resurrection of Lazarus from well over four days of death in a tomb, Jesus's part was to cancel death by restoring life, while the people's part was to obey His command to "take away the stone" so Lazarus could walk out and the people could witness what transpired inside the tomb. (John 11:39) Jesus could have moved, dissolved, or disintegrated the stone, but in His divine providential partnership with mankind, he limits our responsibilities to those things that are in the realm of our physical capabilities. Accordingly, when we commit to obey the Great Commission and preach (witness the gospel), cast out demons, speak with new tongues, and lay hands on the sick, it is assuring to know that God's part will be to actually cast the demons out, help us pray in the Holy Spirit, and heal the sick. (Mark 16:14–20) The following is an example of one of the most extreme cases of power and authority/command prayer I have ever personally experienced.

"Speak to the Wind"
One of my favorite means of exercise is long-distance road-bike riding. I sometimes ride twenty to forty miles at a time but sometimes over seventy. I also periodically ride in the National Multiple Sclerosis Society Bike MS (formerly called the MS 150), which is approximately eighty-five miles per day for two days from St. Augustine to Daytona Beach and back. Sometime after the Lord had placed me into power ministry, I was conducting an MS 150 ride on the way from St. Augustine to Daytona Beach. While traveling

southbound on the A1A, a very strong easterly was blowing against us. At my rate of travel, I surmised I would wind up in Daytona at least an hour and a half behind my usual time frame. Sometime between the first and second hour, the maximum speed of travel I could maintain was between thirteen and sixteen miles per hour, which was down from my usual of between nineteen and twenty-one miles per hour.

As I was struggling against powerful gusts of wind from the Atlantic Ocean, I heard a very still, small voice in the back of my mind saying, "Speak to the wind." I recall repeating what I heard and specifically remembering that it was scriptural and very close to when God commanded Moses to "speak to the rock before their eyes, and it will yield its water; thus you shall bring water for them out of the rock, and give drink to the congregation and their animals." (Num. 20:8) At first the spirit of doubt set in, making me second-guess whether I really heard what I thought I heard. I was trying to simply dismiss it, but the more I struggled, the more I wanted to believe it was true. The Holy Spirit then reminded me that Jesus promised:

> Most assuredly, I say to you, he who believes in Me, the works that I do he will do also; and greater works than these he will do, because I go to My Father. And whatever you ask in My name, that I will do, that the Father may be glorified in the Son. If you ask anything in My name, I will do it. (John 14:12–14)

I was struggling against that wind so much that I had nothing to lose. If I spoke to the wind as directed but nothing happened, then so what? On the other hand, if it worked getting to Daytona at a decent time would be a "breeze."

With this logic in mind, I very silently said words to this effect: "Wind, in the name of Jesus, I command you to shift directions and be behind our backs blowing toward Daytona." Nothing happened, which was not a big deal because I had no expectation that anything would happen. I had previously experienced miraculous healings of people with terminal illnesses and very powerful deliverances from some of the deadliest demons there are but had no experience in this area of power ministry.

Since nothing happened immediately after the declaration, I forgot about it. However, after approximately ten miles, I felt my legs naturally pedaling faster with much less effort than I had been expending over the last two hours or so. I had been riding with my head down and my body tucked, trying to avoid some of the headwinds, so I raised my head a little and noticed the miles per hour were climbing rather rapidly although my efforts were just about the same as they had been since we started. Then I looked up at the trees, and that's when I saw evidence of the miracle. The trees were now blowing back in the opposite direction than they had been all morning! I could not believe it, which sounds peculiar coming from one who has witnessed and experienced so many God-ordained signs, wonders, and miracles. Although I was witnessing a manifestation of Mark 11:22–26, whereby Jesus promises we can command mountains to move and they will obey, it was still kind of difficult to mentally process. I was in complete and utter awe.

No one else has to believe this, but I know as a matter of fact that it happened. The Holy Spirit later spoke to me about the fact that this was a demonstration of mustard-seed faith, which greatly shocked me. I had always (falsely) believed that mustard-seed faith was a great deal of faith. To the contrary, the Holy Spirit let me know that mustard-seed faith is simply obeying God's directives as they come regardless of whether we think they make sense or of what the ultimate outcome will be. Having and maintaining a spirit of obedience with regard to obeying godly instructions will substantially enhance one's ability to hold on to their deliverance.

Praying for an Hour
Early on in my discipleship as a Christian and before I became a minister, I

read *The Hour That Changes the World* by Dick Eastman, who also authored the bestseller *No Easy Road*. The core objective of the book is to value giving God back some of our time and to inspire us to actively pursue doing the same. Eastman defines prayer as "divine communication with our Heavenly Father." He elaborates, "Prayer does not require advanced education," neither is knowledge a "prerequisite to engage in it." He concludes, "Only an act of the will is required to pray."

The book is based upon Peter, James, and John's failure to remain awake to watch and pray after Jesus specifically asked them to do so. It centers on the exchange Jesus had with Peter, James, and John about their inability to obey His command for them to watch and pray with him for an hour while they were at Gethsemane. The actual exchange reads:

> Then He came and found them sleeping, and said to Peter, "Simon, are you sleeping? Could you not watch one hour? Watch and pray, lest you enter into temptation. The spirit indeed is willing, but the flesh is weak." (Mark 14:37–38)

The book inspires believers to learn how to systematically engage in meaningful prayer for an entire hour. I followed the suggested procedure in the book and began the process of periodically taking the time to pray for at least an hour. Whenever I do so, it's usually between 4:00 a.m. and 5:00 a.m. and includes praying naturally and supernaturally in tongues. There is no doubt whatsoever that this type of praying guards the heart, mind, will, and emotions from demonic temptations to sin or to return to old sinful habits from which one has been delivered. Here's an outline from Eastman's book that I often share with those who wish to enhance their prayer life:

Prayer Outline: *"The Hour That Changes the World* Praise
Waiting
Confession

Scripture praying
Watching
Intercession
Petition
Thanksgiving
Singing
Meditating
Listening
Praise

The only addition I use is praying in tongues, which is awesome when coupled with the foregoing prayer guide.

Fasting

Is this not the fast that I have chosen: To loose the bonds of wickedness, to undo the heavy burdens, to let the oppressed go free, and that you break every yoke? Is it not to share your bread with the hungry, and that you bring to your house the poor who are cast out; when you see the naked, that you cover him and not hide yourself from your own flesh? Then your light shall break forth like the morning, your healing shall spring forth speedily, and your righteousness shall go before you; the glory of the Lord shall be your rear guard. Then you shall call, and the Lord will answer: You shall cry, and He will say, "Here I am." (Isa. 58:6–9)

The third and final way that I have found to be exceptionally beneficial in maintaining one's deliverance is through Bible-based fasting. I say "Bible-based fasting" specifically because different people fast for different reasons, many of which are carnal in origin. However, Isaiah chapter 58 makes it crystal clear that fasting serves godly purposes, all of which directly relate to spiritual warfare and caring for the poor, needy, and less fortunate, all of whom are usually ravaged by Satan. I have found fasting to be very powerful both in preparing to take people through deliverance and in being insulated from reverberating demonic attacks thereafter.

Fasting is critical for those who conduct deliverance ministry because there are some demons that are so stubbornly entrenched and deeply rooted into people's family lines through generations that only sincere fasting coupled with prayer can dislodge them so they can be cast out. Mark chapter 9 describes a scenario involving some of the disciples finding it impossible to cast a "deaf and dumb spirit" out of a man's minor son. Feeling completely defeated after witnessing Jesus do with great ease that which they could not do collectively with much effort, the disciples privately asked Jesus, "Why could we not cast it out? So He said to them, 'This kind can come out by nothing but prayer and fasting.'" (Mark 9:28–29)

While there are many different kinds of fasts, the ones that I find most beneficial are those that crucify, mortify, or otherwise subdue the flesh. Man has a natural instinct to survive, and the best way to survive is via repetitive consumption of food and water as often as needed to satisfy hunger and quench thirst. However, when we abstain from such substances, our bodies tend to crave them and revolt against our efforts to hold back from the pleasures of eating and drinking. This is the basic premise of crucifying the natural fleshly desires to satisfy such natural urges.

Taking this principle into consideration, now let's extend it to anything else the physical body desires or has become accustomed to in any particular person's life. There are some people who would not have a problem going on a three-day absolute fast, which entails consuming absolutely nothing for three twenty-four-hour periods; or going seven days with only one meal per day or for twenty-one days as they see fit; or even going forty days with only liquid. However, they may not be able to stop watching their favorite sitcom on television, reading and posting on Facebook for an extended period of time, working out in the gym, power walking, consuming alcohol, smoking cigarettes, and on down the line. Accordingly when it comes down to fasting as a means to assist in one's overall efforts to persevere through trials and tribulations to maintain their deliverance, consulting the Holy Spirit as to what kind of fast to undertake tends to be the best practice. Translation: "If any of you lack wisdom, let him ask of God…" (James 1:5)

Abstaining from food weakens the physical body and consequently allows the spirit to gain strength, for the two tend to run contrary to each other. When one's flesh is in control, the spirit is almost completely subdued and therefore under the direction, power, and sometimes undue influence of the flesh, which has taken control of the physical body with its appetite for all things natural. Conversely, when the spirit of man has been energized and gains headship, the things of God will have preeminence in the person's life. Such a person will not be repulsed by prayer, Bible study, or extending acts of mercy and kindness to the less fortunate. Another benefit of allowing the spirit to be in control of the flesh is a greater ability to be not so easily offended by others, coupled with a supernatural enablement to forgive, admit fault, ask for forgiveness, or even share one's faith with family, friends, loved ones, coworkers, and sometimes complete strangers. Accordingly any one of these godly undertakings would be more than adequate to foster the maintenance of one's hard-fought deliverance from the powers of darkness.

Chapter 15

TESTIMONIES: DOMESTIC MISSION WORKS

So then, after the Lord had spoken to them, He was received up into heaven, and sat down at the right hand of God. And they went out and preached everywhere, the Lord working with them and confirming the word through the accompanying signs. Amen. (Mark 16:19–20)

The final two chapters contain actual testimonies of the demonstrated and awesome power God so freely gives to those who genuinely love Him and obey His commandments. While this chapter covers signs, wonders, and miracles wrought and experienced in domestic ministerial settings, the final chapter (16) addresses the same witnessed in foreign missionary works performed in West Africa in November 2013. The bulk of the testimonies in this chapter (15) are from those who received deliverance ministry (healing, deliverance, or godly assistance) and those who completed one of the spiritual gifts activation classes that are conducted in America. God has instructed and equipped many people over the past decade, some of whom have submitted testimonies particularizing situations that have transpired since their training.

While most of the testimonies in this chapter were sent to me via email, some were posted on my personal Facebook page, recorded on video or audio, or otherwise dictated by those who are not proficient in writing. Due to the delicate nature of this type of ministry, as you can imagine, most of the testimonies are anonymous. However, there are some who feel so thankful for what God did for them that they want their names included because they are not ashamed of the name of Jesus. These individuals are like many in the New Testament who could not remain silent after having experienced God's unfathomable love. Whether their names are revealed or not, each person wants to let the entire world know this undisputed fact: Jesus is still healing the sick, saving lost souls, and setting the captives free, both naturally and supernaturally, in accordance with Luke 4:18–19 and fulfilling Isaiah 61:1–2.

Before we get into the actual testimonies, I was moved by the Holy Spirit to use language from an email I received from the mother of an autistic child to explain why testimonies are so very important in Christianity.

The Importance of Testimonies by Ellen Gardner

> This is what I received in prayer after asking the Holy Spirit for a Word of Wisdom and a Word of Knowledge. Revelation chapter 19 is about "Testimony" and how our testimony is part of the gift of prophecy, the most important of the gifts according to the word of God. "…for the essence of prophecy is to give a clear witness for Jesus." (Rev. 19:10)
>
> Our testimony is absolutely critical because it invites others into the light of Christ and into the immortal life of salvation through Him. How can we accept Christ and offer a testimony to others if we do not accept, respond to, or acknowledge our given name or that we are made in the image of God? Of course, the

enemy doesn't want these individuals who are more sensitive to the Heavenly Realms to respond to their names. Satan wants to rob them of salvation and prevent their amazing, prophetic testimony, all with the goal of preventing the Great Commission from being fulfilled.

Ellen Gardner is the wife of Mitch Gardner, and they are blessed to have been chosen by God to be the parents of a very intelligent nine-year-old autistic child who communicates through typing on an iPad. They have allowed me to minister to their son, who is spiritually gifted on many levels. The Gardners have shown great progress on all fronts since having undergone a few brief sessions of deliverance ministry.

I am very appreciative of the special relationship we all have come to enjoy through the process of deliverance ministry. Ellen understands the importance of releasing one's testimony. In this regard I received her permission to include the word of wisdom and word of knowledge she shared with me about the significance of testimonies. No doubt every Christian should know how Satan particularly attacks those who are motivated to release their testimony. Since becoming so heavily involved in deliverance ministry, I have come to greatly appreciate how much of a powerful effect testimonies have on those who hear others sharing the reason for the hope they have specifically because of what God has done in them, with them, to them, or through them!

Deliverance from Defeatism, Oppression, and Torment by a Happily Married Man, October 3, 2014

I pray that this email finds you all and your congregation blessed. This is Pierre. My wife Drusilla and I are members of West Jacksonville Church of God in Christ. My wife recently attended that anointed class at your church. I am still enjoying this new level of freedom in praising God since my deliverance at the Friday night service you conducted at the end of the class. It would be an honor for you to use my testimony as an example to others of how, when the atmosphere is set and God is exalted, you can be set free and delivered. My desire is to use this new emancipation that I am currently experiencing to break the chains of others. Again I say that I thank God for you, and may God continue to bless you and yours.

Yours in Christ, Pierre

I truly want to thank God for the Spiritual Gifts Activation class taught by Pastor Barlow. I was not a student, just went to support my wife and others who graduated. In order for you to understand how this class revolutionized my life, I must give you a brief picture of what was going on prior to attending that Friday night class. I must also preface this brief testimony by saying that I have been saved, spirit-filled and operating in ministry for over 30 years, so I am not new to this walk. However, I somehow allowed the devil to subtly bind me up for quite a while because of some things that were going on in my wife's life and my adult children's lives. I began to feel like a failure as a husband and a father because I could not do the things I felt a man should do for his family. I had allowed myself to be emasculated to the point that I would not even pray, neither with my wife nor for myself. I was in a serious pity party spirit, just myself and the devil.

I thank God for a praying wife who hung in there with me anyway. Being a woman concerned about her husband, she began to seek help for me, even when I wouldn't do it for myself. I was in critical condition, and it was affecting my relationship with my wife. She began attending the Spiritual Gifts Activation classes at Pastor Barlow's church which lasted through the week with a graduation that Friday night. I decided that I would go and support her and the other graduates who were members of the church we attend. When the service began, Pastor Barlow started to flood and saturate the atmosphere with praise and worship music. The graduates began to pray all around the building, anointing the chairs and binding the enemy and the principalities.

I will never forget when I knelt down at my seat and began to sincerely pray and praise God from my heart, something that I had not done for a long time. The bondage I was in started quite some time ago. I tried to mask it with a smile and church jargon but inside, I was being carried away with condemnation. I knew the Word but could not activate it in my life. I, "the strong man," was bound as the Scripture said. That night something began to happen in me. The sounds of shofars were blowing with the music, and it was like Jesus himself had come down right beside me and told me, "I would never leave you nor forsake you." At that time something broke in me. It was as if chains were falling off of me, it was so real, I was finally free, right there on the spot (THANK YOU JESUS!!!!!!!!).

Well, when the service was coming to a close, Pastor Barlow asked did anyone have a testimony. Remember, I was only there to be a support to my wife and the others. I was not one of the students, so I said I will just keep my mouth closed and just tell what happened to my wife after it was over.

Little did I know that the Holy Ghost encounter that I just had was not going to let me sit there and not say something. Before I knew it, I had gotten Pastor Barlow's attention and asked him if I could testify. He graciously allowed me to, and that's when the tears began to flow. I felt a boldness that I hadn't felt in a long, long time, and to this day it has gotten even stronger. God has restored my marriage, and we are not only praising God together like we were accustomed to doing, but we are praying together like we used to. We are now on the offense for God and not the defense. He has not only risen but He is REAL.

Deliverance from Great Fear and Crippling Anxiety by CMS, a pupil of Spiritual Gifts Activation Class, Fall 2014
As a child I remember being fearful and full of anxiety. As I got older, I did not go places like the store, the mall, the post office, or anywhere by myself. I was perfectly okay when I was with another person. Doctors told me I had social anxiety disorder and that I would need to take medication in order

to remove the feelings that kept me from completing necessary tasks in life. Refusing to take the medication was like refusing to participate in life. I was unable to do a lot of things because of how crippling the anxiety and fear were in my life. I didn't know much about God, but I knew I didn't need a pill to live out my life. I avoided phone calls, people, and conversations. I did not attend my high school graduation or my college graduation because I was gripped with fear and anxiety; the thought of walking on a stage in front of people for the short time it would take was too much for me to even consider.

As an adult, after being saved and beginning my walk with Christ, I was still controlled by these feelings. I got comfortable going to church and could sit amid the crowd. I felt it was a major accomplishment to be able to stand up, praise, and worship God without having a visible panic attack.

While taking the spiritual gifts activation class, I purposely came an hour early to sit in solitude in the parking lot to mentally prepare. I needed to do this to avoid having any visible panic attack in front of or around the other people in the class. During this class I was given a microphone to share a testimony with the rest of the class. I was amazed by God and full of comfort knowing that He had confirmed His Word, and it is only right to testify about His goodness. I stood before the class in tears, with my head in my hands, while trembling and shaking, realizing this was the panic attack I had been trying to avoid and I'm in front of the entire class with no way to escape. For everyone else it was a piece of cake to take the microphone stand before others and talk freely. But for me this was like a deathly plague I had been avoiding my entire life, and I was staring it in the face. So I told myself the only way out of this situation was to give my testimony, and then I could go sit down. So quickly I stated my testimony and rushed back to my seat. I thought it would be over, but I sat there feeling like I was being completely consumed by fear and anxiety in a way that I would never recover from if I left and did not deal with this issue head-on.

After class I went to Pastor Barlow to seek prayer and deliverance. He had me to confess, renounce, and cast fear out of my spirit. After it was all said and done, I remember driving home wondering what had just happened. I felt so strange; I thought something was wrong. I felt like I was floating and so light that I could fly away. I thought, "Okay, something is wrong. I don't know what just happened." I said, "Lord am I okay?" The Holy Spirit reminded me quickly that I had never felt this way before because I had been dealing with the spirit of fear and anxiety since childhood. When it was gone, I did not recognize the freedom because I had never known what it truly felt like. The next day at class, I VOLUNTEERED to walk in front of the class, with the microphone, to share the testimony of this miraculous deliverance. For me to have done this was a miracle!!!!!!!!! I did not cry, shake, tremble, or feel any other way besides free and at ease. In the thirty-three years I've been living, I had never been free from fear or anxiety. I stood in amazement at God's work, and to this day, I still can't believe it's real. I'm free; I can go places alone, hold conversations with people, and go in public places without feeling like my heart is going to break out of my chest!!! I thank God for deliverance!! God is awesome, and I am FREE!!!!

Deliverance from Lust and Fornication by Anonymous

I just listened to the sermon from Sunday. God's message through you really has me spiritually full. This is something that I needed to hear. I was in a dark place as well before. I heard a pastor say how he worries about his members. He wondered if his members were getting the message. He worries about their salvation. Well, let me kill two birds with one stone in this email. I used to worry so much about pleasing people. I now worry about pleasing God. I remember the pastoral discussion we had about the sin that I was in a while ago. You told me that "We all fall; it's not how you start but how you finish." Those words stuck with me. I have been Healed and Delivered from sins of Fornication and Adultery. I asked God to take these away and create in me a clean heart, and He did just that. As Christians we know when

God shows up, He shows out! Before my miraculous Deliverance, I was in so much sin I didn't even recognize myself! I was infected and infested with demonic spirits of Lust and Deception.

I stopped hearing from God at that time, and my life became very difficult because I really needed Him. When I was finally delivered from my rebellious and sinful lifestyle, I saw just what I looked like to God through your eyes as my pastor. Wow, God is so amazing! He showed me myself and what I was doing to Him. Now I fully realize that when I was wallowing in sin, I greatly disappointed my Heavenly Father.

Finally, and most importantly, I am in a different spiritual place today and I truly thank God for bringing me to this new walk with Him! I talk about God to everyone who will listen, even the ones that don't. I love Him and want to continue to be a "sweet-smelling savor to him." Thank you, Pastor Barlow, for doing the things that you do and teaching the way that you teach.

First Time Speaking in Tongues by KG

I attended a spiritual gifts activation class in 2013 with Pastor Barlow. The class went very well even from the very first day. I received a word of knowledge that my left hand would be used to heal. I saw this come to pass the very next class. Moreover, I always wanted to "speak in tongues" so as to have intimate one-on-one prayer sessions with God. I was very humble as I prayed and asked God to give me the gift of speaking in tongues. At the end of the class, we had a healing and deliverance service, at which I received a chance to help with healing a man who had been recently released from prison and was suffering from "double mindedness." I felt the power of the Holy Spirit in the church as we praised God for the healing testimonies. The Holy Spirit was so high that I was still praising God when I went to my car after the service had ended.

I was thanking God for everything that he had ever done for me throughout the course of my entire life. As I began to praise Him alone in my car, I began to speak other languages. I heard these words come out of my mouth as though I knew how to speak these languages. The words just flowed out of my mouth. It was clear that I was speaking to God, and he spoke back to me. He was speaking to my soul. He made me laugh like no one else had ever made me laugh. After that experience I felt a peace that came over me like nothing that I have ever felt. This peace was the comfort of the Holy Spirit. This peace was just what I needed in my life at the time. The spiritual gifts activation class and the healing and deliverance service greatly changed my life. Hallelujah!

Instant Pain Relief from Chronic Spinal Arthritis by S., August 26, 2014

I attended my very first healing and deliverance service, officiated by pastor/attorney Alvin Barlow, and his message was about the power that God has given us. His message was soul-wrenching powerful, and I listened with all the faith and belief that is inside me. I have known God all my life, but I didn't always seek His guidance. Well, the words Pastor Barlow said in his message have changed my life.

I am a proud and happy Episcopalian, and many people believe that the service is DEAD because there is no whooping and shouting. We believe in Jesus, and our pastor delivers a powerful sermon every Sunday that speaks to my heart and soul. He is a masterful teacher of the word, if you listen. I just want to make that part known.

I had to understand that it is important for me to believe and have faith in myself and the power that God has given me. Pastor Barlow reinforced what my pastor has been telling me all along. Then something happened, and God's grace filled me with understanding and the Holy Spirit, and Jesus's love went through my body like a lightning streak. All I could do was cry and praise God for ALL His blessings.

After the message I was led by the Holy Spirit to stand in line for Pastor Barlow to pray for and bless me. I told him that I had spinal arthritis. He touched my neck, shoulders, and all the way to my lower back. He told me that he was not healing me, but if I had faith and belief in God's power within me, the pain would decrease, and when it did, just say, "Thank you, Jesus." Returning to my seat, I started thanking God for all the blessings He gives me. Then I realized that I had NO pain at all. At that point I raised my hands to God and said (out loud): "Thank you Jesus," and I have been thanking Him since Tuesday.

Wednesday I woke up, and I am blessed to say that I had NO pain that inhibited my walking or balance. I am confessing, testifying, and believing in my healing through the power of the Lord Jesus Christ within me. This is my testimony, and I am blessed to share it with you. I give God all the glory for what He has and is doing for me.

Thank you, Jesus, for my healing.
Thank you, Jesus, for my believing.
Thank you, Jesus, for my deliverance.

Spiritual Gifts Activated by CS
I'm writing this now because I went to the Healing and Deliverance Service you held tonight. I am just getting settled in at home, and there are so many things that God did tonight. I felt led to write them down right now and send this to you. Primarily, I have been really struggling with whether or not I am headed in the right direction occupationally or if I just missed God completely, even though I feel like I have received confirmation over and over again. So when I purposed to come to the service, I was seeking clarity on that subject along with some other things, and I summed it up with just feeling stuck.

(1) When I got to the church tonight, immediately it's like my Spiritual Gifts were "activated." I saw visions of multiple chains breaking and exploding simultaneously, and one major demonic ruling spirit being obliterated. Then the song "Break Every Chain" began playing. I felt like just in that moment I was starting to remember what freedom felt like. Then

Fighting in Faith

when you began to speak, you spoke about chains breaking and obliteration of demonic spirits. After the word of God, I sat for deliverance and healing. During that time I was asked about pain in my body, and I said my arms, and during that prayer the Lord had you address my shoulders and neck as well as my arms, and I just had a procedure done on my neck two weeks ago, and it had been bothering me since! I don't know how I forgot about that, but God addressed it during the prayer! Essentially, I felt the Lord strategically had those SPECIFIC people there tonight, and after getting home the more and more I felt like it was a total setup from God for me to be there tonight.

(2) The young lady that sat behind us that was there tonight…oddly enough we recently saw each other this week. Tonight I was wearing the same exact clothes/outfit I had on Tuesday when I saw her. She recognized me and I recognized her. After we finally discovered we had just seen each other at the dentist office where she works, we began talking. So upon walking in the church, initially not really knowing what to expect, the spirit of anxiety never had a chance to bind me. She and I began talking, and it put me at ease although I don't know her. I didn't feel like I was in a room full of strangers. The miracle was that at that dentist appointment, God spoke to me.

(3) My mom had freaked out saying my daughter's top two permanent teeth were coming out. They are super loose, and she insisted they were her permanent teeth. I made an emergency appointment even though I didn't feel like that was right, but for the sake of avoiding confrontation, I just made the appointment. When I called to make the appointment, the lady said, "Those sound like baby teeth." I said, "No, my mom says they are permanent, and there is a really big gap; even if they are baby teeth, we still want her checked out." So I get there on Tuesday, and the doctor says they are officially baby teeth, everything is on schedule, and the gap is a good thing because when the permanent teeth move in they have the room they need.

In that moment God spoke to me, saying that day in the store when my mom freaked out telling me those teeth were permanent…they were always baby teeth, even when she said that they were not baby teeth. The truth never changed. The only thing that changed was my belief of the truth! I knew my child hadn't lost any baby teeth on her top row yet, but instead of "OPENING MY MOUTH" and saying that then, I folded and agreed with an untruth just to avoid confrontation, knowing it wasn't the truth. The Lord said, "Learn how to open your mouth."

So when I saw this lady and we remembered we saw each other at the dentist, boom, I remembered what God had said. Then you spoke about how the devil wants to shut our mouths and keep us quiet.

(4) This morning upon waking, I heard the Lord say, "Stand still… be still." I was really thinking like, "What does this mean, God?" I also have been feeling like I'm neither adequate nor in good enough shape to pray for or minister to others. Then the young man up front spoke about standing still after you had spoken about standing still before a judge while handling a case in court. I remembered these were the same words God said to me this morning. Also, while he was praying for me, the young man mentioned he wondered if he was in the position to be praying for someone else, and He said the Lord told him He was present, and that was enough. The Lord used him to say, "Being present and continuing to hear the word of God is enough," even when you don't feel like you are the one who is supposed to be praying for others. I felt just like that, and it was like God spoke directly to me with that as well. This was one of the issues I have been dealing with lately.

(5) When I attended the Spiritual Gifts and Activation class, the same woman God used to speak just one word to me about my future occupation was there tonight as well. It was like God was saying I already confirmed with the word "Chaplain," the direction I am headed in, and just seeing her was His way of addressing my concerns about being uncertain in that regard. It brought me instant clarity; when I saw her, she said, "I told

you what you were supposed to be doing already."

(6) I have been feeling like I haven't really been hearing God speak lately, but you and the man in the front row confirmed what I heard God say this morning, the lady behind me reminded me of what God said to me on Tuesday, and the woman that testified about her friend's healing reminded me of when God spoke to me last October. Clearly God is still speaking to me, and He had all those people there to point that out.

(7) I gave an offering tonight; I emptied out everything I had in my wallet, and before I walked out of the church, a woman handed me back the same amount I had put in the offering, so at this point I'm like, really, God? I have been stingy on my offerings lately because I'm not working, and I was trying to be "wise," but the Lord cleared that up for me tonight as well. Wisdom is letting him do what He does best, taking a little and turning it into enough!

(8) Driving home, I felt like I did the first time I went through the deliverance there; God showed me what freedom felt like, this time I recognized it and knew I felt free!

OK, that was all my miracles from God on tonight. I was excited and encouraged that God is still with me, and just like the teeth, the truth hasn't changed. I am grateful to God, and I thank you for your obedience, and every one of those people that were there probably have no idea how God used them just through their presence.

OK, that's all, hope it all makes sense!

Good evening, Pastor and First Lady Barlow,

CS

Deliverance Poem: "Spiritual Self-Defense" by Candace Spicer
Control, manipulation, deception, wasn't clear
But I did acknowledge always bringing up the rear
Filled with bitterness and anger, resentment and disdain
Blaming everyone around yet, only I could feel the pain

As long as I believed that I never played a part
The enemy could slowly infiltrate my heart
We know what's in the heart, will come out in what we say
I had decreed and I declared, that my life would stay this way
Now please don't get me wrong, I love the lord, I love to pray
But the devil is truly seeking to devour whom he may
About the time I realized, that Jesus had won the fight
I decided I would not lose any sleep…not another night
I told God that I would stand for Him, if He would show me how
And the Bible says the Holy Spirit, with Him, He will surely endow
So I said yes to God, to His will, and to His ways
And I immediately received, my requested, training days
He led me to a course, I said yes sir, I will go
Taught by an earthen vessel…Pastor A. W. Barlow
God used this man to show me, to confess, and to renounce
To break off all agreements…and cast unclean spirits out
In Jesus's name of course, we want God to get His glory
This training set me free and so I need to share my story
The anger and the fear and every hindrance that I had
No longer had the power, to frustrate me, or make me mad
This freedom comes with maintenance, so when faced with some oppression,
I can tell these spirits where to go and teach them all a lesson
I now walk in the authority, given to me by my Christ Jesus
To God be all the Glory, because He's the one that frees us!

Daughter Takes Mother Through Deliverance After Taking Spiritual Gifts Activation Class by CS and CS

Good evening, Pastor Barlow,

I know it is late, but I was excited to share another testimony with you. I witnessed something I never thought I would see happen! Earlier today, I was on the phone with my mother as I was driving and running some errands. I can't recall how we began talking about her and the need for deliverance. Either way, by the time I got home, my mother and I sat in the living room. I prayed and allowed the Holy Spirit to take over. My mom wanted to go through the deliverance process (that I learned in the Spiritual Gifts Activation Class), and I discerned she was ready to do so.

We sat for about four hours or so through the process. Although I was semi hesitant, I took confidence in God that He was going to do whatever needed to be done. My mother and I have never had a good relationship. As matter of fact, if she were neither my mother nor I her child, I'm certain we would have left each other a long time ago. Anyway, after her deliverance session had ended, I asked my mom if she wouldn't mind writing how she felt, and a testimony of the process and all. This is what she had to say:

> In the past I have always been in control. I have always had to or had the feeling of always having to put out the fires of all the issues that came up from all the people around me. It started in my early childhood and continued throughout life. There was a time around twenty-nine years ago where it seemed like people would bring me their problems. Ranging from people I knew to people I didn't know. I was developing a pattern of becoming the shoulder everyone leaned on. I had not realized that I was carrying the weight of other people's burdens. I had not realized that resentment, anger, bitterness, and hatred and a number of other things had developed in my heart, and that this was only adding more to the weight already on my shoulders.
>
> My daughter and I both took the Spiritual Gifts Activation, Healing, and Deliverance class offered by Pastor A. W Barlow. After the second night of the training, I was at home in my room praying, and I began to speak in Tongues and had an energy that I had not had in years. A couple weeks after the training was over,

my daughter began talking to me about areas that I was still in need of deliverance and that she was willing to walk me through the process when I was ready.

However, the history between me and my children, and more specifically this particular daughter, has been one that has left me feeling pain, anguish, frustration, bitterness, detachment, impatience, and probably led to my having a hardened heart. I made the decision that I would trust God to work through my daughter and that I would receive total deliverance.

My daughter held my hands, and for the first time we prayed together as she led in prayer. We began the deliverance process as taught by Pastor Barlow. The Lord revealed forty-one areas of unrighteousness that needed to be addressed. It was while renouncing and breaking agreement with unforgiveness that I began to cough, and I felt a tightening and a squeezing in my throat. After forgiving a list of people from my past and present, I began to feel something like an intense electrical current running through my legs, my arms, and my entire body. As the deliverance process continued, I became more and more relaxed. I confessed to a number of things that were hindering me from truly experiencing God and His love.

After the process was completed, I felt calm and at peace, a NEW kind of peace that I HAD NEVER FELT! I could tell the weight that had accumulated in my life that I was carrying around for forty-three years had been lifted instantaneously! A few hours after the process, I was talking with my daughter. I realized that my daughter and I were having the first conversation we have had in twelve years without any anger or tension. She asked me if I could describe how I felt in one word, what word would I use, and I said well…calm…relaxed…peaceful…so if I have to choose just one word I would say FREE!

I THANK God for the training given by Pastor Barlow, I thank God that Elder Freeman from our church invited me to the training, and I thank God for my daughter! Who would have ever guessed that one of the people I disliked the most would be who God used to bring about my deliverance! To God be the Glory!"

Healed of Fibromyalgia by Kathleen

To Whom It May Concern,

My name is Kathleen. I attended one of Pastor Barlow's healing services in September of 2014. I had been given a diagnosis of fibromyalgia as far back as 1990. I was told it has no known cure and that I would have to adjust my life to accommodate this debilitating disease, as well as take a prescription drug for the rest of my life to just try to manage the excruciating pain it causes.

While at the service, Pastor Barlow asked if anyone was suffering with pain. My hand shot up without my even realizing I had even responded. He asked me to come forward and take a seat or stand if I preferred. He asked me where the pain was located. I told him it went from my neck and into my entire back. We prayed, he prayed, and then he laid hands on my affected area of my back. It was swollen and the pain was constant; however, while his hand was on me and he prayed, I felt something similar to little tiny needles all through my back and neck. I literally felt the swelling go away. I could move and had no pain for the first time in many, many years. Jesus has healed me, and I no longer require medication, and the inflammation that previously would show up on a blood test (similar to rheumatoid arthritis) is GONE.

I praise the Lord for leading me to a true Jesus-believing Pastor who still knows that we are able to call on His name and be set free from any negative thing that evil would have us believe.

In Christian Love,
Kathleen, Jacksonville, Florida

Blessing and Praying for "Enemies" by Anonymous

I was recently threatened by someone to whom I owed a certain sum of money. Although I told this person I would pay it as soon as I could, I was stalked and repeatedly threatened with great bodily harm and even death if I didn't pay the money ASAP. I consulted with Attorney Barlow for counseling and advice and was quite surprised with his response. I was advised that the person threatening me needed salvation and was being spiritually tormented. The counsel was that I should start praying for this person. I was specifically told to pray that this person's spiritual eyes would be opened to the fact that Satan was using him to his own detriment. Finally, he said I should pray for this person's soul so that this person would be delivered from permanent separation from God in Hell and ultimately the lake of fire.

To be honest, this was not the kind of response I expected from an attorney and counselor-at-law. However, I reluctantly obeyed his advice. To my great surprise, I was soon thereafter approached by this same person with a completely different mindset and disposition. The same person who previously wanted to hurt or even kill me is now telling me how sorry he is for having threatened me and how much he genuinely cares for me. The bottom line in this situation is that there is tremendous spiritual power in blessing those who curse you and praying for those who spitefully use you. If I had not experienced this situation myself, I would not have believed it. I thank God for using Attorney and Minister Barlow to serve Him by ministering to me in such a unique and powerful way.

Mammogram Examination Testimony by Cassandra D. Barlow, May 27, 2014

GOD STILL HEALS, Hallelujah!

A month ago I had my annual mammogram, and my doctor's office called me to say there was "suspicious" tissue on my right breast X-ray, and to return for a breast deep tissue ultrasound exam. That night I performed a self-exam, and I felt two lumps on the right breast that I had not noticed before. I then recalled feeling slight pain in that breast a few weeks earlier but ignored it. Well, it was six days between the call and the follow-up exam. During that time, I only told one or two prayer warriors (named Tony and Jewel Salter and one or two others) to go before God's throne with me. I fasted, prayed, and my husband, Alvin Wellington Barlow Sr., anointed me with Holy Oil and called on Jesus as Jehovah Rapha, to heal me, and we TRUSTED GOD!

A day later I went to bed and tried to sleep on my stomach, but that lump made it impossible. So I cried and barely slept that night. Those were the longest six days of my life. I had the faith that God was going to heal me but through chemotherapy or, if necessary, mastectomy. I believed He was going to heal me; I had faith that this cancer was leaving me with man's help. Two days after we anointed me, I still felt these two lumps, and I was very sad. My husband told me to stop examining myself and to hold on to my faith. Well, can you say Jehovah Rapha, the God who heals? When I returned in six days for the exam, I was nervous but strong in faith that this "cancer" was going to be healed, but through medicine. Well, after the X-ray, I was told to wait for the doctor to call me back to view my X-rays.

When they called me back, they said, "Here are your X-rays from two weeks ago, and here are your X-rays from today." There was an obvious enlarged something on the first X-ray and a very clean, beautiful, spot-free X-ray the second time." The doctor said it was negative and therefore it must have been a false reading.

So I went home and performed the self-exam again. Need I tell you that the two lumps were gone, that God moved them? I know in my heart that God healed me of breast cancer, and it was from fasting, praying, and believing and the fact that the lumps were totally gone! It was not a false reading but a true healing! God did it without modern medicine, wow! God is awesome and full of surprises. It felt like Christmas morning to me. God has such an engaging personality. He surprised me really good with this one. I had to look up at Him and smile. He wants our time and attention, just like our significant others do! He wants to show Himself mighty through us. Please give Him access to your heart!

Delivered from Death While at the Hospital by Anonymous

I was involved in an accident that left me near death. My body was all messed up, and my kidneys were failing. I was near the end, given my pre-existing condition of being HIV positive. I had been checked into the hospital, and they were beginning to treat me. I was totally messed up, in very bad condition due to the accident, AIDS, failing kidneys, and a myriad of other serious conditions.

Surprisingly, Minister Barlow showed up in my hospital room. He anointed me with oil and prayed for me after having asked my doctor what was wrong with my body. The doctors told him that I had only a very short time to live.

God moved! I totally recovered, was in good shape, and left the hospital within a few days after the healing and deliverance session. I had been in the hospital for about two weeks before he showed up. All of my conditions turned around for the good after Minister Barlow anointed my head and prayed. I was near death! Without God intervening through Minister Barlow, I probably would have died, just like the doctors were telling me before God delivered me. To God be the Glory!

The Ministerial Side of This Awesome Testimony by Pastor A. W. Barlow

This is one of the many deliverances that I have been blessed to perform that will always be dear to my heart. This one actually took place many years before I became a pastor. It is significant, particularly because it demonstrated how God providentially sends us to those who are in need. This is the same young man who is mentioned in chapter 13 and whom God used me to lead to confess faith in Jesus as his personal savior and to later take through deliverance from the spirit of homosexuality.

My wife and I wanted to take our daughter (who was between four and five at that time) to a theme park. Our choices were Disney World, only two hours from our home, or a theme park in another state that's well over a four-hour drive. Our daughter had already been to Disney World, so we thought it might be a good idea to take her to the other park. Within approximately two hours from the time we left home, I received a call from this young man telling me he was in a hospital and the doctors were saying he had only a very short time to live. In this regard he was calling family and close friends, saying his final goodbyes. It just so happened we were travelling to the same city where he was hospitalized. Let me stop right here and rebuke Satan in the name of Jesus for moving me to write what I just wrote. As you will shortly discern, it was not by happenstance or coincidence that we were traveling to the same city where he was hospitalized but by God's divine providence!

I specifically recall the Holy Spirit restraining me from telling him I just happened to be headed to the very city where he was. Although it was particularly difficult, I obeyed the Holy Spirit and did not tell him. The Holy Spirit further instructed me to continue to talk to him periodically on the phone and encourage him but to spend quality time with my family the rest of that day (which was a Friday) and all day Saturday, but then pay him a surprise visit early Sunday morning before returning to Florida. This was some very wise advice that allowed me to not detract from our family trip, which I'm sure could have caused some issues had I allowed his situation to pull me away from my family when we were on a family getaway. I really appreciate the word of wisdom from the Holy Spirit on this very important matter.

Word of Wisdom

As previously stated, a word of wisdom is spiritual advice, direction, or instruction from the Holy Spirit to bring about godly and righteous results. It is through such means that God orders our steps and directs our paths to achieve His righteous purposes. In this particular case, God was spiritually advising me to continue having fun and relaxing with my family. In other words, He was letting me know that He would not allow this young man to die before I had a chance to minister to him on Sunday before it would be time for me to return home. I have to admit that my first mind was to interrupt our plans, immediately go to that hospital upon our arrival, and minister to him. However, as I reflect back, the same would have interrupted our plans, probably put me in a less-than-festive mindset, and therefore hindered our plans to simply relax and have fun together as a family. Fortunately I obeyed the Holy Spirit's directives, refrained from telling him I was headed his way, and just enjoyed quality time with my family.

Sunday Morning
I arose very early that Sunday morning and prayed. My plans were to go to the hospital, minister to the young man, and return in time to make the designated time to check out of our hotel. Upon leaving the hotel, I went to a nearby grocery store and purchased a bottle of virgin olive oil. Just prior to driving out of the parking lot, I opened the bottle and stuck my right index finger in the top of the bottle until the tip of my finger touched the oil and the opening of the bottle was tightly wrapped around my finger so that no oil could escape. I then prayed in the spirit (tongues) all the way to the hospital, which was no less than fifteen miles or so away. I located his room, walked in, and greatly surprised him. For a minute I thought he was about to go into cardiac arrest, as he was just that shocked that I was actually in his hospital room. I then explained the godly providence of the entire weekend in that I was on the way to that particular city to spend the weekend there when I received his call two days prior. I also explained that the Holy Spirit told me not to worry because he would still be alive on Sunday—and he was.

A Conversation with the Treating Physician
As we talked, his main treating physician arrived to check on him. I asked for and received permission from him to speak with the doctor about his diagnosed conditions and why she believed he was dying. Receiving his authority to speak with the treating physician was very important for the type of deliverance ministry I was planning to perform on him. His doctor said the main issues were that he was HIV positive and that his immune system was insufficient to protect him from bacteria and other matters that were negatively affecting his system. As a consequence, she said, just about everything was shutting down in his system, which would ultimately lead to his death within a very short period of time. She said it could range from forty-eight hours to a week or two at the very most. I asked the doctor about her faith. While pointing upward, she said she believes the "man upstairs" controls everything and has the last say. Although she said this, I discerned that she was not at all comfortable with expressing her personal views on God, religion, or her personal faith—for which I had respect back then and still do now. However, the Holy Spirit was moving me to ask the doctor these questions for strategic reasons.

The Intervention of the Holy Spirit
The Holy Spirit moved within me to ask the doctor a few very specific questions, write down the answers, and then declare and decree the same over this young man's life, which would allow him to live. This was a very specific word of wisdom and a prophecy. The word of wisdom was for me to inquire of the doctor, write down the answers, and then declare and decree them over his life. The prophecy was that the result of having done so would be that he would live.

After having heard the word of wisdom and the prophecy, I spoke these words: "Doc, if you could speak to each and every area of his body that's not functioning properly and command them to do what they need to do so that he would live, what would you say?" She went down a laundry list of where each of his vitals should be, such as his heart rate, blood pressure, glucose, and several others, all of which I cannot recall. Unfortunately I no longer have that list, or I could share the rest. I meticulously jotted down everything she said. After she finished with him and left the room, I immediately placed the sheet of paper with the notes on his chest, opened my Bible, pulled out the olive oil, and asked for and received his permission to both anoint and pray over him. This was very important because it is by the volitional exercise of our free will that we can either be blessed by God or cursed by Satan and his demons.

A Word of Knowledge—The Presence of Unconfessed Sin
Before attempting to be used by God to affect any healing in the man, the Holy Spirit moved me to first address all unconfessed sin in his life. This was a very powerful word of knowledge informing him that a great part of his problems was due to the vestiges of un-renounced sin. In brief review, a word of knowledge is a fact or specific information that is either in the past or the present as opposed to the future, which would be pure prophecy.

After having received this word of knowledge about the presence of unconfessed sin in his life, I specifically asked if he had any sin in his life either in the past or the present which he had yet to confess, renounce, and break agreement with. I specifically informed him that unconfessed sin blocks blessings, hinders healing, and delays deliverance! I quoted 1 John 1:9–10, in which God solemnly promises, "If we confess our sins, He is faithful and just to forgive us our sins and to cleanse us from all unrighteousness. If we say that we have not sinned, we make Him a liar, and His word is not in us."

He then specified many areas of sin and unrighteousness in his life, the chief of which was having lived a lifestyle of prideful homosexuality. This was the chief cause of him being HIV positive, which in turn caused his bodily functions to be in such rapid decline that it was facilitating his demise. Under the very tender guidance of the Holy Spirit, I had him confess, renounce, break agreement with, and cast out every previously unconfessed sin the Holy Spirit brought back to his remembrance. This part of his deliverance session entailed him saying the following:

"I confess that I have sinned by _____."
"I renounce the sin of _____."
"I break agreement with the sin of _____."
"Sin of _____, come out in the name of Jesus."

In my opinion, it is a critical error to try to minister healing of sickness or disease without first at least inquiring of the Holy Spirit (in prayer) as to whether any unconfessed sin is anchored in the person's soul. By the way, in the "things of God," disease simply means "dis-ease" of whatever the world, the flesh, and/or the devil is manifesting in one's life. Concerning mental illnesses, there is "dis-ease" of the mind, will, and emotions until God delivers His peace that surpasses our very limited understanding. With regard to physical illnesses, one is placed "at ease" when healing is effectuated through God's awesome, miraculous, and unlimited power.

With the ultimate goal of allowing one to maintain their deliverance, it is of vital importance to address whether there are any sinful propensities, stubborn negative habits, or wicked proclivities that could potentially move a person to revert back to sin after they have experienced a healing or deliverance breakthrough. Such negative circumstances often lead to much worse symptomology and can often lead to the person's death. (See Matthew 12:43–45 and Luke 11:24–26.)

Power Ministry via Prayer Command
Once the deliverance segment of ministry was completed, I quickly transitioned to the healing segment. Speaking out loud, I read everything the doctor said needed to change and the specific level at which it needed to be

for him to live. Each declaration was either preceded or followed by these very powerful words and Holy Bible–based declaration: "In the name of Jesus." I never asked God, Jesus, or the Holy Spirit to do anything. To the contrary I was being specifically obedient to several passages of Scripture where God promises that we can perform signs, wonders, miracles, healings, and deliverances "in Jesus's name." (Mark 9:38–39, Mark 11:22–26, Mark 16:15–20, Luke 9:49–50, Luke 10:17–20, and Acts 1:8)

Although I can't recall the specific blood pressure level the doctor said he needed to have in order to live, I commanded it to be at the level she specified. For example, it would have been like this: "Blood pressure, in the Holy Name and through the righteous shed blood of Jesus of Nazareth the Christ, I command you to be at __ over ____, no more and no less." I methodically went down that entire list until each and every thing the doctor stated had been declared and decreed out loud into the spirit realm. In particular I had Luke chapter 10 verses 1–20 and Mark chapter 16 verses 15–20 in my mind as I was ministering in such a way as I had never been used by the Holy Spirit before this very unique scenario.

The Miraculous Healing and Deliverance

After completing both the deliverance and the healing ministry, I left the hospital, went back to the hotel, checked out, and drove back home, which took approximately five hours. Within about an hour after we got home, the young man called asking, "What did you do to me?"

I said, "What do you mean? You were right there; you saw everything I did."

He then said, "I want to know what you did because I feel so different than I did before you came." He went on to say that he had energy that he had not had before he went through that prayer session.

The bottom line is that he went from having been pronounced all but dead to having made a complete recovery in a few days, after which he was discharged from the hospital. That was well over ten years ago, and this middle-aged man is still alive, living a very healthy, Christian, heterosexual (albeit celibate) life and praying for a wife!

God's Awesome Providence
God's providence was surely at work in this very unique case. After his healing, deliverance, and restoration, I was able to retrospectively see God's awesome providence at work. The reality of what happened is that this man had been in the hospital praying for God to intervene and heal him. In the process of answering his prayers, God moved me to travel to that particular state and that particular city for a brief getaway with my wife and daughter. God then moved him to call me to say goodbye while we were on our way to the very city where he was lying in a hospital bed waiting to die. All I can say is, God is awesome!

The last testimony in this chapter exposes how Satan attacked the editor of this book for having been Holy Spirit–led to take on this spiritually challenging project. Since this book contains practical means by which Christians can put our faith into active operation to break up fallow ground, tear down demonic strongholds, and therefore experience true deliverance or freedom from demonic influence, Satan viciously attacked my editor. Please recall that I warned readers in the introduction that in order to handle the content of this book, one needs to have faith (belief plus trust) in Jesus; to have a desire to obey God regardless of what others think; to have been filled with the Holy Spirit; and to have already been delivered from doubt, fear, pride, and unbelief. As you will now discern, this caveat also applied to the person God selected to edit this book. Fortunately she's a strong believer in the resurrected Savior, Jesus of Nazareth, the Christ. Her faith (belief + plus trust) in Jesus is what saved her from Satan and his demons that certainly came to try to destroy her.

Delivered from Evil while Editing This Book by Laurie Visher, Editor
As soon as I read in Pastor Barlow's third email on August 12, 2015, that he

was "lead" to send the introduction to me, I heard the "fingernails on the blackboard" and knew I had to tell him that he was "led," not "lead." Then I opened the introduction and God addressed my one misgiving about this project: am I too afraid to have another battle with Satan? No, I'm not. I have never backed down from a confrontation with the old snake, and I won't now. So it was not surprising that one thing after another happened to try to discourage me from editing this book.

Just a few days after I started working on this, my husband took me out to lunch, and I bit down on something that broke off a crown in the very back of my mouth. Because it was a Saturday, I sought help from an emergency dental office. Rather than spend lot of money repairing a tooth that nobody would ever see anyway, I opted to have the tooth pulled that day. Everything went fine until I had been home for several hours and the bleeding became a problem. I started to gather my things for a trip to the emergency room, then became aware that I might bleed out before I even got there.

My mouth was continually filling with blood, and I was feeling like I was about to lose consciousness. My mind was floating on the edge of unconsciousness, and I saw something I had seen once before, during a severe asthma attack many years ago. I saw a "cloud of witnesses," a gathering of loving spirits which included my parents, my grandparents, and other family members who had passed on, going way back into the mists of time. The procession seemed to have no end. I also saw my son, who had died as a young man twenty-two years before, but he was looking away as if somewhat embarrassed.

That was when I realized that when I got to Heaven, my family would ask me how I had died, and I would have to tell them—what? That I had had one tooth pulled—one tooth—and bled to death? What would my son say? I could just see him rolling his eyes, as he did when he was a teenager. What would my parents think as they looked away, embarrassed to admit they knew me? And what about all the other family members who had

Fighting in Faith

gone before—people who had all died of serious illnesses or fatal accidents? Oh no, I thought. I can't let this happen. I can't bleed to death over one tooth. It would just be too embarrassing.

So I pulled myself away from the vision and told my husband that I needed him to lay hands on me and pray to make the bleeding stop. He did so, in the name of Jesus, and the bleeding slowed dramatically, though it took several days to completely stop. Meanwhile I emailed Pastor Barlow about what had happened, and he advised me to "be prepared for these types of challenges. Please remain humble, prayed up, and biblically read up while we are completing this project. My wife and I will also start praying God's protection over you, your husband, and family."

Throughout the rest of the project, numerous lesser problems arose: my computer crashed, so I switched to my old laptop, which had electrical problems and kept dying; my Word program acted up and refused to work with me. As I had progressed to the point in the book in which Pastor Barlow instructs people on deliverance, I screamed at the demon inside my computer and ordered it to go away and leave this place, in Jesus's name. It did.

When I came to the chapter about ministering to women, I felt prompted to advise Pastor Barlow to add a section about ministering to mothers who have lost a child. He did so after having consulted the Holy Spirit, but then I became very depressed while editing it. I mentioned to him that I had lost my son, my husband at that time, and both of my parents all within just a few years, and while editing the chapter, I was reliving how devastated and alone I had been. He wrote back to me that the Holy Spirit had spoken to him about me and told me that I had not been alone—that I had a friend who had stuck closer to me than a brother, and that friend was Jesus.

This shocked me, because I had just a few hours earlier received an email from my long-lost brother, who had turned his back on me during my hard times and then dropped out of my life, leaving no forwarding address. I went back to Pastor Barlow's email and tried to find the part about the friend who had stuck closer to me than a brother, but I couldn't find it, so I asked him if he could find it and resend it. He looked and could not find it anywhere. Then he wrote back to me:

> I am being reminded that the Holy Spirit told me to tell you that Jesus has replaced everything you "lost" in every person who has gone on to glory. However, I seem to recall wanting to look up the passage of Scripture before including that truth in the email. I apparently forgot to look it up and come back to include it in the information I sent. If this is the case, I never actually included it, albeit the Holy Spirit specifically instructed me to do so.
>
> Moreover, if I in fact did not send it, do you understand what this means? This would mean that the Holy Spirit miraculously allowed you to read what I intended to type but unfortunately forgot! If neither of us can find it, then this is a sign, wonder, and a miracle that God really wanted you to receive this message about how much Jesus loves you.

And that is the message of this book: that Jesus loves me—and you, and all of us. The veil between the natural world and the spirit world is very thin, and Jesus is never far away from us. He is much closer to us than we realize, and every now and then, when we are fighting our battles against evil and most need a friend, He reminds us in a miraculous way that He is right beside us on the battlefield.

CHAPTER 16

TESTIMONIES: FOREIGN MISSION WORKS

"[Y]ou shall receive power when the Holy Spirit has come upon you; and you shall be witnesses to Me in Jerusalem, and in all Judea and Samaria, and to the end of the earth." (Acts 1:8)

While chapter 15 consists of testimonies from the perspectives of those who received ministry from God through me, this chapter entails exceptionally powerful signs, wonders, and miracles that I personally witnessed while ministering and teaching a spiritual gifts activation class in Ouagadougou, Burkina Faso, West Africa, in November 2013. Accordingly this chapter covers experiencing the wielding of God's Divine Power from the perspective of one who is being used by God to perform the signs, wonders, and miracles Jesus promised would be worked by those who believe and obey Him.

During the summer of 2013, I was blessed with a unique opportunity to minister to a full-time missionary who was back in the States on a brief vacation from the mission fields of West Africa. She was referred to me through two doctors (one a chiropractor, the other a doctor of philosophy), both of whom received training through one of the spiritual gifts activation classes I conduct a couple of times per year. Missionaries in foreign countries often suffer demonic attacks from witches, warlocks, witch doctors, Satan worshippers, and/or those who do rootwork and voodoo on those who threaten their control in certain realms of spiritual power, authority, and influence. Accordingly it is very common for foreign missionaries to be ravaged by the plots and wicked wiles of demons who go for the jugular with these people because they tend to be well rooted in their faith in Jesus and very knowledgeable that their very presence is a serious threat to the power Satan has over the minds, wills, and emotions of the people they serve.

I provided the foreign missionary an appointment to take her through deliverance ministry at the church where I pastor. I had just celebrated the end of my first year as pastor prior to meeting with this missionary. She arrived on time, accompanied by one of the doctors who referred her and by the vice president of ministries of Go To Nations, which was formerly named Calvary International. The vice president of ministries is responsible for the health, safety, and welfare of the missionaries. In this regard I discerned that the VP came to make sure the missionary was not coming to some quack of a minister who would do more harm than good. The Holy Spirit gave me a word of knowledge concerning the reason the VP of ministries showed up with the missionary and the doctor who holds a PhD.

I took the missionary through a deliverance session that lasted approximately two and a half hours. She received major breakthroughs in several significant areas. The vice president of ministries witnessed the session and experienced the awesome power of God being wrought during the missionary's deliverance session. As they were leaving, the vice president told me there are other missionaries who are suffering the same kind of attacks on mission fields around the entire world. I let her know that God had shown me dreams of me conducting deliverance ministry and teaching spiritual gifts activation classes in foreign countries. She then invited me to consider attending a short-term mission trip to West Africa in November of that year. I told her I would pray, asking the Holy Spirit to let me know if I should go, and would get back to her with an answer. Needless to say the Holy Spirit released me to go. In fact the answer was so powerful that it reminded me of when God said, "Fool, pray!" the day He very gently ushered me into the healing side of deliverance ministry. This time it was as if God was saying, "Of course, I want you to go to Africa; now get going!"

Ouagadougou, Burkina Faso, West Africa

Accordingly I made contact with the vice president of ministries, who put me in contact with the missionary's husband, both of whom just happened to be in charge of Go To Nations' missionary operations in Ouagadougou. Having witnessed how his wife had been blessed through the deliverance session, he understood the effectiveness of such power ministry firsthand. He informed me that the African pastors could really use someone to teach them how to conduct deliverance ministry in a way that was practical and effective. He further informed me that deliverance ministry is greatly needed in West Africa due to the widespread practice of the occult by voodoo priests who control the people through witchcraft. He further explained that they really needed someone who would not just teach what the Bible says about healing and deliverance ministry but would perform it and most importantly actually show the Africans, the American missionaries, and the missionary interns how to perform it as well.

Healing and Deliverance Ministry in West Africa Before I Went There

I shall never forget the missionary's husband's explanation as to why it was so important to bring this type of training to West Africa. He explained that when people become overpowered by demons in that particular part of West Africa, the African pastors would tie the demonically victimized person to a tree and allow them to spend the night in that condition and then release them when they were no longer under the power of demons. As you can imagine, this process is so embarrassing and inhumane that most people would not want to subject either themselves or their loved ones to it. Accordingly Satan and his demons were reigning supreme in that part of West Africa.

With this in mind, I explained how I both perform healing and deliverance ministry and teach others how to do the same. I informed him that the method I have been trained to use completely disarms demons before casting them out. I further explained that I have the victim confess, renounce, and break legal agreement(s) with the specific sinful misconduct that had allowed Satan to take over their minds and thereby control their bodies. This was in accordance with Jesus's teaching: "No one can enter a strong man's house and plunder his goods, unless he first binds the strong man. And then he will plunder his house." (Mark 3:26–28)

Confessing sin is basically agreeing that God is right when his Holy Word declares, "[A]ll have sinned and fall short of the glory of God." (Rom. 3:23) Renouncing sin establishes a mindset that one has an earnest desire to turn away from sin and thereby make a commitment to refrain from continuing in sin. This is what breaks the power of sin over the mind, will, and emotions and thereby weakens the influence demons have in our lives. These professions and commitments subdue demons, which makes it much easier to extract them in the name of Jesus.

The missionary's husband said he would speak with a few of the pastors in the city and the "bush pastors" (who ministered in the bush country areas of West Africa) and get back to me with their responses and what they might need from me. Bush pastors are gospel preachers who live and minister in the bush country. They hold church in areas of the rugged countryside where there are none of the amenities that many take for granted, such as electricity, indoor toilets, and well-built structures in which to live. Bush pastors had become very near and dear to me before I ever went to Africa because I quickly discerned that they minister under some of the most extreme conditions and circumstances imaginable yet continue to serve God with strong faith and the joy of Jesus in their hearts.

Ministerial Plan of Action for Burkina Faso, West Africa

The missionary's husband followed up with me as promised. He discussed my trip with several of the most well-known and influential pastors in the city of Ouagadougou and with many of the bush pastors in the surrounding countryside of Burkina Faso. He let me know that they were all very excited about the possibility of an American pastor coming to both teach and perform healing and deliverance ministry. One of the pastors from the city had specifically asked if I merely taught this type of ministry or if I both taught and actually performed it. I would later be told by him that he wanted to know the answer because they were tired of teachings on deliverance ministry that were not accompanied by actual demonstrations of the power of God being manifested along with the instruction. Here's what I sent back to them via email:

> I am very flexible in terms of where I can be used. For information purposes, my general instructional gifting lies in converting general biblical principles into ACTIVE and PRACTICAL APPLICATION under the aid, guidance, and counsel of the HOLY SPIRIT, as opposed to man's finite wisdom. Looking forward to serving you all wherever I can." (November 5, 2013, at 7:46 a.m. EST)

Based upon their concerns, they gave me three options, each of which involved instruction followed by actual application of the principles that would be taught in each session. I selected the option that had me teaching from 8:00 a.m. to 12:30 p.m., followed by healing and deliverance services at five churches around the city of Ouagadougou from 6:00 p.m. to 9:00 p.m. or until the last person was served, which usually turned out to be around midnight. I would be the lead teacher and minister at a different church each night while other pastors, who would receive the teaching, would lead services at the other churches. After the preaching was completed, healing and deliverance ministry would be conducted both by the lead preacher and those who took the class. Those who took the class would be divided up among the five churches and minister to individuals in small groups of two to four people. Here's a rendering of the actual spiritual gifts activation seminar and corresponding ministerial schedule:

Tuesday, November 19 – Arrival of village pastors from thirty villages (up to eight hours away)

Wednesday, November 20
7:30 a.m.–8:00 a.m. Worship and prayer
8:00 a.m.–10:00 a.m. Teaching: Session 1
10:00 a.m.–10:30 a.m. Break
10:30 a.m.–12:30 p.m. Teaching: Session 2
12:30 p.m.–3:00 p.m. Lunch break
3:00 p.m.–5:00 p.m. Prayer/intercession
5:00 p.m.–6:00 p.m. Break
6:00 p.m.–9:00 p.m. Deliverance ministry

Thursday, November 21
7:30 a.m.–8:00 a.m. Worship and prayer
8:00 a.m.–10:00 a.m. Teaching: Session 3
10:00 a.m.–10:30 a.m. Break
10:30 a.m.–12:30 p.m. Teaching: Session 4
12:30 p.m.–3:00 p.m. Lunch break
3:00 p.m.–5:00 p.m. Prayer/intercession
5:00 p.m.–6:00 p.m. Break
6:00 p.m.–9:00 p.m. Deliverance ministry

Friday, November 22
7:30 a.m.–8:00 a.m. Worship and prayer
8:00 a.m.–10:00 a.m. Teaching: Session 5
10:00 a.m.–10:30 a.m. Break

10:30 a.m.–12:30 p.m. Teaching: Session 6
12:30 p.m.–3:00 p.m. Lunch break
3:00 p.m.–5:00 p.m. Prayer/intercession
5:00 p.m.–6:00 p.m. Break
6:00 p.m.–9:00 p.m. Deliverance ministry

Accordingly the testimonies you are about to experience are from instructional sessions in the mornings and actual healing and deliverance ministry sessions that took place in the evenings over a three-day period from November 20 through 22, 2013, plus a miraculous event that took place on Saturday, November 23, which was my last day. Although the Spiritual gifts activation class/seminar and corresponding healing and deliverance services thereafter were only three days, I spent a total of fourteen days in West Africa. Over this span of time, I was very blessed to minister to American missionaries and instruct missionary interns. I also was used by the Holy Spirit to perform many feats of power ministry. As will be shortly revealed, some of the work God performed through me involved the working of special miracles, not only through me but also through the apostles, deacons, evangelists, missionaries, prophets, pastors, teachers, and even two laypeople to whom I ministered between November 10, 2013 and November 23, 2013.

As part of the instructional process, I allowed those being trained in the art of healing and deliverance ministry to give testimonies at the beginning of the morning classes on the second and final days, particularizing the signs, wonders, and miracles they had personally experienced the night before. As you can imagine, testimony time was one of the best parts of the class because it allowed the entire body of believers to hear about the wonderful works that God had performed through each of them as they put their training into active practice within just a few short hours of having received it. At the start of the second day of instruction, we heard pastors who had never laid healing hands on anyone before testifying that God had worked miracles through them involving the following:

> Formerly paralyzed people walking
> Formerly blind people seeing
> The chronically sick receiving healing for the very first time
> A minor child instantly delivered who suffered from an "incurable" disease (dis-ease) that forced her to urinate every five minutes. In fact, it was the Go To Nations' interns (whom I instructed in very abbreviated sessions my first week there) that God used to work this awesome miracle.

Time and space requirements do not allow me to detail every miracle I either personally experienced or was made aware of through those who received training from the Holy Spirit through me in the art of healing and deliverance or power ministry. Accordingly I have selected a few of the ones that impacted me the most and will forever remind me of how awesome, wonderful, just, loving, and supremely powerful God can be when we submit and allow Him to use us in whatever ways that please Him.

Teaching Session 1: Tongues and Interpretation of Tongues, Wednesday, November 20, 2013
There was an African gentleman whose native language was Mòoré. He sat in the first row at every session, so he was always within my sight as I taught. I had to use two translators—one to translate my English into French, which is the official commercial language of Burkina Faso, and one to translate from French to Mòoré, which is their native tongue. As I taught I had to pause to allow both translators to translate before moving on to the next point. If I said something humorous, there would be a delay before the audience would laugh because what I spoke would need to be translated first into French and then into Mòoré. However, I always noticed that this one particular African gentleman, the one who sat in the front row, would smile, laugh, and respond

before the translators started speaking. It was quite clear to me that he was comprehending my English very well, while everyone else had to wait for the translators before they could say amen, laugh, or otherwise appropriately respond. The last healing and deliverance service that I conducted was at the church he attended. After the service was over, I used a translator who spoke both English and Mòoré to tell him my observations about him during the instructional sessions and how he seemed to understand what I was saying before the other Africans. In reply he confirmed that he could understand what I was saying very well as I spoke it. He then said that a week or so before the conference, God had been showing him in dreams how the man from America would teach him in English but he would understand it in his native language. He also testified that the Lord had shown him the camera setup and the arrangement of the area where the teaching would take place before the event was organized.

First Healing and Deliverance Service: Power Encounter with a Demonized Man

When conducting such healing and deliverance ministry services, I usually preach and teach for thirty to forty minutes, then try to seamlessly move into the ministry portion, which takes the longest time. It is not uncommon for me to preach for thirty minutes but then minister for well over four hours afterward. What's so amazing is that no one leaves, because everyone wants to witness and/or personally experience the miracles and hear the powerful testimonies of the people who are being healed, delivered, and set free from Satan and his demons. This is the case whether in the United States or in a foreign country. It is quite evident that the Holy Spirit ushers in a revival that no one was expecting, which makes such experiences so special and priceless.

As fate would have it, Satan sent a demonized man (one who was under the direct power and influence of demons) to challenge my authority and ultimately disrupt the service. This was a very bold attempt to prevent people from experiencing the awesome power of God as a sign and a wonder to receive healing, deliverance, and most importantly soul salvation. This man showed up at the very first healing and deliverance service that was conducted on Wednesday, November 20, 2013. He was being very disruptive and made audible outbursts that were in express disagreement with what I was preaching. He appeared to be very deranged.

I first tried to ignore him until I realized that the audience was being distracted. In a bit of righteous indignation toward the demons (not him), I very loudly dared any demon to speak through him and warned if any did so I would cast them out in the name of Jesus! I noticed that the ushers were surrounding him and were about to escort him out, but I asked them to let him stay. I specifically told the audience that the man needed deliverance from the demons that were motivating him to disrupt the service. I further explained that the man was present to hear the Word of God and get delivered, but the demons within him were trying to prevent him from being delivered. Accordingly the ushers allowed him to remain.

After I resumed preaching, about five minutes elapsed before the demons spoke through him again. Before I realized it, the Holy Spirit moved me to shout these words at the very top of my lungs: "Shut up, in the name of Jesus!" His mouth shut in middle of a sentence, and there was complete silence for a few moments. The silence was eerie because this was an outdoor service. Absolutely no sound whatsoever could be heard for a few moments. The next sound that came was someone shouting "HALLELUJAH!" in reference to God having shut the man's mouth, which caused the audience to shout praises to God and clap their hands. By now you should be pondering this question: was it biblical to tell that man to shut up in the name of Jesus? The answer is yes, as explained below.

I did so inspired with a Word of Wisdom from the Holy Spirit. See I Corinthians 12:8

"Jesus rebuked him, saying 'Be quiet and come out of him.'" (Mark 1:25)

This was the first of what would be many power encounters with demons I would experience while ministering in West Africa on my very first overseas mission trip. This first power encounter was a public spectacle whereby demons were trying to intimidate me and prevent the power of God from reigning in that particular service. The demons knew a stranger from another nation had arrived in their territory, and they sent someone to let me know I was trespassing in their territory. This was akin to how the man with the legions of demons immediately confronted Jesus when he got off the boat in the country of the Gadarenes. Matthew 8:28 reads, "When He had come to the other side, to the country of the Gergesenes, there met Him two demon-possessed men, coming out of the tombs, exceedingly fierce, so that no one could pass that way." This is the nature of the situation I experienced during the very first healing and deliverance service I conducted in Africa. As usual, God prevailed!

Looking back on what happened, I can clearly discern that it was a very critical moment. If I had allowed the demons within the man to go unchecked, it could have negatively impacted the healing, deliverance, and most importantly the potential salvation of many people who came to be blessed by God. It could also have potentially moved many of those who were actively being trained in the spiritual gifts activation class to either quit or take the training lightly. However, God would have absolutely none of that! After the audience witnessed how the name of Jesus shut down those demons, the people's faith increased and their hearts were filled with joy, wonder, and expectancy. No doubt this powerful and public display of God's awesome power beat down a spiritual path of expectancy that paved the way for the major healings, deliverances, signs, wonders, and very special miracles of which you are about to read.

Demonic Spirit of Infirmity
A mother brought her daughter to the service for deliverance from an anomaly that caused her to cough uncontrollably. In fact she could not stop coughing. The Holy Spirit moved me to lay hands on her back and forehead and then

apply the blood of Jesus to her cough by saying, "I apply the blood of Jesus to you, cough, and further command you, cough, to wither, dry up, and die, in Jesus's holy and righteous name." I then commanded the coughing to stop, in name of Jesus. The girl coughed a few more times, but then the coughing completely ceased.

Refusing to Break a Soul Tie
A lady came up, saying her relationship with her husband was not going well. She explained that spirits have sex with her in her dreams and cause her to climax, which leaves her in such a state that she has absolutely nothing left by the time her husband comes home from work and wants to have intercourse with her. Through a divinely inspired word of knowledge, the Holy Spirit revealed that she had a devilish soul tie with the man with whom she had broken up to marry her husband. It was further revealed to me that she was still very much in "love" (really lust) with that man and enjoyed fantasizing about him and what they used to do. As you can imagine, she was quite startled as she heard such accurate information coming from a complete stranger from another country whom she had never met before that evening. No doubt the Holy Spirit revealed this to me to arrest her attention so she would be receptive to the next revelation, which was a word of wisdom informing her what must be done to break the soul tie and set her free from Satan's stronghold over her life and marriage. This very precise word of wisdom called for her to confess her feelings for her ex-boyfriend as sinful, renounce and break legal agreement with those feelings, and ask God to forgive her for continuing to fantasize over the former intimate relationship she had had with her ex-boyfriend. In essence she was committing spiritual adultery in her heart, which authorized demons of lust to keep her in bondage through nightmares. Jesus deals with this in Matthew 5:28, which says, "But I say to you that whoever looks at a woman to lust for her has already committed adultery with her in his heart." I informed her that the soul tie must be broken in order for the dreams to stop.

She was reluctant to break the soul tie. Unfortunately she was torn between wanting to be set completely free to please her husband and the desire to continue to fantasize about the sexual relations she had previously had with her ex-boyfriend. After spending a great deal of time waiting for her to decide, I asked her to sit down, pray about it, and come back to me again if she wanted to break the soul tie so the tormenting dreams would stop. She went and sat down for a few moments but ultimately left without returning to break the soul tie. This is a classic case of a person wanting to have their cake and eat it too. God blesses us with free will. In fact I personally believe our God-given free will is second only to the free gift of salvation in Christ Jesus because we exercise free will to accept salvation. However, far too many people fail to appreciate the doctrinal fact that God will hold us accountable for the stewardship He gives us to exercise our free will.

With respect to this particular woman, she was not serious enough about wanting deliverance from the power Satan wielded over her life through lust, which is a very powerful demon. In fact this is the demon that deceived Eve and got both her and her spiritually weak husband kicked out of the Garden of Eden. To the contrary she wanted the dreams to stop, but she wanted to continue to fantasize about the former intimate relationship she had experienced with her ex-lover while still trying to satisfy her spouse. God was trying to show her that harboring lust in her heart for her ex-lover was offensive not only to her husband but also to God. The conclusion of this matter was that she did not want to be "made whole," as Jesus sometimes inquired of some people just prior to ministering to their heartfelt needs. Far too many of us want the fish, loaves, leeks, onions, and melons but not that God-given manna from Heaven. Translation: real soul food.

Healings and Deliverances from Pain

That first healing and deliverance service attracted many people who presented themselves for deliverance from sundry anomalies manifesting in chronic pains in multiple areas. People were complaining of severe migraine headaches and pain in their arms, legs, and joints. These anomalies and ailments were manifestations of the power Satan and his demons were evilly exercising over those people. Amazingly God healed and utterly eradicated pain in every person who submitted to deliverance ministry. To God's glory, many of them experienced relief through the obedience of the apostles, deacons, evangelists, missionaries, pastors, teachers, and laypeople who had received just a few hours of training earlier that morning.

Second Healing and Deliverance Service: Several Special Miracles, Thursday, November 21, 2013

"Just Snap Your Fingers"

I conducted the second healing and deliverance service at another West African church the night after the first service. After preaching for approximately thirty minutes, I stepped down from the platform and walked out into the audience to minister healing and deliverance. I had two translators standing with me as I called for people to stand in line to receive ministry. As one approaches for prayer, I often ask, "What would you have the Lord Jesus do for you?"

One lady who came up for prayer replied, "I want to be able to hear out of both ears." Through a translator, she explained that she could hear quite well in her left ear but was completely deaf in her right ear. I was on her left side as she informed me of her problem, so I moved around to her right. I cupped my hands around her ear and was about to whisper, "Ear, I command you to open up and receive sound in the name of Jesus." However, before I could touch her or even had a chance to speak, the Holy Spirit spoke these words to my mind, "Just snap your fingers." Without doubting or second guessing, I placed my left hand close to her right ear and snapped my fingers in immediate obedience, which caused the lady to immediately blink as if something had startled her. While publicly testifying about this experience, she said "I heard a popping sound in my right ear." Amazingly, when I snapped my finger, God's divine *dunamis* opened up her right ear.

"Fear of Singing in Church"
A lady came up for prayer, saying she has a gift from God to sing. She complained that she can sing very well everywhere except before people in church. She explained that while in church, she gets so nervous that she freezes up and can't sing very well at all. Through a word of knowledge from the Holy Spirit, I informed her that Satan had put the spirit of fear in her to control, hinder, and ultimately "kill" her gifting from God. (John 10:10) She allowed me to take her through a power and authority deliverance prayer that culminated in casting the spirit of fear out of her mind, will, and emotions in the name of Jesus. The Holy Spirit then gave me a word of wisdom to have her sit down and quietly sing through an entire song, and when she finished singing that song, she would be completely delivered from the spirit of fear. She obeyed and returned, giving God the glory that she had become completely delivered from the spirit of fear. However, unbeknownst to either one of us, God would shortly allow her to powerfully demonstrate the awesome success of her deliverance from the spirit of fear, as He was about to use her to deliver another person who was under Satan's evil power.

"Deaf in Both Ears and Delivered via Singing"
A lady came up saying she had lost just about all hearing in both ears approximately five years prior. Her complaint was that everything sounded like a muffled hum, which prevented her from being able to distinguish various sounds. The Holy Spirit quickly provided a "Word of wisdom to call back the lady with the singing gift and have her sit down with this lady and sing into her ears. The Holy Spirit specifically instructed me to have the singer sing an entire spiritual song in this lady's right ear and then sing an entirely different spiritual song into her left ear. I had the singer cup both hands around the lady's ears as she sang the songs. I further declared that "in Jesus's name" the lady would be able to hear when she finished singing. They sat

down to do what God instructed. I later found them both praising God because the lady could clearly hear out of both ears. She was slowly beginning to relearn how to hear again. Her ears had been closed for so long that she was trying to remember how sound sounded. Hallelujah!

Just think about the singer for a second. Within about thirty minutes, God took this lady from being deathly afraid of singing in church settings to becoming a powerful woman of God who could not only sing in church but also be used by God "to destroy the works of the devil" in the lives of others. (1 John 3:8) This is a classic case of the fulfillment of Matthew 17:20, in which Jesus solemnly promises, "If you have faith as a mustard seed, you will say to this mountain, 'Move from here to there,' and it will move; and nothing will be impossible for you." Finally this testimony also fulfills Acts 1:8, which says: "[Y]ou shall receive power when the Holy Spirit has come upon you; and you shall be witnesses to Me…," and Mark 16:20, which declares, "And they went out and preached everywhere, the Lord working with them and confirming the word through the accompanying signs. Amen."

"Congregational Miracle"
God gave me a special word of knowledge telling me that many people had made up their minds that the only way they would be healed, delivered, or blessed would be if the man of God from the United States would either lay healing hands on, touch them, or individually pray with them. The problem with this fallacy was that it would lead to sinful idolatry, as they would give more credit for their healing to the man of God instead of the God in the man.

In response to this devilish work of demonic origin, the Holy Spirit provided me with a very unique word of wisdom to solve this problem. God had me stop the entire service, organize the people, and give them some specific instructions that I have never heard performed in a healing and deliverance service. This was a very specific prescriptive cure for a unique satanic problem. I had everyone whom God had already blessed, delivered, and/or healed in any way come up front and form a line. I placed myself as the last person in that line. I asked every person in the building who had prayer requests to form a line at the very back of the church. I then told them to walk up one by one and shake the hand of each person in the line, after which they would proceed out of the back door of the church, walk outside the church along the outside wall, and then return through the front door of the church. The word of wisdom the Holy Spirit had me speak was: "When you walk back into the church from the front door, you will be healed, delivered, and set free!"

In obedience to that directive, they formed a line, walked up, shook our hands, and walked out the back door. However, and unfortunately, many never returned through the front door. Many people walked out the back door in unbelief and never returned that night. Fortunately about half of the people obeyed the instructions with childlike faith and received some of the greatest blessings imaginable, to which many of them publicly testified. As you can imagine, I was a bit taken aback that so many people left. I'm quite sure spirits of doubt, fear, pride, and unbelief went into demonic overdrive trying to block these people's deliverance and freedom. This was one of the worse cases of demonically driven hindrances I have ever seen in all of the time I have been in healing and deliverance ministry. However, God was glorified in that He miraculously separated the sheep from the goats that night.

The Holy Spirit confirmed that this exercise was specifically prescribed to weed out the people who just wanted some quick fix from God from those who were very serious about wanting God to transform their lives. This was a comforting word for me because it is not my desire for some to get healed or some to get delivered or some to get saved. When I minister it is my sincerest hope and expectation that everyone present will experience the resurrection power of Jesus, be saved (receive *sozo*), and be transformed and therefore never be the same again. However, we all have God-given free will, which means we can either accept or reject God and all of the blessings He has for u—but we will give account on Judgment Day for how we have exercised our free will! Note: There is only a single *e* in the word *judgment*, which is one of the first things taught in law school.

Deep Emotional Healing: Deliverance from "Dry Bones," Friday, November 22, 2013

A few hours before I would conduct the third and final healing and deliverance service at yet another West African church, God blessed me to experience one of the most unique and personally fulfilling ministerial sessions I have ever conducted. At about 5:00 p.m., I was asked to pray with a particular lady. As we sat down across from each other, I could tell that she was seriously depressed in her spirit, so much so that she looked as if she wanted to die right then in my presence. I asked, "What would you have the Lord do for you today?"

"Peace" was the reply she delivered through a translator.

The Holy Spirit spoke to me and said, "Look into my eyes," so I immediately said to her, "Look into my eyes." While I am ministering, the Holy Spirit often speaks the exact words to me that I am to speak verbatim to the person to whom I am ministering.

This is why I repeated exactly what I heard the Holy Spirit speak to me, which was "Look into my eyes." She initially looked at me but then immediately turned her eyes away. I said, "Look at me," and she briefly looked into my eyes but then quickly looked down toward the floor. Her spirit was so depressed and damaged that she simply could not maintain eye contact with me for more than a few seconds. Unfortunately her soul was so tormented and ravaged that she could not look me directly in the eye for as much as five seconds before returning to a downward gaze toward the floor.

"What makes you happy?" The Holy Spirit registered these words in my mind, which I immediately spoke to her.

This question immediately generated a smile as she opened her mouth and began to share how much she really enjoyed cooking, spending time with her children, and doing things around the house. She said these things were very relaxing and made her very happy. However, she went on to say, "This all changes as soon as my husband comes home." She explained that he yelled at her, berated her, and called her dumb and stupid. While looking toward the floor, she further said he constantly puts her down. Just as quickly as that nice smile came when she began to speak on what makes her happy, the sadness, gloom, and depression quickly returned when she recalled how badly her husband treated her. She was deeply depressed, wounded, and downtrodden spiritually, emotionally, and psychologically—literally living in a state of mental hell.

Word of Knowledge from Ezekiel 37

Out of the blue, the Holy Spirit said to me, and I repeated to her, "Are you familiar with Ezekiel 37?" Her eyes lit up as she excitedly said yes. I then asked her to tell me what Ezekiel 37 is about. She proceeded to accurately tell me that it's about dry bones and God breathing his spirit on them, which allows the bones to live again. The Holy Spirit confirmed to my spirit that Ezekiel 37 was her favorite Scripture. Having been given this very accurate and precise word of knowledge, I then employed a legal skill and asked this leading question: "Isn't it true that Ezekiel 37 is your favorite scripture?" to which she replied yes with a tiny smile on her face. This was the first time I had seen her with this much positivity in her spirit. She proceeded to voluntarily explain that she read it all the time because it made her feel good. The Holy Spirit asked, and I repeated, "Why is Ezekiel 37 your favorite Scripture?"

She then said, "Because I want God to remember me one day and make me live again."

The Holy Spirit asked (and I repeated), "Why didn't you tell me that reading Ezekiel makes you happy when I first asked what makes you happy?"

She looked kind of puzzled and said, "I forgot."

To this I replied, "But someone remembered that Ezekiel 37 is your favorite Scripture in the entire Bible, and it makes you happy and feel good, right?" She said yes. Then I asked her who remembered it was her favorite.

She said, "You remembered," but I told her it was not me because I did not know Ezekiel 37 was her favorite Scripture. Then I looked deeply into her eyes and could tell that the eternal light of the truth was sinking in that it was God who had remembered her favorite Scripture, despite the fact that she had forgotten. I then told her, "God remembered you and reminded you of something very important that you forgot, namely that Ezekiel 37 gives you great comfort, as you continue to have hope that God will remember you—which He has!" I delicately informed her that God remembered so much that it was better than her own memory. When she forgot about the importance of Ezekiel 37 and how much comfort it brought to her soul and spirit, God loved her enough to remember and then remind her. Upon hearing this she released a big smile for the very first time. I could tell that God was actively delivering her from a severely broken heart at that very moment.

Prior Ministry Opportunities
This lady almost missed the opportunity to receive ministry. She was merely sitting down in a chair in the room near another person to whom I ministered, and when I asked if anyone else needed prayer, she said nothing. It was only later that she reluctantly spoke up and requested assistance. She also confirmed that on many prior occasions throughout her adult life, she either went to an event or to a church for prayer but always thought, "They won't pray for me," then left. I told her that was the voice of Satan, stealing, killing, and destroying her hope that God would remember her woes and deliver her from the powers of darkness.

Third and Final Healing and Deliverance Service: Muslim Lady Confesses Jesus as Savior

The last healing and deliverance service I conducted was by far the most dramatic, dynamic, and powerful of them all. While I have yet to mention the salvations that were experienced, there were significant numbers of people who professed faith in Jesus during those three nights of ministry that took place at five different African churches throughout Ouagadougou. As a matter of fact, during the first day of the spiritual gifts activation seminar, I heavily emphasized that the ultimate purpose of signs, wonders, and miracles is to authenticate the eternal veracity of the gospel of the kingdom of God to deliver lost souls from Hell and ultimately the lake of fire. Accordingly there was a heightened emphasis on offering salvation in the name of Jesus after recipients of ministry had received healing, deliverance, a sign, a wonder, or a miracle in Jesus's name. The emphasis came due to something God taught me when I first took a spiritual gifts activation class in 2004. Back then our class was experiencing so many powerful healings, deliverances, and accurate words of knowledge and prophecies that we were beginning to miss that the true significance of signs, wonders, and miracles is to authenticate the veracity of the gospel to save lost souls. God warned me of the issue in a dream, which I shared with the instructor, who then had me share it with the class. Accordingly from that time on, it has been my chief objective to intensely focus on the end goal of these classes and deliverance ministerial sessions, which is to lead people to a saving knowledge of Jesus of Nazareth, the Christ!

After I preached for thirty-five to forty minutes, I asked people to stand if they needed Jesus do to anything for them. The first lady to whom I spoke renounced Islam, which is the dominant religion in Burkina Faso and all of West Africa, and professed faith in Jesus of Nazareth, the Christ. This was a major blow to Satan and his demons that took place right in their territory. Through a translator, she kept saying she didn't know how her husband was going to receive this when she went home. This sister's conversion in and of itself was worth the entire two weeks that I spent in West Africa. However, believe it or not, this was just the beginning of what would be a very productive night of God's power dominating and casting out the powers of darkness from that church.

Dreams of Healing the Sick—but Then Death

Next, one of the ladies told me she believed God had gifted her with the supernatural ability to heal the sick, but she was afraid to actually lay hands on people because of recurring nightmares. She explained that during these dreams she would lay her hands on sick people, who would be immediately healed. However, just before she awoke, the dream would turn into a nightmare as each person died. Through a word of knowledge from the Holy Spirit, I affirmed that God had in fact gifted her in not only healing but also deliverance ministry, which involves casting out malevolent spirits that we commonly identify as demons. I further explained that demons were trying to hinder her from stepping out in faith in obedience to God and that she was dishonoring God but reverencing Satan by failing or otherwise refusing to do what God wanted her to do. This was clearly one of those situations the Apostle Paul explained in Romans chapter 7 with these words:

> I find then a law, that evil is present with me, the one who wills to do good. For I delight in the law of God according to the inward man. But I see another law in my members, warring against the law of my mind, and bringing me into captivity to the law of sin which is in my members. O wretched man that I am! Who will deliver me from this body of death? I thank God—through Jesus Christ our Lord! (Rom. 7:21–25)

This was a very hard case specifically because she had absolutely no faith that she could be used by God to perform this powerful ministry. I was so angry at Satan for what he and his demons were doing to this lady that a very healthy dose of righteous indignation bubbled up in me. Instantaneously I was in lockstep with the Holy Spirit and found myself on spiritual autopilot, which athletes call being "in the zone." I started receiving a series of instructions from the Holy Spirit for her. Surprisingly but very pleasantly, she obeyed every one of God's instructions through me without any hesitation whatsoever, which means the Holy Spirit had her in the exact same zone. She was exercising immediate obedience, and God richly blessed and rewarded her for the same. I asked her to come up on the platform and stand next to me before the entire church. Please keep in mind that this is a layperson who has never done anything like this before. In fact when everything was over, she had ultimately done things that night that few apostles, bishops, deacons, evangelists, priests, prophets, ministers, missionaries, pastors, or teachers had done.

As we stood on the platform, I had her standing to my immediate right with the pulpit to her right. I asked if there was anyone in the audience who had any kind of sickness or disease or was in any kind of serious pain. One lady came forward who said she was sick and in pain. I had the sick lady stand in front of us. I then asked the lady who was having the dreams to stand directly in front of the lady with the sickness. I asked her to put her right hand on the lady's head and repeat after me, which she did. I told the audience that I would repeat whatever I heard from the Holy Spirit, the lady with the dreams would repeat after me, and the sick lady would be healed in the name of Jesus, which was a very bold prophecy. Frankly I can't recall the actual words the Holy Spirit spoke through me, but we basically declared and decreed healing in Jesus's name.

After the words stopped coming from the Holy Spirit, I stopped speaking, and she followed suit. I then asked her to remove her hand from the lady's forehead. As soon as she removed her hand, the lady started shaking and wincing as if she was in great pain. This lasted approximately five to ten minutes. She later testified that she was experiencing a great deal of heat going throughout her entire body as God was healing her. The manifestation was very remarkable to witness. She lit up the entire church with glee as she started praising God at the top of her lungs, repetitively thanking God and saying, "I'm healed! I'm healed! I'm healed!"

Demons Manifested in Another Person

As soon as God started manifesting healing in this lady's body, a demonized boy managed to work his way to the platform directly behind where we were standing. I had been introduced to this young man before the start of the service by someone who said the boy was there to be delivered from either a sickness or demons that caused his legs to be stilted and feel like wood. Because of this condition, he could barely walk. His back and legs were hard and felt just like wood. The demons in him were using his vocal cords to shriek very loudly, trying to divert the people's attention toward him and away from the miraculous healing that was taking place in the woman who came up for prayer. This was specifically designed to glorify Satan by instilling great fear and dread in the hearts of the people who had previously been watching God bless the lady who was being healed before the entire congregation. In other words, Satan was trying to steal glory from the King of Glory, who had just healed a lady and was receiving His due credit/glory for the same. (Psa. 24) Hence, in true smoke-and-mirror form, Satan was trying to distract people from what God was doing with the lady by riling up the demonized boy. Under Holy Spirit guidance and inspiration, I shouted out loud, commanding the people to stop looking at the demon-possessed boy and refocus their attention on the lady who was experiencing God's healing, which they did.

This boy was stilted in both legs, which made it impossible for him to walk no matter how hard he tried. He stumbled and fell behind the pulpit and almost knocked over an infant who was sitting in a baby chair. I asked the audience to leave him on the floor until we finished hearing the testimony of the lady God was still healing before us. I can imagine this appeared somewhat harsh, but that's how the Holy Spirit led me at that time. After she finished testifying, I had the same lady whom God had used to heal the sick lady lay that same right hand on the demon-possessed boy as he was still on floor. I walked her through a two-pronged power and authority deliverance prayer. The first prong entailed her appropriating Jesus's name to cast out every demon within him. The second prong involved proclaiming healing in the name of Jesus, which she did. We left the young man lying on the floor, and I went back to ministering. However, before ministering to others, I asked the lady if she had felt anything either when she laid her hand on the lady who was now healed or on the young man for whom God used her to cast demons out of him. She said, "No, I didn't feel anything." I then asked her if either of them had died, to which she had to again say no.

I finally asked, "Now do you believe that God has given you the awesome power to heal people and that they will not die when you lay hands on them?" She replied yes.

After a few minutes, the Holy Spirit said, "Look toward the back of the church." I quickly looked toward the back door and noticed the young man who had been delivered from demons pulling up his trousers (which were falling down) while hurriedly walking out of the church without any difficulty whatsoever. Pointing toward the back of the church, I shouted out loud to the entire church to see how God had delivered the boy who was stilted and could not walk without assistance at the start of the service. It was clear that there were some remaining demons in him that did not want God to receive the glory for his healing, because he tried to quietly leave the church unnoticed while everyone's attention was centered on the lady God was still healing before our very eyes. However, the Holy Spirit would have none of it. When the crowd witnessed him hurriedly walking out the back door on his own power and without assistance from anyone, everyone glorified God because they knew this meant Satan was leaving the church with his tail between his legs!

Lady with Envy, Jealously, Bitterness, Anger, and Resentment

The final miracle on the final night's service involved a lady who was delivered from anger, bitterness, envy, jealously, and resentment, all of which are demonic spirits who take up residence in the mind, will, and emotions. After the above-referenced salvation of a former Muslim woman—a major healing and casting out of demons coupled with the formerly possessed boy's healing—there were a few people who appeared to be angry about what was transpiring. These few people were by no means happy for the other people God was healing and delivering from the powers of darkness.

One particular lady's facial expression looked as if she had so much anger and rage inside that she could kill at the drop of a dime. The Holy Spirit had me take a few photos of her and the other frowning people with my cell phone. They had no idea what was about to happen, but neither did I. The Holy Spirit then focused my attention on the lady who looked like she was mad enough to kill. I zeroed in on her, approached, and said, "Look at me," which she did. I then asked her if she was happy for the others in the church whom God had healed from sickness and delivered from Satan. Although a yes came from her mouth, the nonverbal expression on her face and her overall body language said, "Hell no."

The Holy Spirit then had me use the photo I had taken of her to show her how her facial expression looked to everyone in that church. Upon seeing her very own hard, stone-faced countenance, she immediately smiled in heartfelt conviction and surrender as if to say, "God, you've caught me." The Holy Spirit had used her own photograph to show her how guilty she was of the anger, bitterness, envy, jealously, and resentment she was harboring in her heart. Without any false condemnation from Satan whatsoever, the Holy Spirit powerfully brought her to genuine repentance, which allowed her to renounce and cast out every one of those defiling sins of the heart.

After the service was over, she approached and publicly thanked me for having had the nerve to confront her so publicly with her sin, especially in the delicate manner in which it was done. I admitted to her that I really hadn't known how it would turn out, but I was determined to settle for her being angry with me rather than God being angry with me for refusing to confront her as He moved me to do. She then confessed one more sin of her own volition. She told me that she had really wanted a one-on-one session with me earlier that day, but I had spent so much time with another lady that it was time to go by the time I finished. As I recalled the place and time, I realized she was referring to the lady God had miraculously delivered through a word of knowledge concerning that lady's favorite Scripture, which was Ezekiel 37. This lady with the former anger issue admitted that her anger, bitterness, envy, and jealousy issues started earlier that day when I finished with the other lady but did not have the time to minister to her in the specific way she both wanted and expected. In this regard she was thanking God for being so loving and patient in giving her the relief she wanted but truly did not deserve; such humility is a miracle in and of itself.

Final Miracle, Saturday, November 23, 2013
It was finally my last day in Burkina Faso. I woke up that morning and started packing up for a flight back home that would not depart until 9:10 p.m. All of the spiritual gifts activation class instruction, the healing and deliverance ministerial services, and the one-on-one prophetic sessions were over—well, that's what I thought. Unbeknownst to me at the time, the Holy Spirit had one final test for me that would arguably produce the greatest miracle of the entire missionary trip to West Africa. There was a divine setup awaiting me, the likes of which I had never experienced nor even heard of having occurred in evangelistic ministry. The last encounter is proof positive that we must be ever ready to preach, teach, and minister to the lost, sick, destitute, and deceived "as we go." (Matt. 10:7)

While visiting a special camp for teenage boys who were predominantly Muslim, I met a young man who was crippled. His mode of transportation was a little apparatus that appeared to be a hybrid between a wheelchair and a reverse bicycle that was pedaled with the hands instead of the feet.

His condition was quite critical, and he was the only person in the camp in that state. His condition was so serious that it really burned me to see him in such a pitiful state of being. With a heavy heart over his condition, I prayed, asking the Holy Spirit for an opportunity to minister healing to him. I was moved with such compassion that I really wanted to see him healed and set free from his crippled condition before I returned home. Surely, I reasoned, if God has worked so many other miracles over the last three days, He could certainly heal and deliver this poor young man from his crippled condition. Mind you, this was not the Holy Spirit speaking to me but my own personal desire to see that young man walking, running, and playing with all of the other boys in that camp who took such godly grace for granted. While my motives were pure and my compassion was not misplaced, I would soon discover that God had much bigger plans for this young man.

The Awesome Power of God
There was a young African minister who had started preaching shortly after I arrived at the camp. The teaching topic was God's awesome and unlimited power. Unfortunately the young minister chose a natural means by which to try to demonstrate God's awesome power, and it literally backfired. I surmise what he did was what those pastors meant when they said they were "tired of teachings!"

After having preached on God's awe-inspiring power, he took a two-liter bottle of Diet Coke and dropped several Mentos candies in it. One of the missionaries who was familiar with such demonstrations expressed doubt as to how Diet Coke would work as opposed to regular Coke, which was what he said was normally used. Mind you, having just experienced all kinds of miraculous healings, deliverances, and wonderful works of God over the past two weeks, I wondered just how the chemical reaction from dropping candy into soda could convey the kind of awesome works I had been witnessing while teaching and ministering. Unfortunately when the young preacher dropped the Mentos into the bottle, there was a very small fizzle, which caused the soda to slowly run over the top of the bottle and down to the ground. With all humility and candor, it was the poorest demonstration of what had been touted as "the awesome power of God" that I had ever heard of or seen.

After witnessing this very poor demonstration of God's power, the Holy Spirit quickly spoke these words to my mind, which I immediately repeated several times out loud: "What just happened?" The Holy Spirit then proceeded to answer His own question in my mind with these words:

> Unfortunately the opposite message has been conveyed to these children. Instead of God's awesome power being demonstrated, this suggests that God is not as powerful as the preacher's words suggested during the sermon. Now these young boys, whose faith background is Islam, question whether the "god" this young minister represents is the real God or not.

Upon having received this word of knowledge, I quickly discerned that the young minister had generated the demonic spirit of confusion, whose job is to cause a state of double mindedness with the specific goal of preventing one from making a decision either way. The problem with such a scenario in this particular setting is that it made it difficult for any of these boys from an Islamic faith background to make the decision to abandon Islam for salvation in Christ Jesus. With this going through my mind, quite a bit of righteous indignation rose up in my spirit. To be perfectly honest, I was very angry! My indignation, however, was not directed at the young preacher but at Satan for having deceived the preacher, which resulted in exactly what Satan desired—God receiving no glory whatsoever from this so-called demonstration of His awesome power.

There is no doubt in my mind whatsoever that demons orchestrated that entire demonstration to impugn God by making Him look weak, ineffective, and incapable of being all powerful as the preacher had been claiming in the sermon before the demonstration. If nothing else this mishap demonstrated how man should not employ natural means to demonstrate God's omnipotent supernatural power. In other words, God's power is awesome and unlimited! In this regard He authorizes us to deploy signs, wonders, and miracles under the tutelage of the Holy Spirit of Christ Jesus to accurately demonstrate His divine power. This is the kind of awesome godly power I have been experiencing since I first laid Holy Spirit–guided "healing hands" on myself to be cured by God of a migraine and since I cast a demon out of a church member, before I ever knew anything about healing and deliverance ministry. Such works were supernatural demonstrations of God's awesome and unlimited divine power.

"I Hate Jesus"
In my state of righteous indignation after this demonstration, I quickly made up my mind to defend the God of the Holy Bible! In my view God had just been belittled and defamed in the presence of at least fifty young men of the Islamic faith and several adults, most of whom were foreign missionaries and several missionary interns whom I had trained on an abbreviated basis the week prior. It appeared that no one else was bothered by the real message that poor demonstration was sending out in both the natural and supernatural realms. No doubt my discerning of spiritual gifting kicked in to alert me of this very unfortunate situation. Accordingly I asked one of the missionary interns if she wanted to demonstrate the real power of God, and she said yes. I then asked her if she believed that God had the power to heal that young man who was crippled. Again she said yes. I then asked her to follow me as I approached the young man. I asked the intern to lay her hands upon him, and she did. However, he quickly pushed her hand away. I spoke about God having the power to heal him of his condition in the name of Jesus. Upon hearing those words, he immediately shouted out loud, "I hate Jesus!"

This totally shocked everyone, but especially the director of the program, as she had believed this young man was already saved and loved Jesus. Apparently he had been attending the camp, eating, fellowshipping, and "receiving" biblical instruction for quite some time, all the while masking his true feelings about the God of the Bible and His only begotten son, Jesus. Fortunately the Holy Spirit used me to expose the truth during this event, which quickly turned into a power encounter between the forces of darkness and the light of God's Holy Truth. The question quickly became which force would ultimately prevail in what was becoming a great public spectacle, the likes of which I had never witnessed before nor experienced since that fateful day.

God's Awesome Power Displayed
One of the missionaries approached me with a bit of anger in her eyes and warned me that I should not publicly embarrass that young man because he was from a particular tribe of people in West Africa who do not like to be publicly shamed. Before I even realized it, these exact words came out of my mouth in a very loud and stern voice: "Jesus said if you deny me before men, I will deny you before my father in Heaven!" (Matt. 10:23) To my knowledge, no one translated this into that young man's native language. However, after what would soon take place afterward, I am absolutely positive the Holy Spirit somehow communicated this to his mind.

As you can imagine, it was a bit chaotic after the young man shouted that he hated Jesus and I shouted a Holy Bible–based warning about the consequences to anyone who would publicly deny the Christ of the entire world who died on the cross, was buried, was resurrected from the grave, and ascended back into Heaven thereafter. After all, this was in the middle of preaching and teaching from the Holy Bible about God's awesome power, yet it was apparently having no positive effect on this young man who was publicly rejecting God's resurrected Son, Jesus. This event became so strange that to the untrained and unspiritual eye, I can imagine that it probably seemed as if I was way out of line and had caused things to become indecent and out of order.

However, this was a very dynamic work of the Holy Spirit to achieve two important objectives: First, to repair the damage that had been unwittingly rendered to God's character and awesome nature. Second, to demonstrate God's true divine power so the witnesses present could differentiate between this and the poor demonstration that had just occurred with the Coke and Mentos candy. God was about to release His divine power to perform a miracle that everyone present would not soon forget.

After the young man publicly expressed his true feelings about Jesus, I remained by his side and shared lunch with him. We partook of an African tradition whereby several people eat from the same pot with only their hands. No forks or spoons are involved in this tradition. You simply stick your hands (clean or dirty) into the pot, pick up the food, and place it in your mouth. By the way, my wife, who is the proverbial "Queen of Clean," didn't like that photo of me eating with them like that. While we ate, the Holy Spirit had me use my digital camera to take pictures of the young man and his friends and allow them to see the photos on the camera's review screen. This allowed him to calm down and relax. After we finished lunch, the boys then went across the yard to play. After about twenty minutes, I saw a young man motioning with his hands for me to come to him and the crippled young man who had said he hated Jesus. The young man who was calling for me pointed to the crippled boy and then placed his hands together as if praying to let me know that the crippled boy wanted me to pray either with him or for him. All of this was taking place nonverbally, because these boys could not speak English and I could not speak their native language, which made what was transpiring even more special.

Sensing that the Holy Spirit had convicted this young man's heart after he so publicly denied Jesus before many people who had incorrectly believed he loved Jesus, I immediately obeyed the other young man's nonverbal cues for me to come to them. As I approached, the other young man again placed his hands together as if praying, pointed at me, and then pointed at the young man with the disability. At that point it was clear that the young man who was crippled had asked his friend to get me to pray for him. I was very excited, as I believed that God was about to manifest one more powerful miracle before I left Africa. I was particularly excited because, as previously stated, I wanted to see that young man healed and able to walk, run, and play with the rest of his friends.

Salvation

Although I wanted to see the young man walk, it was more important for him to be saved and delivered from the powers of darkness that had already crippled his soul and had it on a trajectory toward Hell and ultimately the lake of fire. Through a translator I asked if he believed that Heaven is real, and he replied yes. I then asked if he believed Hell is real, to which he responded likewise. From memory, as guided by the Holy Spirit in fulfillment of what Jesus promised believers in John 14:26, I then quoted the following: "[A]ll have sinned and fall short of the glory of God," followed by "the wages of sin is death, but the gift of God is eternal life in Christ Jesus our Lord." (Rom. 3:23, 6:23) And finally:

> [I]f you confess with your mouth the Lord Jesus and believe in your heart that God has raised Him from the dead, you will be saved. For with the heart one believes unto righteousness, and with the mouth confession is made unto salvation. For the Scripture says, "Whoever believes on Him will not be put to shame." (Rom. 10:9–11)

I asked if he understood these words, and through the translator he said yes. By this time quite a few people had gathered around to witness what was taking place. I then asked if he believed the words I spoke to him, and again his reply was, "Yes, I believe." At that point I had him repeat the basic "sinners' prayer" paraphrasing Romans 10:9–11, which he did, thereby confessing his sins, including having publicly denied Jesus within that same hour. He gladly accepted Jesus as his personal savior.

The witnesses were in total awe as they watched this young man who had so publicly denied Jesus now publicly confessing faith in Jesus within what seemed like the same hour! Without any doubt whatsoever, this was the kind of awesomely divine power that God wanted to be displayed that day. This powerful and very public profession of faith in Jesus by one who had shortly before declared that he hated Jesus completely annulled and overshadowed that poor attempt to use natural means that were devised through man's wisdom to display the unfathomable and omnipotent power of Almighty God!

I then proceeded to pray over the young man for him to be healed of his physical afflictions. However, to my great surprise, the Holy Spirit confirmed that the miracle was his publicly receiving salvation after shortly having rejected Jesus. He then reminded me that it was *I* who had wanted the boy healed, but God never told me that He wanted the boy physically healed (at that particular time) from his physical condition.

Accordingly I had mixed emotions about what had just transpired. On one hand I was in complete awe after having witnessed how God so powerfully saved that young man's soul in such a public and dramatic way. In so doing God literally snatched that boy's soul from Satan's grip in front of our very eyes. On the other hand, however, I was saddened that the young man was still physically crippled and therefore could not walk, run, and play as all of the other kids could. Despite this I humbly and obediently accepted God's perfect will for that young man's life by abandoning my will and what I personally wanted to see happen that particular day. After all, as God solemnly declares, "[A]s the heavens are higher than the earth, so are my ways higher than your ways, and my thoughts than your thoughts." (Isa. 55:9)

This miraculous series of events took place on my last day in West Africa at a time when I thought I was done ministering and was just relaxing in preparation to return to the United States. However, God tested me by walking me into a very unique situation to see how I would respond. I sincerely hope and pray that I met God's expectations, not only that day but throughout my entire missionary trip to Ouagadougou, Burkina Faso and will do so throughout the rest of my natural life on the Earth that He created "in the beginning…" (Gen. 1:1)

Conclusions and Questions
In closing let's revisit the two primary objectives of *Fighting in Faith* that are specified in the introduction. The first is to demonstrate how to utilize the Holy Bible to teach God's eternal truths about how Satan and his demons operate in our daily lives—whether we believe it or not. The second is to provide very practical means by which to both activate and operate our faith in God to engage and completely conquer demonic forces through Bible-based spiritual warfare. After having read the entire book, has each objective been achieved in your view? Have you gained a better or clearer understanding of the Holy Bible with respect to the awesome and omnipotent power God, in the person of Jesus of Nazareth and the Holy Spirit, authorizes Christians to wield?

Finally, and most importantly, please be ever mindful that each and every sign, wonder, and miracle shared in this book was actually worked by God through willing vessels who were simply believing in Jesus, trusting His promises, and appropriating them in childlike faith. I solemnly promised in the introduction that if you have and maintain mustard-seed faith as you read through this book, by the time you are done reading and completing the practical exercises, the Holy Spirit will have fully equipped you to "move mountains" as Jesus promised every believer in Mark 11:22–26. Well, my friend, has God equipped you to move mountains? If so, what in Heaven are you waiting for?

ACKNOWLEDGMENTS

Thank you, God, for calling me out of darkness into Your marvelous light! Thank you, Jesus of Nazareth the Christ, for dying on the cross and having been raised back to life to pay my sin debt. Thank you, Holy Spirit of Christ Jesus for equipping, enabling, and empowering me to evangelize around the world through power ministry.

I also thank the evangelist who witnessed to me and led me to the first knowing confession of my sins and my faith in Christ Jesus in my parents' front yard circa 1981 while I was home on a break from college. I will never forget how boldly he walked up and down the streets of a neighborhood full of people of a different race and culture, looking for anyone who would hear the gospel message. God not only used him to lead me to my very first genuine confession of faith in Christ; God also blessed me to receive the mantle of courage and spiritual boldness that evangelist wielded. No doubt these two spiritual attributes have enabled me to successfully minister in some of the most difficult environments and situations imaginable, both here in the United States and in Africa.

Thank you very much, Cassandra D. Barlow, my God-given wife, for living a godly life before me from the day I met you in college back in 1983 to the present. Your lifestyle enabled me to see God working in you well before He drew me into His kingdom, majesty, glory, dominion, and power!

Thank you, Rev. Dr. Joseph W. Rigsby, pastor of Woodlawn Presbyterian Church, for being a servant leader whose life demonstrates what it means to serve, bless, and disciple Christians to be all God created us to be. I have modeled many of my pastoral duties after you and the way you are so very dedicated to serving God by blessing His flock.

Thank you, Pastor Frederick D. Newbill of First Timothy Baptist Church, for having blessed me with so many opportunities to serve God under your tutelage. Under your pastoral leadership, I learned the significance of evangelism and marketplace ministry. I also learned the art of door-to-door evangelism, which enables me to be bold in my witness for Jesus both domestically and internationally.

Thank you, Prophetess Cheryl Schang, for accurately prophesying what thus said the Lord, Jesus, with respect to my life back in 2002. Your very accurate prophecies back then, many of which are particularized in this book, are still coming into fruition well over thirteen years later. Please know that your godly work has impacted hundreds of thousands of people both domestically and internationally and will continue to do so through this book.

To my editor, Laurie Visher, who "heard fingernails on a blackboard" when I sent my third email to her and knew she had to help me, I can't thank you enough! God blessed me to have you edit this book that He wrote through me. Our Heavenly Father powerfully gifted you in the accurate utilization of diction, grammar, and the construction of sentences and paragraphs. Thanks to you, I now know that I was led (not lead) by the Holy Spirit to select you to edit this work. ☺

AUTHOR BIOGRAPHY

A. W. "Al" Barlow is married, has three children and two grandchildren. He has practiced law for over thirty years, having earned Bachelor of Arts and Juris Doctor degrees from the University of Florida. He holds bar membership in Florida and Georgia. God surprisingly called him into the ministry, which ultimately led him to pastor a nondenominational church from 2012 to 2020. He transitioned into street ministry where he preaches the gospel to and serves the heartfelt needs of the homeless. He actively operates in spiritual gifts activation and healing and deliverance ministry. Advancing clients' heartfelt interests in courts of law and communicating with jurors from all walks of life uniquely qualifies him to be an effective evangelist for the cause of Christ. He ministers both nationally and internationally. He fully embraces the move of God in the marketplace by which he ministers outside the four walls of the church. Al Barlow has ministered in the United States as well as in Africa, where he teaches spiritual gifts activation courses to apostles, prophets, evangelists, teachers, pastors, missionaries, deacons, and laymen.

Pastor A. W. "Al" Barlow, Esquire
PO Box 26098
Jacksonville, FL 32226
Email: 1Cor311Publishing@gmail.com

REFERENCES

Eastman, Dick. 1978. *The Hour That Changes the World*. Baker Books.

Gunatilake, Ravindu and Avinash S. Patil. 2015. "Drug Use During Pregnancy." *Merck Manuals*.

Holy Bible: New King James Version. 1982. Thomas Nelson Bibles.

Holy Bible: King James Version. Thomas Nelson Bibles.

Llamas, Michelle. 2013. "Study: Autism Linked to Antidepressant Drug Use During Pregnancy." Drugwatch.com, May 10. https://www.drugwatch.com/news/2013/05/10/antidepressant-use-pregnancy-autism/.

Strong, James. 1996. *The New Strong's Exhaustive Concordance of the Bible*. Thomas Nelson Bibles.

Strong, James. 2001. *The New Strong's Expanded Dictionary of Bible Words*. Thomas Nelson Bibles.

The Amplified Bible. 2015. The Lockman Foundation.

SCRIPTURE INDEX

Scripture	Page	Scripture	Page
Introduction			
Matthew 16:18-19	ix	1 John 4:4	x
John 10:10	ix	James 1:25	xii
1 John 3:8	x	Mark 11:22-26	xii
Chapter 1			
1 John 4:18	1	Proverbs 16:18	3
2 Corinthians 4:3-4	2	Exodus 20:17	3
John 12:40	2	James 4:10	4
James 1:7-8	3	Hebrews 11:6	4
2 Timothy 1:7	3	Matthew 21:22	7
Chapter 2			
Matthew 18:18, 19	9, 11	1 Timothy 6:12	14
John 8:32	10	2 Thessalonians 2:12	14
John 10:10	10	Matthew 4:1	14
John 8:34	12	Matthew 3:17	14
John 10:10	13	1 John 2:16	15

Genesis 3:6	15	Genesis 4:8	16
Genesis 3:5	16		

Chapter 3

Exodus 3:1, 2, 3	17, 18	Galatians 5:22, 23	23
2 Peter 1:4	19	1 Corinthians 12:8	23
Deuteronomy 10:21	22		

Chapter 4

1 John 2:27	25	Matthew 17:20	36
Hebrews 11:6	27	Mark 3:13-15	38
1 Corinthians 12:8-11	28	Luke 10:17-20	38
Hebrews 13:2	33	Mark 16:15-20	39
Colossians 3:9-11	35	1 John 4:4	39
Luke 4:23	36		

Chapter 5

Romans 12:6	41	1 Corinthians 14:1-4	48
1 Corinthians 10:7-10	43	2 Corinthians 10:5	49
Exodus 3:1-3	44	1 Corinthians 6:19	49
1 Corinthians 12:8	45		

Chapter 6

Mark 16:17	51	1 Corinthians 14:21-22	59
1 Corinthians 14:5	52	Acts 8:36	61
2 Corinthians 4:3-4	52	1 Corinthians 14:22	61
John 7:38	53, 54	Acts 10:44-47	61
Acts 2:38	53, 54	Acts 9:1-6	61
Luke 11:13	54	1 Corinthians 12:10	62
Mark 5:17	57	1 Corinthians 14:22	62
Hosea 4:6	58	1 Corinthians 4:4	63

Psalm 11:9	63	John 10:10	66
1 Corinthians 14:5	64	John 14:26	68
Matthew 18:18	65	Judges 7:7-12	70
Hebrews 12:2	65		

Chapter 7

1 Corinthians 2:1-5	71	Isaiah 14:12-17	80
Matthew 16:16, 17	72	Ezekiel 28:1-19	80
Matthew 16:16-19	73	Ezekiel 28:12	80
Matthew 16:22, 23	73	Isaiah 14:13-14	81
Romans 6:16	74	John 8:32, 10:10	81
2 Timothy 2:15	76	Ezekiel 28:17	82
Luke 17:14	76	James 4:7	83
Matthew 20:34	76	Leviticus 11:44	83
Mark 1:41	76	1 Peter 1:16	83
Luke 17:14	76	2 Samuel 24	85
Matthew 20:34	76	1 Samuel 17:45	85
Mark 1:41	76	1 Samuel 16:13	86
Luke 8:46	76	1 Samuel 17:46-47	86
Genesis 1:26	78	Exodus 17:8-16	87
Mark 6:5	79	1 Samuel 16:13	87
1 Corinthians 14:11	79	Judges 3:9-10, 6:34, 11:29, 14:19	88
Matthew 9:6	79		
Matthew 21:23	79	2 Corinthians 4:4	89
2 Corinthians 10:8	79	John 10:10	89
Genesis 2:7	79		

Chapter 8

Luke 14:18-19	91	2 Thessalonians 5:23	92
Matthew 16:24	91	Matthew 10:28	92
Hebrews 12:2	91	John 6:26, 27	93

Acts 14:12	94	Luke 9:1-5	102
John 1:1-3, 6:63	94	2 Timothy 4:5	103
2 Corinthians 4:4	94	1 Corinthians 2:2	103
John 10:10	94	John 8:32	103
1 John 3:8	95	2 Timothy 3:7	103
Matthew 4:23-24	95	2 Timothy 3:5	104
Matthew 1:23	96	Acts 4:13	104
Luke 1:37	96	Acts 3:6	104
Mark 9:23	96	Acts 3:2	104
Matthew 19:26	96	Psalm 24	104
Matthew 17:20	96	1 Corinthians 1:27-29	105
Luke 17:7	97	Luke 9:49	106
John 5:5-9, 5:14	97	Philippians 2:9	106
Luke 2:47, 4:1	98	Matthew 7:22-23	106
John 2:11	98	1 Corinthians 1:26	106
Luke 4:28-29, 31-32	99	Ephesians 4:10-13	107
Luke 4:1-2, 14-19, 35-36	100	Ephesians 4:12	108
1 John 3:8	100	1 Corinthians 15:4	109
John 3:15	101	John 8:32	109
Matthew 9:35-38	101	Luke 10:1-9	110
Mark 3:13-15	102	Luke 10:17-22	111
Matthew 10:1-8	102		

Chapter 9

Mark 16:15-18	113	James 1:7	116
Matthew 28:18-20	113, 114	John 10:10	116
Luke 24:45-49	114	Ephesians 5:17-21	117
Luke 11:14-23	115	Acts 3:31	117
Mark 9:23	116	James 4:7	118
Matthew 17:20	116	John 20:22	119
Luke 17:6	116	Genesis 2:7	119

John 20:22	119	Luke 1:1-2	122
Genesis 1:1-2	120	Luke 1:15	122
Acts 1:5, 2:1	120	Luk 1:41	122
Luke 24:49	120	Luke 1:67	122
Mark 16:17	121	Luke 1:63-65	123
Acts 2:17-18	122	Ephesians 4:30	124
Joel 2:28-29	122	James 4:17	124

Chapter 10

Genesis 1:26	127	Mark 4:13	130
Genesis 1:26, 2:7	128	Matthew 10:21	131
Luke 4:6	129	Matthew 10:19	131
John 19:30	129	Mark 4:19	131
2 Timothy 3:7	130	Matthew 18:18-19	134
2 Corinthians 10:4-5	130		

Chapter 11

Psalm 106:36-38	135	Genesis 3:16	143
Genesis 1:27	136	1 John 1:9, 10	143
Genesis 1:28	137	Matthew 10:37	143
Exodus 20:13	138	Genesis 5:24	147
Deuteronomy 5:17	138	2 Kings 2:1	147
Matthew 5:21-22	138	2 Corinthians 5:8	148
Proverbs 22:6	143	Genesis 2:18	149
Genesis 1:28	143	Genesis 2:24	149

Chapter 12

Proverbs 22:6	153	Isaiah 57:3	161
Matthew 18:6	154	Revelation 22:15	162
Ephesians 5:18	161	Revelation 21:8	163
Jeremiah 27:9	161	Matthew 7:7-8	164

John 14:26	165	Deuteronomy 28:28	167
John 16:8	165	1 Corinthians 4:3-4	167
Isaiah 5:14	165	2 Corinthians 11:14	167
Revelation 21:8	165	Luke 4:1-13	169
1 Corinthians 12:10	166	1 Corinthians 12:8	169
John 10:10	166		

Chapter 13

1 Corinthians 6:9-11	173	Mark 9:23	182
Proverbs 23:7	174, 175	John 9:7	182
Romans 1:24-25	176	Matthew 6:8	182
Revelation 6:10	177	John 9:35-38	183
James 4:17	177	Ephesians 6:12	185
John 9:1-3	178	John 4:8	186
John 2:16	178	Matthew 6:14-15	187
Genesis 3:14-19	178	Matthew 18:21-35	187
Matthew 17:20	180	Matthew 5:43-45	188
John 9:6-7	181	2 Timothy 2:15	188

Chapter 14

Luke 11:24-26	191	John 14:15	197
Matthew 12;43-45	191	John 23:24	197
Hosea 4:6	192	1 Peter 1:3-5	198
1 Samuel 15:22-23	192	2 Timothy 2:15	198
Leviticus Chapter 26	192	Mark 14:38	199
Deuteronomy 11:26-28	192	James 5:14-15	200
Hebrews 4:15	192	Deuteronomy 32:30	200
Luke 4:13	192	Hebrews 3:7-11	201
Matthew 12:34-45	196	Matthew 7:7-8	202
Luke 12:24-26	196	Proverbs 9:10	202
Romans 6:23	197	Matthew 18:19	203

Proverbs 6:17-19, 15:33	203	John 11:39	207
Romans 12:3	204	Mark 16:14-20	207
Proverbs 16:18	204	Numbers 20:8	208
Acts 4:29-30	204	John 14:12-14	208
Ephesians 6:19	204	Mark 11:22-26	209
Matthew 18:18	205	Mark 14:37-38	210
Mark 11:22-26	206	Isaiah 58:6-9	211
Exodus 14:15-18	207	Mark 9:28-29	212
Exodus 17:6	207	James 1:5	213
Numbers 20:8	207		

Chapter 15

Mark 16:19-20	215	Mark 9:38-39	240
Luke 4:18-19	216	Mark 11:22-26, 16:15-20	240
Isaiah 61:1-2	216	Luke 9:49-50, 10:17-20	240
Revelation 19:10	216	Acts 1:8	240

Chapter 16

Acts 1:8	245	Psalm 24	267
Mark 3:26-28	248	Ezekiel Chapter 37	271
Romans 3:23	248	Matthew 10:7	271
1 Corinthians 12:8	254	John 14:26	277
Mark 1:25	254	Romans 3:23, 6:23	277
Matthew 8:28	255	Romans 10:9-11	277, 278
1 John 3:8	260	Isaiah 55:9	278
Mark 16:20	260	Genesis 1:1	279
Ezekiel Chapter 37	263, 234	Mark 11:22-26	279
Romans 7:21-25	266		

www.ingramcontent.com/pod-product-compliance
Lightning Source LLC
Chambersburg PA
CBHW070634160426
43194CB00009B/1456